S0-BBY-871

JOURNAL FOR THE STUDY OF THE OLD TESTAMENT SUPPLEMENT SERIES
181

Editors
David J.A. Clines
Philip R. Davies

Executive Editor
John Jarick

Editorial Board
Richard J. Coggins, Alan Cooper, Tamara C. Eskenazi,
J. Cheryl Exum, John Goldingay, Robert P. Gordon,
Norman K. Gottwald, Andrew D.H. Mayes, Carol Meyers,
Patrick D. Miller

Sheffield Academic Press

Theory and Method in Biblical and Cuneiform Law

Revision, Interpolation and Development

edited by
Bernard M. Levinson

Journal for the Study of the Old Testament
Supplement Series 181

BS
1199
.L3
L48
1994

Copyright © 1994 Sheffield Academic Press

Published by
Sheffield Academic Press Ltd
Mansion House
19 Kingfield Road
Sheffield, S11 9AS
England

Typeset by Sheffield Academic Press
and
Printed on acid-free paper in Great Britain
by Bookcraft
Midsomer Norton, Somerset

British Library Cataloguing in Publication Data

A catalogue record for this book is available
from the British Library

ISBN 1-85075-498-5

Contents

ABBREVIATIONS

AASOR	Annual of the American Schools of Oriental Research
AbB	*Altbabylonische Briefe im Umschrift und Übersetzung*, F.R. Kraus (ed.), Vols. 1- , (Leiden: Brill, 1964)
AfO	*Archiv für Orientforschung*
AJSL	*American Journal of Semitic Languages and Literatures*
AnBib	Analecta biblica
ANET	J.B. Pritchard (ed.), *Ancient Near Eastern Texts*
AnOr	Analecta orientalia
AOAT	Alter Orient und Altes Testament
AOS	American Oriental Series
ARM	Archives royales de Mari
ArOr	*Archiv orientální*
AS	*Assyriological Studies*
BA	*Biblical Archaeologist*
BETL	Bibliotheca ephemeridum theologicarum lovaniensium
Bib	*Biblica*
BM	Cuneiform tablets in the collection of the British Museum
BO	*Bibliotheca orientalis*
BWANT	Beiträge zur Wissenschaft vom Alten und Neuen Testament
CAD	*The Assyrian Dictionary of the Oriental Institute of the University of Chicago*
CAH	*Cambridge Ancient History*
CahRB	Cahiers de la Revue Biblique
CBQ	*Catholic Biblical Quarterly*
CH	Codex Hammurabi. Cited after G.R. Driver and J.C. Miles (eds.), *The Babylonian Laws*, 2 vols. (Oxford: Clarendon, 1955)
EstBíb	*Estudios bíblicos*
FLP	Cuneiform tablets in the collection of the Free Library of Philadelphia
HL	Hittite Laws. Cited after H.A. Hoffner, *The Laws of the Hittites* (Brandeis University PhD; Ann Arbor; University Microfilms International, 1963)
HUCA	*Hebrew Union College Annual*
IEJ	*Israel Exploration Journal*
JANESCU	*Journal of the Ancient Near Eastern Society of Columbia University*
JAOS	*Journal of the American Oriental Society*
JCS	*Journal of Cuneiform Studies*

JESHO	*Journal of the Economic and Social History of the Orient*
JNES	*Journal of Near Eastern Studies*
JPOS	*Journal of the Palestine Oriental Society*
JQR	*Jewish Quarterly Review*
KBo	*Keilschrifttexte aus Boghazköi*
KD	*Kerygma und Dogma*
KUB	*Keilschrifturkunden aus Boğazköi*
LE	Laws of Eshnunna. Cited after R. Yaron (ed.), *The Laws of Eshnunna* (Jerusalem/Leiden: Magnes Press/Brill, 1988)
MAL	Middle Assyrian Laws. Cited after G.R. Driver and J.C. Miles (eds.), *The Assyrian Laws* (Aalen: Scientia Verlag, 1975).
MANE	Monographs on the Ancient Near East
MIO	*Mitteilungen des Instituts für Orientforschung*, Berlin
MVAG	Mitteilungen der Vorderasiatisch- ägyptischen Gesellschaft
OBO	Orbis biblicus et orientalis
OLZ	*Orientalistische Literaturzeitung*
Or	*Orientalia* (Rome)
PRU	*Le Palais royal d'Ugarit*
PWCJS	*Proceedings of the World Congress of Jewish Studies*
RlA	*Revue d'assyriologie et d'archéologie orientale*
RB	*Revue biblique*
RA	*Reallexikon der Assyriologie*
RS	Cuneiform texts excavated at Ras Shamra, Syria
SBS	Stuttgarter Bibelstudien
SD	Studies and Documents
SEb	*Studi Eblaiti* (Rome: Istituto di Studi del Vicino Oriente, 1977–)
StudBib	Studia Biblica
TCS	Texts from Cuneiform Sources
TLZ	*Theologische Literaturzeitung*
TRE	*Theologische Realenzyklopädie*
TRev	*Theologische Revue*
TWAT	G.J. Botterweck and H. Ringgren (eds.), *Theologisches Wörterbuch zum Alten Testament*
UF	*Ugarit-Forschungen*
UM	Cuneiform tablets in the collection of the University Museum at the University of Pennsylvania in Philadelphia
VT	*Vetus Testamentun*
VTSup	*Vetus Testamentum*, Supplements
WO	*Die Welt des Orients*
WZKM	*Wiener Zeitschrift für die Kunde des Morgenlandes*
YOS	Yale Oriental Series, Babylonian Texts, Vols. 1-, (New Haven, Yale University Press, 1912-)
ZA	*Zeitschrift für Assyriologie*
ZAW	*Zeitschrift für die alttestamentliche Wissenschaft*
ZEE	*Zeitschrift für evangelische Ethik*
ZTK	*Zeitschrift für Theologie und Kirche*

INTRODUCTION

The academic study of the Hebrew Bible is currently in a state of ferment. All conventional models for understanding the formation and development of the Pentateuch have been opened to question.[1] On the one hand, increasing numbers of scholars, eschewing conventional diachronic analysis as atomistic and sterile, embrace the 'literary approach' that views the text as synchronically coherent, even as the product of a single author.[2] By concentrating exclusively on the final form of the text, these scholars attempt to demonstrate the meaningfulness of its composition. On the other hand, many scholars powerfully challenge classical source criticism from within, retaining the diachronic method yet drastically revising conventional assumptions about the sequence, dating, scope and redaction of the documentary sources and proposing new models for the formation of the Pentateuch. Renewed consensus remains elusive. As one scholar wrote, perhaps unconsciously echoing Dostoevsky on the death of another certainty: 'With regard to written sources, the rejection of the Documentary Hypothesis simply increases the range of possibilities'.[3]

The essays in the present volume focus on two areas of discussion that have been given short shrift in the current debate. First, even the most innovative work has devoted little attention to biblical law and

---

1. For the best introduction to the current state of Pentateuchal studies see A. de Pury (ed.), *Le Pentateuque en question* (Le monde de la Bible; Geneva: Labor et Fides, 2nd edn, 1989), with the title essay by de Pury and T. Römer, pp. 9-80.

2. For recent assessments see B.M. Levinson, ' "The Right Chorale": From the Poetics to the Hermeneutics of the Hebrew Bible', in *'Not in Heaven': Coherence and Complexity in Biblical Narrative* (ed. J. Rosenblatt and J. Sitterson; Bloomington: Indiana University Press, 1991), pp. 129-53; J.-L. Ska, 'Le "Nouvelle Critique" et L'Exégèse Anglo-Saxonne', in *Recherches de Sciences Religieuses* 80 (1992), pp. 29-53; R.P. Carroll, 'The Hebrew Bible as Literature—a Misprision?', *Studia Theologica* 47 (1993), pp. 77-90.

3. R.N. Whybray, *The Making of the Pentateuch: A Methodological Study* (JSOTSup, 53; Sheffield: JSOT Press, 1987), p. 236.

the legal and cultic institutions that were associated with it.[1] In contrast, when the now challenged consensus was first forged in the final third of the last century, the situation was precisely the opposite. Abraham Kuenen framed the issue trenchantly: 'But what then? Must the law stand with the narratives, or must the narratives fall with the laws? I could not hesitate for a moment in accepting the latter alternative.'[2] During the first two-thirds of the nineteenth century, source criticism, based primarily on analysis of the pentateuchal narratives, held the *Grundschrift*, that is, the Priestly stratum, to be the earliest source. Although both Reuss and Vatke had previously suggested the idea, it was Graf and especially Kuenen who then forged the radical position that the priestly stratum was, to the contrary, the latest of the pentateuchal sources.[3] Their claim was based on the analysis and relative dating of the Bible's legal and cultic material, and it was given decisive confirmation by the brilliant work of Julius Wellhausen.[4] Any adequate new theory of the composition and formation of the Pentateuch must come to grips with the data that the likes of Reuss, Graf, Kuenen and Wellhausen marshalled in support of their models.

Secondly, the current theoretical debate proceeds curiously

1.   The focus is clearly narrative in R. Rendtorff, *The Problem of the Process of Transmission in the Pentateuch* (JSOTSup, 89; Sheffield: JSOT Press, 1990 [1977]); E. Blum, *Die Komposition der Vätergeschichte* (WMANT, 57; Neukirchen–Vluyn: Neukirchener Verlag, 1984); *idem*, *Studien zur Komposition des Pentateuch* (BZAW, 189; Berlin: de Gruyter, 1990); T.B. Dozeman, *God on the Mountain: A Study of Redaction, Theology and Canon in Exodus 19–24* (SBLMS, 37; Atlanta: Scholars Press, 1989).

2.   A. Kuenen, *An Historico-critical Inquiry into the Origin and Composition of the Hexateuch* (2 vols.; London: Macmillan, 1886), I, p. xxii.

3.   E. Reuss, *L'histoire sainte et la loi (Pentateuque et Joshue)* (2 vols.; Paris: Sandoz & Fischbacher, 1879); W. Vatke, *Die biblische Theologie wissenschaftlich dargestellt*. I. *Die Religion des Alten Testamentes nach den kanonischen Büchern entwickelt* (Berlin: Bethge, 1835); K.H. Graf, *Die geschichtlichen Bücher des Alten Testaments: Zwei historisch-kritische Untersuchungen* (Leipzig: Weigel, 1866).

4.   J. Wellhausen, 'Die Composition des Hexateuchs', *Jahrbücher für deutsche Theologie* 21 (1876), pp. 392-450, 531-602; 22 (1987), pp. 407-79, published as a book in 1885 and now as *Die Composition des Hexateuchs und der Historischen Bücher des Alten Testaments* (Berlin: de Gruyter, 4th edn, 1963); *idem*, *Geschichte Israels* I (1978), published from the 2nd edn (1883) on as *Prolegomena zur Geschichte Israels* and translated as *Prolegomena to the History of Ancient Israel* (Edinburgh: A. & C. Black, 1885).

untainted by due consideration of literary and editorial phenomena in cuneiform literature; some biblicists engaged in the current debate continue to treat the Pentateuch as if Israelite authors had written in an intellectual and literary-historical vacuum. Of course, the older consensus was also forged without benefit of Near Eastern literary parallels, chiefly on the basis of immanent literary analysis. Because rapid developments in Semitics and archaeology were already overtaking this approach, 'Wellhausen's *Prolegomena* appeared at the last moment at which its method and its conclusions could have seemed sound'.[1] Yet even the newer theories of pentateuchal formation generally fail to deal with the comparative data that have come to light since Wellhausen's day.[2]

By correcting the double omission—both of legal and of comparative material—the contributors to this volume attempt to move current research on the Pentateuch forward.[3] Each author

1.   J.D. Levenson, 'The Hebrew Bible, the Old Testament, and Historical Criticism', in R.E. Friedman and H.G.M. Williamson (eds.), *The Future of Biblical Studies* (Atlanta: Scholars Press, 1987), pp. 19-59, at p. 34.

2.   The valuable collection of essays edited by J.H. Tigay, *Empirical Models for Biblical Criticism* (Philadelphia: University of Pennsylvania Press, 1985) is not really an exception. The aim of the volume's authors is to provide extrabiblical evidence for diachronic literary criticism, which they do successfully. They presuppose the classical documentary hypothesis, whose various revisions are not at issue in the volume.

3.   Other scholars, working from analysis of the biblical legal corpora and their redaction, have also engaged the current ferment in pentateuchal theory. See S. Amsler, 'Les documents de la loi et la formation du Pentateuque', in de Pury (ed.), *Le Pentateuque en question*, pp. 235-57; A. Cooper and B.R. Goldstein, 'The Festivals of Israel and Judah and the Literary History of the Pentateuch', *JAOS* 110 (1990), pp. 19-31; *idem*, 'Exodus and *Maṣṣôt* in History and Tradition', *Maarav* (Stanley Gevirtz Memorial Volume) 8 (1994), pp. 15-37; *idem*, 'The Cult of the Dead and the Theme of Entry into the Land', *Biblical Interpretation* 1 (1993), pp. 285-303; E. Otto, 'Del libro de la Alianza a la Ley de Santidad: La Reformulación del derecho israelita y la Formación del Pentateuco', *EstBib* 52 (1994), pp. 195-217; R. Rendtorff, 'Two Kinds of P? Some Reflections on the Occasion of the Publishing of Jacob Milgrom's Commentary on Leviticus 1–16' and J. Milgrom's 'Reply', *JSOT* 60 (1993), pp. 75-81, 83-85. Generating new models of redactional or exegetical relation between the legal strata, see I. Knohl, 'The Priestly Torah versus the Holiness School: Sabbath and the Festivals', *HUCA* 58 (1987), pp. 65-117; *idem*, *The Sanctuary of Silence: The Priestly Torah and the Holiness School* (Minneapolis: Fortress, 1994); B.M. Levinson, *The Hermeneutics of Innovation: The Impact of*

provides an analysis of fundamental issues involved in the study of biblical law and thereby helps restore to pentateuchal theory its original theoretical and methodological anchor. The consistent focus is on the prerequisites for a sound theory concerning the composition and interpretation of the legal collections.

The volume originated in a special session of the Biblical Law Group of the Society of Biblical Literature, organized by Martin Buss, which took place on November 24, 1991, at the Annual Meeting in Kansas City, Missouri. At that session, which Alan M. Cooper chaired, Martin Buss, Samuel Greengus and Bernard M. Levinson responded to Raymond Westbrook's keynote paper, 'What is the Covenant Code?' The members of the Law Group subsequently decided that the issues raised by the discussion had an essential bearing on the discipline of biblical studies and warranted publishing. Having originally proposed the session, I was asked to edit the volume. I then invited a number of additional colleagues to contribute to the volume, Law Group members (Victor H. Matthews, William S. Morrow, Dale Patrick) as well as international scholars with compatible specializations (Sophie Lafont and Eckart Otto, now himself a member). While some of the contributors reflect specifically upon the original keynote paper, others formulate their arguments independently.

The contributors to the volume investigate a fundamental issue: whether the biblical and cuneiform legal corpora underwent a process of literary revision and interpolation and whether, more broadly, these legal collections show evidence of legal-historical development. Raymond Westbrook throws down the gauntlet, arguing that the empirical evidence afforded by the cuneiform legal collections requires that diachronic analysis be rejected for both the Covenant Code and the cuneiform legal collections. Instead of explaining apparent redundancies or inconsistencies in terms of legal development,

Centralization upon the Structure, Sequence, and Reformulation of Legal Material in Deuteronomy (Ann Arbor: University Microfilms International, 1991); E. Otto, 'Vom Bundesbuch zum Deuteronomium: Die deuteronomische Redaktion in Dtn 12–26', in G. Braulik, W. Gross and S. McEvenue (eds.), *Biblische Theologie und gesellschaftlicher Wandel: Für Norbert Lohfink SJ* (Freiburg: Herder, 1993), pp. 260-78; *idem*, 'Rechtsreformen in Deuteronomium XII–XXVI und im Mittelassyrischen Kodex der Tafel A (KAV 1)', in *Congress Volume of the XIV International Organization for the Study of the Old Testament Congress, Paris 1992* (ed. J.A. Emerton; VTSup; Leiden: Brill, 1995).

interpolation or revision, these phenomena require an explanation in terms of specific judicial issues which explain the apparent difficulties. From this perspective, it becomes clear the extent to which the legal collections are coherent compositions free of both legal-historical and textual development.

Taking up the challenge from the perspective of biblical law, I argue that, despite the claim of empirical grounding, Westbrook's interpretations often find no direct basis in the actual biblical text but rather supplement or revise it. Diachronic analysis, I maintain, more coherently accounts for the biblical text. Samuel Greengus, working from the perspective of cuneiform law, counters two of Westbrook's fundamental postulates: his assumption of a single, coherent 'common law' embracing the ancient Near East and Israel and his denial of legal-historical development. Martin Buss applies the distinction between natural and positive law to the question of whether or not the biblical and cuneiform legal collections were normative and binding and, if so, why they were not cited in contemporary documents.

Sophie Lafont systematically reexamines what biblical scholars presuppose when they speak of 'law', 'legal code', 'casuistic' or 'apodictic' law, and 'interpolation'. Arguing for cultural pluralism and against Westbrook's notion of a uniform 'common law' in the ancient Near East, she introduces new evidence for the creation of law by demonstrating the transformation of a private royal ruling into a general legal principle. Victor H. Matthews offers a social-scientific analysis of the institution of slavery in the ancient Near East and of the slave laws in the biblical text. He employs this model to argue that legal-historical development took place in ancient Israelite law, until canonization, as a necessary consequence of changes in the social world. William Morrow analyzes the origins of the second-person genre of legal formulation in the Covenant Code. He argues that it points to the combination of provisions from different legal traditions and thus to legal-literary development. Dale Patrick argues that important conceptual development did take place as Israelite authors developed their own systems of law and ethics. Form criticism, drawing on rhetorical theory, helps explain why the Covenant Code was composed. Finally, Eckart Otto provides an independent statement of the issues. He systematically marshals the evidence for legal-historical development and for literary revision within each of the cuneiform legal collections as well as within the Covenant Code and

Deuteronomy. He points to redactional structures that reveal extensive textual revision in the service of legal, ethical and theological ends.

I have received much help in editing this volume. Ms F. Rachel Magdalene, J.D., M.Div., expertly copy edited several of the papers, with an extraordinary eye for detail and a sensitive ear for language. Professor Martin Oosthuizen generously helped revise the English translation of Sophie Lafont's article, which I then further edited. Professor Victor H. Matthews incorporated editorial revisions into several articles, assisted with correspondence, and frequently helped discuss editorial matters. I am very grateful to all.

Bernard M. Levinson
Chair, Biblical Law Group
Society of Biblical Literature

WHAT IS THE COVENANT CODE?

Raymond Westbrook

It has long been recognized that the 'Book of the Covenant' (Exod. 20.22–23.19) forms a separate entity that has been inserted into the surrounding narrative. While the whole entity consists of normative provisions, it is easy to recognize a further section within it which may more properly be described as a law code, in that its norms are justiciable in a human (as opposed to divine) court and carry sanctions enforceable by such a court. The section in question is usually taken to extend from Exod. 21.1 to 22.16, but I would include the provisions of 22.17-19 since, although religious in character, they are likewise amenable to normal human jurisdiction, with corresponding sanctions. It is this section, the 'Covenant Code' strictly so called, that is the subject of this study, although many of the opinions that will be considered have been expressed in terms of the wider entity.

Legal interpretation of the Code's provisions is fraught with difficulties. Contradictions appear to abound between the various laws and even within them, while abrupt changes of form and syntax seem to break the thread of discourse. Even distinctions made by the laws themselves are hard to appreciate: why should the penalty for theft of an animal vary according to whether the thief has it alive in his possession or has slaughtered or sold it? Traditional commentaries employed numerous devices and rationalizations to arrive at a logical and systematic legal corpus; but the consensus of modern scholars is that the explanation for these discrepancies is historical. They are the result of a long and complex legislative process whereby the original text suffered repeated amendments and accretions in order to take into account developments in the law. Numerous studies of both the Code as a whole and of individual provisions have adopted this approach, which may be illustrated by the following examples.

Biblical scholars have, inevitably, applied to the Covenant Code the methods developed with respect to other genres of biblical literature such as psalms and narratives, in particular that of form criticism.[1] The fundamental study remains that of Alt, who distinguished between two types of laws on the basis of form: casuistic and apodictic.[2] The former, characterized by an if-clause ('If men fight. . . ') were taken to derive from the cuneiform law code tradition, via putative Canaanite codes, whereas the latter, characterized by concise commands ('Whosoever strikes a man and he dies shall be put to death'), were the indigenous product of ancient Israel. The two types of laws differed not only as to source but as to character, casuistic laws being dry, practical, and secular, apodictic laws being emotional imperatives dealing with religious and moral issues. More important still is their difference in substance. For example, the casuistic law of homicide took into account the culprit's intention, the apodictic law imposed talionic punishment.

Alt's claim of Israelite uniqueness for apodictic law has not been universally accepted, but his basic distinction has, together with the notion that the two forms are somehow different in source and content.[3] Furthermore, the existence in the Covenant Code of both forms closely intermingled and sharing features that were supposedly unique to one or the other (as, for example, the use of YHWH in a casuistic law in Exod. 22.10) obliged Alt to assume a complex process of redactional fusion, with secondary insertions and with deletions.[4] Again, this 'patchwork quilt' image of the law code has remained a necessary element in the historical explanation of its provisions.

Thus Otto in a recent monograph attributes to the two forms different origins within the internal history of Israelite law.[5]

---

1. See B. Baentsch, *Das Bundesbuch* (Halle: Niemayer, 1892); A. Jepsen, *Untersuchungen zum Bundesbuch* (BWANT, 41; Stuttgart: Kohlhammer, 1927); A. Jirku, *Das Weltliche Recht im Alten Testament* (Gütersloh: Bertelsmann, 1927).

2. A. Alt, 'Die Ursprünge des israelitischen Rechts' (1934), reprinted, *idem*, *Kleine Schriften*, I (Munich: Beck, 1959), pp. 278-332.

3. See T. Meek in *ANET*, 3rd edn, p. 183 n. 24; G. Mendenhall, 'Ancient Oriental and Biblical Law', *BA* 17 (1954), p. 30; J. Williams, 'Concerning One of the Apodictic Formulas', *VT* 14 (1964), pp. 484-89.

4. Alt, 'Ursprünge', pp. 294, 302-11.

5. E. Otto, *Wandel der Rechtsbegründungen in der Gesellschaftsgeschichte des antiken Israel* (Leiden: Brill, 1988); 'Interdependenzen zwischen Geschichte und Rechtsgeschichte des antiken Israels', *Rechtshistorisches Journal* 7 (1988), pp. 347-67.

Apodictic law arises from the jurisdiction of the paterfamilias within the family or clan. He has power to punish individual members, if necessary with the death penalty. The apodictic form, then, reflects the curt commands of the paterfamilias.

Casuistic law, on the other hand, arose from disputes between families within a tribe. It was not concerned with individuals although the dispute may have been triggered by individuals. Jurisdiction was that of the local court, which acted as an arbitrator. It had no coercive powers, since settlement of the dispute ultimately depended on the agreement of the two families. Accordingly, all judgments were compensatory in nature, with the exception of blood vengeance, where the parties took justice into their own hands. The casuistic form, then, reflects a series of precedents as to when compensation is appropriate.

With the advent of the monarchy, society became more complex, and according to Otto, this led to two developments. Patriarchal jurisdiction was taken over by the courts, which thereby developed a casuistic criminal law. The law of theft, for example, moved from simple compensation to twofold to four- and fivefold payment as the courts' jurisdiction became more penal. Secondly, casuistic law, which formerly had dealt with disputes between families on an equal footing, now had to deal with vertical disputes between rich and poor, which it achieved by developing a social law to protect the latter.

At the end of the process, therefore, there existed several independent bodies of law—casuistic civil law, casuistic criminal law, apodictic criminal law and casuistic social law—which came together under the jurisdiction of the local court. Their ultimate fusion is reflected in the Covenant Code, which interweaves these various sources.

For example, the group of laws from Exod. 21.33 to 22.14, which all contain the phrase 'he shall pay' (*yšlm*), can be seen to alternate between simple compensation and multiple compensation (= penalty).[6] An even more complex scheme of editing is proposed by Otto for 21.18-32.[7] Its core comprises two laws concerning a fight (vv. 18-19 and vv. 22-25). Both originally ended with payment, reflecting the early casuistic law's function as a compromise settlement. The interpretation of 'life for life' in v. 23, however, gave v. 22 a new role: it introduced the death penalty into casuistic law, giving the local

---

6. Otto, *Wandel*, pp. 12-14.
7. Otto, *Wandel*, pp. 28-30.

court the power of punishment. The interpolation of rules on the killing and the wounding of slaves (vv. 20-21 and vv. 26-27 respectively) after the two core laws added the dimension of social law. The interpolation of the talionic wounding rules (vv. 24-25) replaced compensation with punishment in all but a few special cases such as v. 18.

Other scholars have drawn different conclusions from the logic of legal development. In considering the theft provisions of Exod. 21.37–22.3, Daube points out that the passage comprises three rules which are not in their logical order: (a) the thief who slaughters and sells, (b) the right to kill a thief breaking in, (c) the thief who has not yet slaughtered and sold.[8] The logical order would have been for (c) to precede (b).

The logical order was not followed, however, because originally the law consisted of the two provisions: (a) and (b), while (c) is a later amendment. It was appended and not inserted, as logic would require, because the law was too well known in its traditional order.

The reason for adding the later provision, according to Daube, was a development in the law of evidence. The original law contained a crude, objective test—theft was not proven until the stolen object had been used. Later, a more sophisticated test developed whereby the subjective intentions of the thief were considered. If it could be ascertained that he had the intention to misappropriate, then possession alone would be sufficient to establish theft.

Similarly, Jackson attributes various features of the law concerning a pregnant woman to the incorporation by editors of reforms in the general law.[9] Thus the singular form 'you shall give' in v. 23 was interpolated to restrict liability to a single individual, *wntn bpllym* in v. 22 was interpolated to restrict the husband's claim by assessors, and, most subtly of all, the talionic wounding provisions in vv. 24-25 were added to change the context of the word *'swn* and thus shift its meaning from the death of the fetus to the death of the mother, without changing the original wording.

Finally, in his recent monograph dedicated to the Book of the Covenant, Schwienhorst-Schönberger proposes for the Covenant Code

8.   D. Daube, *Studies in Biblical Law* (Cambridge: Cambridge University Press, 1947), pp. 74-101.
9.   B. Jackson, *Essays in Jewish and Comparative Legal History* (Studies in Judaism in Late Antiquity, 10; Leiden: Brill, 1975), pp. 75-107.

the model of a pristine casuistic code, the provisions of which underwent expansion at three stages by different redactors, the first being secular, the second religious, and the third the Deuteronomist.[10] Each stage reflects legal and social developments, but is achieved only by interpolation in the previous text, not by amendment.

Thus, for example, in the deposit law (22.6-14), the pristine provision dealt only with injury or death to an ass, ox, or sheep entrusted or loaned (vv. 9, 10, 13).[11] The first redactor added the question of theft of goods deposited and a divine verdict procedure that included the aforementioned animals (vv. 6-8), while in v. 11 he covered for both categories the unresolved case of the depositee's responsibility where he is not the thief. The second redactor replaced the divine verdict with the YHWH oath (vv. 9-10), adding (*inter alia*) the generalizing words 'any animal' so as to change the meaning of v. 8 from divine verdict to oath by giving it a new context. As with Jackson, Schwienhorst-Schönberger ascribes great subtlety to the biblical redactors.

The above authors and the many others who espouse a historical explanation of the Covenant Code differ greatly as to the details of historical development and its reflection in the text. Their method, however, is uniform. It is based on no empirical evidence but upon identification of allusions in the text itself by the application to it of certain basic premises. Those premises are difficult to formulate because they are more usually assumed than stated and they are not shared to the same degree by all scholars.

I would suggest that the following three represent the widest consensus:

1. The Israelite legal system underwent radical development from 'primitive' law to a relatively sophisticated model.
2. The process is visible in the Covenant Code because the forms of its provisions are indicative of their content and/or source.
3. The process is also visible because of the manner of the Code's editing. The pristine text, although it reflected primitive law, was clear and logical. The present text is

---

10. L. Schwienhorst-Schönberger, *Das Bundesbuch* (BZAW, 188; Berlin: de Gruyter, 1990), esp. pp. 234-38.

11. *Bundesbuch*, pp. 194-211.

neither, because the radicalism of its redactors in matters of content was matched by their conservatism in matters of form. It was possible to add to, or rearrange, existing laws, but difficult to delete any part of their text, and simply to redraft them was out of the question.

Let us now consider whether, in the light of evidence available, these premises are justified.

1. *Primitive Law and Development*

Legal historians of the nineteenth century attributed various 'primitive' features to early law.[12] The most salient of those features were:

a. law exists between families, clans or tribes, not between individuals;
b. redress for individual wrongs took the form of feud between the groups to which the culprit and victim belonged;
c. the courts acted as arbitrators between such groups, seeking to find a just settlement but without power to enforce their judgments;
d. liability was strict, with no consideration of the culprit's intentions (so-called *Erfolgshaftung*).

Propositions of this kind constantly recur in scholars' analyses of the Covenant Code, without discussion of the evidence for them; they are taken as axiomatic.

It is not my purpose to enter into a general discussion of their validity, but merely to question whether the picture of early law that they present is at all applicable to the Israelite legal system, at least within the termini for composition of the Covenant Code.

Thanks to cuneiform records, evidence for the history of law in the ancient Near East now extends back to the early third millennium. The very earliest records, however, already reveal a highly organized legal system, whose courts have full coercive power and whose individuals have the capacity to make contracts. Nor are third millennium sources ignorant of the significance of intention in

12. See H. Maine, *Ancient Law* (Tucson: University of Arizona Press, 1986 [1861]).

determining liability.[13] As is well known, the Sumero-Akkadian civilization that produced this legal system spread throughout Western Asia through the medium of cuneiform writing. Its influence is already attested in Syria in the third millennium, at Ebla, and legal documents drafted in Akkadian from Alalah and Hazor show that not merely the writing but the legal culture itself was established in Syria-Palestine by the early second millennium.[14]

The implications for Israelite law are clear. Any primitive stage must either have predated the second millennium (at the very least) or reflect early Israel's total isolation from the surrounding societies. The first is a chronological impossibility and the second, inherently improbable, is all the more so in the context of the Covenant Code.

Some earlier commentators such as Morgenstern sought to deny any connection between the Covenant Code and the cuneiform law codes, but their position has become untenable in view of the accumulation of parallels.[15] More than half of the Covenant Code's provisions have some parallel in one or more of the cuneiform codes, whether in the form of the same problem addressed or distinction applied, a similar rule, or an identical rule.[16] It is difficult to see how provisions that are so closely associated with an outside source can at the same time be the product of internal development from an earlier primitive version.

The difficulty is seen by Otto, who by way of answer suggests that the cuneiform element in the Covenant Code is due not so much to direct influence as to the fact that Israelite law was part of a common legal culture of the ancient Near East. That culture merely forms the framework within which the Israelite and other legal systems develop.[17]

Otto's answer raises the whole question of legal development in ancient Near Eastern law. At first sight, it may seem obvious to

13. CU 7 (ed. F. Yildiz, 'A Tablet of Codex Ur-Nammu from Sippar', *Or* 50 [1981], pp. 92, 96). The adulterer's ignorance of the woman's married status relieves him of liability.

14. D. Wiseman, *The Alalakh Tablets* (London: British School of Archaeology in Ankara, 1953); W. Hallo and H. Tadmor, 'A Lawsuit from Hazor', *IEJ* 27 (1977), pp. 1-11.

15. J. Morgenstern, 'The Book of the Covenant, Pt. 2', *HUCA* 7 (1930), p. 68 n. 70.

16. See S. Paul, *Studies in the Book of the Covenant in the Light of Cuneiform and Biblical Law* (VTSup, 18; Leiden: Brill, 1970), pp. 43-105.

17. Otto, 'Interdependenzen', pp. 366-67.

assume that legal systems would change and develop considerably over hundreds, indeed thousands, of years. That, however, is an attitude derived from our own culture, where constant changes in technology, social structure, and ideology raise concomitant demands for reform of the law, demands which are met by the investment of considerable intellectual effort on the part of trained specialists.

The most striking feature of the cuneiform legal material, on the other hand, is its static nature. The basic pattern of contractual transactions found in Sumerian legal documents of the third millennium survives, differences of detail notwithstanding, throughout the cuneiform record.[18] Some contractual terms, indeed, survive even longer, passing into Aramaic and Demotic documents.[19] Continuity is no less evident in the law codes, where the same rules, tests, and distinctions recur in codes separated by hundreds of years. Of course, there are also discrepancies between the codes, but discrepancies do not necessarily betoken a significant development in the law.

It should be remembered firstly that the codes do not give anything approaching a complete account of their legal system or even of any given area of law. It is dangerous, therefore, to argue from the silence of a code on a particular point of law for its absence from that legal system.

Secondly, the circumstances of two cases are seldom the same. In applying rules to an amorphous set of facts, a court will have any number of distinctions to make, as to status, wealth, intention, causation, remoteness of damage, etc. Casuistic codes cannot put into their paradigmatic cases every possible circumstance and will inevitably tend either to blur all distinctions if they are too general or to emphasize one distinction to the neglect of others if they are more

18. See D. Edzard, *Sumerische Rechtsurkunden des III. Jahrtausends* (Munich: Bayerische Akademie der Wissenschaften, 1968), No.43 (24th century); M. Schorr *Urkunden des Altbabylonischen Zivil- und Prozessrechts* (Vorderasiatische Bibliothek, 5; Leipzig: Hinrich, 1913), No.79 (18th century); H. Petschow, *Mittelbabylonische Rechts- und Wirtschaftsurkunden der Hilprecht Sammlung Jena* (Berlin: Akademie-Verlag, 1974), No.1 (14th century); T. Kwasman and S. Parpola, *Legal Transactions of the Royal Court of Nineveh*, Part I (State Archives of Assyria, 6; Helsinki: Helsinki University Press, 1991), No. 98 (7th century); M. San Nicolo and H. Petschow, *Babylonische Rechtsurkunden aus dem 6. Jahrhundert v. Chr.* (Munich: Bayerische Akademie der Wissenschaften, 1960), No.17 (6th century).

19. J. Muffs, *Studies in Aramaic Legal Papyri from Elephantine* (Studia et Documenta ad Iura Orientis Antiqui Pertinentia, 8; Leiden: Brill, 1969).

specific. Patterns of emphasis may be seen in certain codes: between classes of society in Codex Hammurabi, between classes of animal in the Hittite Laws. Rudiments of the same distinctions can be seen in all the codes; differences between them are a matter of degree of emphasis.

Thirdly, differences between the codes may be more apparent than real. As an example I would cite the difference between physical and pecuniary punishments, which has long been seen as signalling the dividing line between primitive and developed law. The earlier view was that a change from physical to pecuniary punishments marked the crucial development from feud to law.[20] It was supported by the appearance of the former in Codex Hammurabi and the latter in the Hittite Laws. It was challenged when earlier codes than Codex Hammurabi were discovered, Codex Ur-Nammu and Codex Eshnunna, which contained only pecuniary punishments. The development was then said to be from civil law (pecuniary) to criminal law (physical).[21]

There remained, however, the question of what line of development was followed. A general development of ancient Near Eastern culture could not apply because the movement was not chronological—the Hittites retained the 'older' system of civil law. For the same reason, there could be no question of a slow and imperceptible development (as opposed to deliberate reform). In any case, the Hittites undoubtedly knew the text of Codex Hammurabi and Codex Eshnunna predates Codex Hammurabi by about forty years only.[22] The answer was to make value judgments upon the civilizations in question: the Sumerians, Eshnunnans, and Hittites were more 'primitive' than the Babylonians or the Assyrians.[23] Such judgments, however, were based solely on this one difference in their respective law codes; our knowledge of those cultures would demand no such conclusion. Imposing a developmental model on apparent differences between law codes entails assumptions about the surrounding culture and society

20. G. Driver and J. Miles, *The Babylonian Laws,* I (Oxford: Oxford University Press, 1952), pp. 501-502.

21. A. Diamond, 'An Eye for an Eye', *Iraq* 19 (1957), pp. 151-55.

22. G. Cardascia, 'La Transmission des sources juridiques cunéiformes', *Revue International des Droits de l'Antiquité* 7 (1960), pp. 43-50.

23. Diamond, 'An Eye for an Eye', pp. 154-55; Cf. J. Finkelstein, 'Ammi-saduqa's Edict and the Babylonian "Law Codes"', *JCS* 15 (1961), pp. 96-99.

that are not warranted by the empirical evidence. There is empirical evidence, however, that (in the guise of revenge and ransom) physical and pecuniary punishments could be two sides of the same coin, and on this basis we have argued elsewhere that the societies in question all enjoyed the same system of punishment throughout.[24] Where they differed was in the exact limits to be imposed on revenge and ransom—as represented in the codes by physical and pecuniary punishments respectively—and whether the latter was to take precedence over the former in the particular case. No evolution was involved, therefore, but an exercise of discretion that could vary from case to case, from court to court and from system to system.

Fourthly, consideration must be given to the nature of the law codes themselves. If they were legislation in the modern sense, then they could be expected to furnish reforms as part of their intrinsic purpose. It has been persuasively argued, however, by Kraus and others that the law codes were essentially academic documents, which may accurately have described the law but did not prescribe it.[25] They were, therefore, conduits of tradition rather than of change.

Furthermore, with one important exception (the Hittite laws, to be discussed below), there is no consciousness of reform in the law codes. The kings who are their supposed authors do not boast of changes made in the system by the codes, nor is there any indication of their rules being valid from a particular point in time. The codes have a timeless quality, as perhaps befits an academic document. External evidence likewise gives no hint of awareness of the code's impact. The often monumental reforms posited by scholars find no echo in inscriptions, letters, or legal and administrative documents.

Given the fragmentary state of textual evidence, the preceding statement might be considered an unacceptable argument from silence were it not for the fact that we have ample evidence that a different genre of legal text was consciously seen as reforming the law. The royal edicts both proclaimed themselves as reforms, changing legal rules from a particular point in time, and were regarded in contemporary documents as having such an impact, with corresponding

---

24. R. Westbrook, *Studies in Biblical and Cuneiform Law* (CahRB, 26; Paris: Gabalda, 1988), pp. 39-77.

25. F.R. Kraus, 'Was ist der Codex Hammurabi?', *Genava* 8 (1960), pp. 283-96; J. Bottéro, 'Le "Code" de Hammurabi', *Annali della Scuola Normale Superiore di Pisa* 12 (1982), pp. 409-44.

reactions from persons affected by them.[26] Such edicts, however, were remarkable for the narrowness of their scope. Only three categories of reform are recorded in them: retrospective cancellation of debts, reorganization of the royal administration, and the fixing of prices (which in this context also means pecuniary penalties, including fixed limits on ransom). Any reforms, therefore, that are attributed to differences between law codes will only be credible if they fall within those three categories, pending further empirical evidence to the contrary.

This hypothesis as to the limits of reform can be tested by reference to the Hittite Laws, which contain two special features. Firstly, unlike the other codes, they do exhibit some consciousness of reform. The most common expression thereof is the much-repeated phrase 'formerly they gave x shekels, now he shall give y shekels' in respect of payments by way of penalty.[27] It thus falls within the category of price-fixing and may possibly be recording the provision of an edict or edicts to that effect, especially in view of the other expression of reform, which actually narrates the legislative history of the measure.[28] In paragraph 55 we are told that the king's father in the assembly had altered the status of certain feudal tenants in response to their petition. This reform falls squarely within the category of administrative reorganization.

Secondly, we possess one tablet of the law code (KBo VI 4) that, by

26. See the literature cited in Westbrook, 'Cuneiform Law Codes and the Origins of Legislation', *ZA* 79 (1989), pp. 214-16.

27. See para. 9, where the king also relinquishes his share of the payment. Cf. the Edict of Uru'inimgina (ed. J. Cooper, *Sumerian and Akkadian Royal Inscriptions* [New Haven: American Oriental Society, 1986], No. La 9.3 i-iii).

28. Para. 92 replaces revenge for theft of bee-hives (by stinging) with a fixed ransom. This combines price-fixing with the court's function of setting a limit on revenge and ransom, which may sometimes lead it to give fixed ransom precedence over revenge. On the other hand, para. 166 replaces a ceremony whereby a man and oxen are killed with a sacrifice of sheep as substitutes. This would appear to be a purification ritual, unconnected with revenge, and the reform is therefore of a religious nature (cf. paras. 196, 199). The scope of reform in the religious sphere is a question that requires separate study. It should be noted, however, that the possibility of substitution of an animal for the culprit in the sacrifice was an integral part of the system, as attested in the biblical scapegoat and even in early rabbinic sources. See P. Segal, 'Postbiblical Jewish Criminal Law and Theology', *Jewish Law Annual* 9 (1989), pp. 107-18.

its language, appears to be later than the version recorded in the other copies. It contains numerous differences from the main version and the question thus arises whether those differences represent substantive reforms.[29]

The major difference again lies in the scale of payments by way of penalty. In some cases, the medium of payment has also been changed—from slaves or land into silver—but that is a matter of accountancy rather than law, since it must always have been possible to pay in silver as well as in kind. Where the amount of silver payable has been changed, however, we might seem to be in the presence of a substantive reform. Nonetheless, it is no more than price-fixing.

The second difference takes the form of additional circumstances not covered by the original protasis. They consist of variations, such as in the type of property lost,[30] the type of tax payable,[31] the type of victim[32] or the type of land on which the offense was committed,[33] or of distinctions, such as those between provocation and negligence[34] or between temporary and disabling injury.[35] These variations and distinctions are not reforms at all, but scholarly refinement, using the characteristic academic method of the codes, of extrapolating variants from the original cases. Some of these variants, indeed, are themselves found elsewhere in the earlier version.

The third difference consists of omissions. Such is the fate of the phrase *parnassea suwaizzi* ('he shall push/peep(?)' to his house), which occurs frequently in the apodosis of paragraphs in the earlier version,

---

29. In an earlier study, following (uncritically) the opinion of A. Goetze (*Kleinasien* [Munich: Beck, 2nd edn, 1957], pp. 110-11), I did indeed assume that the references to reduction of penalties in the Hittite Laws and the existence of KBo VI 4 in particular indicated substantive law reforms (Westbrook, 'Biblical and Cuneiform Law Codes', *RB* 92 [1985], pp. 255-56). While rejecting that assumption here, I retain the view espoused by my earlier study that the law codes could have a practical application. I would only emphasize that they functioned as consultative documents rather than authoritative legislation. For the latter distinction, see Bottéro, 'Le "Code" de Hammurabi', pp. 435-38 and Westbrook, 'Cuneiform Law Codes and the Origins of Legislation', p. 202.

30. XXXV (= 45 of the older version), cf. III (= 5).
31. XXXVII (= 47).
32. IX (= 10).
33. IV (= 6).
34. III (= 5), V-VII (= 7-8).
35. X-XI (= 11-12).

but only once in the later version.[36] Both the meaning of the phrase, however, and the rationale for its being appended to specific laws remain obscure.[37] No conclusions can therefore be drawn as to the legal import of its omission from later parallels. In two instances an alternative circumstance is omitted from the protasis, thereby eliminating a distinction made by the earlier version. In the first instance, the case of a merchant killed abroad (as opposed to one killed in Hatti),[38] it is of no legal significance, but the second, concerning the month of pregnancy in which a miscarriage was caused, might signal a change in the law.[39] Since the sole consequence of the distinction, however, lay in the amount payable by way of penalty, we are once more in the realm of price-fixing.

The fourth difference consists in additional legal consequences. Thus where the earlier version mentions only that the offender is deemed a thief, the later version adds the penalty applicable.[40] For all we know, the same penalty may have been applicable in the earlier version, and if not, it is again a question of price-fixing. In the second example of this type, the king is granted a discretion over the amount of a certain type of feudal due.[41] If this were an innovation, then it falls within the sphere of administrative reform.

In summary, the Hittite Laws, which afford us a unique diachronic view of a cuneiform legal system, provide little evidence of substantive change and such evidence as they do provide lies within the narrow categories of reform found in royal edicts.

This image of a static legal system should be less surprising if regard is had for the nature of the society that produced it. From the mid-third millennium to the end of the Bronze Age, the Near East saw no major advance in technology nor any radical change in social or

36. XII (= 13).

37. R. Haase suggests that the phrase gives the judgment creditor the right to 'look into the house' of the judgment debtor, i.e., to distrain upon his property ('Gedanken zur Formel *parnasseia suwaizzi* in den hethitischen Gesetzen', *WO* 11 [1980], pp. 93-98). This theory does not explain, however, why a procedural facility which should in principle be available to any judgment creditor is expressly mentioned in only a limited number of delicts, nor why any law reform should wish to remove it in some, but not all, cases.

38. III (= 5).

39. XVI-XVII (= 17-18).

40. XXXV (= 45).

41. XXXIXb (= 47b).

political structure. Intellectual expression was dominated by Mesopotamian 'science', a form of logic severely handicapped by inability to define terms, create general categories, or reason vertically from the general to the particular.[42] A legal system cannot be more advanced than its social and intellectual environment: the social environment was hostile to change, while the intellectual environment lacked the tools to give legal expression to anything more than superficial reforms.

Beginning in the seventh century, the intellectual revolution documented in the Greek sources led to sweeping changes in the way that law was conceived and ultimately provided it with the intellectual tools for reforms to match the radical changes in social and political structures. The system that emerged remains the norm for us today. Its Near Eastern predecessor, on the other hand, was already a mature system when it first becomes accessible to us in Sumerian sources of the third millennium. The intellectual revolution that produced it lies further back in time, at a turning-point about which we can only speculate, whether it was the smelting of bronze, urbanization, or even the agricultural revolution. The common legal culture of the ancient Near East would not, then, have provided a framework for legal development in the Covenant Code.

The later biblical codes—the Deuteronomic and Priestly codes— share something of the intellectual ferment of contemporary Greek sources and thus some taste also of their new legal conceptions. The Covenant Code, on the other hand, although it cannot be dated with any confidence, looks back to the cuneiform codes of the second and third millennia. It is in the light of that long and stable tradition that the two remaining premises as to its form and composition are to be judged.

2. *Forms in the Covenant Code*

The predominant form in the Covenant Code is casuistic, as is characteristic also of its cuneiform predecessors. Seven laws are in apodictic form, grouped in two blocks: 21.12, 15-17 and 22.17-19. The question that concerns us is whether the difference in form is of *legal* significance, either because the laws derive from a different

---

42. For the application of Mesopotamian science to law, see Bottéro, 'Le "Code" de Hammurabi', pp. 425-35, and Westbrook, *Studies*, pp. 2-5.

jurisdiction (foreign, patriarchal, sacral, etc.) or because they represent different stages of legal development.

It has been pointed out by scholars that apodictic forms, as defined by Alt, do occur in the cuneiform codes, albeit rarely.[43] Alt's hypothesis of a purely Israelite origin for apodictic law cannot, therefore, stand. Furthermore, it is hard to discern any pattern in the isolated instances of apodictic form in the cuneiform codes. In Codex Hammurabi, it occurs in paragraphs 36-40, all of which concern limitations on the rights of tenants over their feudal holdings. It might, therefore, be argued that its use is connected with its original function—administrative orders from the palace concerning its feudal tenants, especially since the only apodictic form in the Hittite Laws (paragraph 56) also concerns feudal tenants.[44] On the other hand, there are many similar provisions in the two codes which concern feudal tenants but are drafted casuistically. Codex Eshnunna, paragraphs 51-52, concerning slaves entering and leaving the city, might have some connection with the city administration, but no such connection is apparent in paragraphs 15-16, which place restrictions on the commercial activities of slaves and sons. The same can be said of the only apodictic provision in the Middle Assyrian Laws (A 40), listing the classes of woman who must or must not veil themselves in public. In sum, there is no obvious common factor in these diverse provisions in source or content and certainly no indication that they might represent types of jurisdiction or levels of legal development.

If the apodictic forms furnish no special rationale for their occasional use in the law codes, perhaps our inquiry should be in the opposite direction, namely as to why the *casuistic* form came to be the dominant form of the codes. It is not, after all, a natural form for a source of law. Judgments are based on actual, not hypothetical, facts and are rendered with reference to the parties in the case, in the form of a specific order. Such is the case, for example, in the various literary accounts of trials from Nippur, which, it has been suggested, may be sources for the law codes.[45] Royal decrees would also tend to

43. See n. 3 above.

44. Cf. R. Yaron, *Laws of Eshnunna* (Jerusalem: Magnes Press, 2nd edn, 1988), p. 108. Mainly on the basis of form, Yaron divides the provisions of Codex Eshnunna into two groups: those derived from a decree and those based on precedent, while admitting the speculative character of the enterprise (pp. 106-13).

45. C. Locher, *Die Ehre einer Frau in Israel* (OBO, 70; Freiburg,

be in the form of direct, if more general, orders. That is indeed the dominant form in administrative and debt-release edicts and in instructions to officials.[46] Price-fixing, on the other hand, would simply be by lists of the goods or services and their corresponding price, usually expressed as a statement of fact. Apart from the latter then, all sources of law would tend to be expressed in some kind of apodictic form.

The casuistic form was the quintessential 'scientific' type of Mesopotamian literature, as attested in the omen and medical texts. It was the means whereby raw data could be cast into a generalized, objective form, stripped of any connections with circumstances irrelevant to their universal application. It was the nearest Mesopotamian science could come to expressing principles. The casuistic form, therefore, far from reflecting any particular source of law, was itself a process of editing, creating a uniform body of rules indifferent to their origins.

It would be naive, however, to conclude that a non-casuistic form always betokens an original legal source. The bulk of law in ancient Near Eastern societies was traditional law handed down from time immemorial. It was, however, regarded as having come from specific judgments, orders or the like, an assumption that could be expressed by giving a traditional rule the form of one of those sources.[47] This is why the apodictic rules of the cuneiform codes cannot be assigned to legal categories. The choice of form for the individual paragraphs of what was essentially a literary document, belonging (as we have argued above) to the genre 'academic treatise', was not a legal one but depended on other factors, perhaps pedagogical or rhetorical. The casuistic form, for all its scientific credentials, was not always the ideal vehicle for the latter purposes, nor did all the cuneiform codes share the same desire for uniformity. Codex Hammurabi is the most extreme, placing even price lists in casuistic form, although the result

Schweiz: Universitätsverlag, 1986), pp. 93-109.

46. See e.g., the Edict of Ammiṣaduqa (ed. F. Kraus, *Königliche Verfügungen in Altbabylonischer Zeit* [Studia et Documenta ad Iura Orientis Antiqui Pertinentia, 11; Leiden: Brill, 1984], pp. 168-83) and the Hittite Instructions to the Commander of the Border Guards (ed. E. von Schuler, *Hethitische Dienstanweisungen* [*AfO* Beiheft, 10; Osnabruck: Biblio-Verlag, 1957], pp. 41-52).

47. See Codex Hammurabi, Epilogue, col. 47:1-5 and compare Exod. 21.1 itself, which attributes the code to judgments (*mšptym*) given by God.

is clumsy and unsuitable (268-277), while Codex Eshnunna (1-4, 7-8, 10-11, 14) and the Hittite Laws (178-185) present their tariffs as bald statements. At the other end of the spectrum, Codex Eshnunna presents a mixture of styles, which may more accurately represent the 'peripheral' tradition to which the Covenant Code belongs. In contrast to the 'core' tradition of southern Mesopotamia, which is a direct heir to Sumerian civilization, the Akkadian-speaking areas of northern Mesopotamia share with the rest of the fertile crescent, where cuneiform learning was acquired primarily through the medium of Akkadian (Susa, Nuzi, Hatti, Emar, Ugarit, Hazor, etc.), a tradition of legal drafting that is less austere and more heterogeneous.[48]

Turning to the apodictic laws of the Covenant Code, we see that they are no less diverse in content than their cuneiform counterparts, covering murder, striking or cursing parents, kidnapping, witchcraft, bestiality and heretical sacrifice. The only unifying factor is that they are all very serious offenses, requiring the death penalty, but then so does the casuistically formulated case of the goring ox (Exod. 21.29). Two of the offenses involve inner-family relations, which is a slim basis on which to conclude, as Otto does, that the apodictic form had its origins in inner-family jurisdiction.[49] The first group comprises private delicts involving a victim, while the second consists of victimless crimes, in which the public interest is engaged.

A further test of their unique status is whether these provisions have an equivalent in the cuneiform codes and if so whether those equivalents form any special category. Two laws, cursing parents and heretical sacrifice, have no equivalent, which might give them special status were it not for the other five.

The homicide rule of Exod. 21.12, 'He who strikes a man and he dies shall be put to death', is directly paralleled by the casuistically formulated paragraph 1 of Codex Ur-Nammu: 'If a man kills, that man shall be put to death'.[50] The Sumerian law is couched in the same stark tones as the biblical law, with no mention of the question of intention—which is, I hasten to add, no evidence that intention was not taken into consideration.[51] Much has been made of the fact that the

48. See Muffs, *Studies*, pp. 17-23.

49. Otto, *Wandel*, pp. 31-33.

50. Ed. Yildiz, 'A Tablet of Codex Ur-Nammu', pp. 91, 95.

51. Codex Ur-Nammu is particularly laconic, leaving out details that are supplied by parallels from later laws. For an example, see Westbrook, 'Adultery in

question of intention in the biblical law is couched in casuistic form immediately following upon the above apodictic rule, thereby opening the door to a distinction between the 'primitive' strict liability of the apodictic law and the more enlightened casuistic law.[52] I would view the proposed distinction with skepticism, in the light of the *casuistic* cuneiform law above and in the light of paragraph 40 of Tablet A of the Middle Assyrian Laws. The latter begins with a series of apodictic commands concerning the veiling of women, which reveal themselves, however, to be no more than the necessary preamble to the casuistic part of the law, which lays down punishments for men who fail to report infringements of the veiling regulations. In the same way, the apodictic rule of Exod. 21.12 can be seen as the necessary preamble to the casuistic rules of vv. 13-14, which distinguish between intentional and non-intentional homicide.

The cuneiform codes likewise furnish casuistic parallels for kidnapping (Codex Hammurabi 14: death), striking a parent (Codex Hammurabi 195: cut off hand), witchcraft (Middle Assyrian Laws A 47: death) and bestiality (Hittite Laws 187-188, 199-200: death or no liability, depending on animal). There is nothing in these parallels to suggest that they come from a special source or contain a special legal content. I conclude that the same must apply to the biblical provisions. As we have seen with the apodictic rules of the cuneiform codes, the reason for their formulation does not lie with legal considerations. Depending on the literary tradition, the same rule may be drafted casuistically, apodictically, or in some other fashion.

3. *The Text of the Covenant Code*

The idea of a conservative editing of the text, by exclusion, addition, and interpolation in order to make it comply with changes in the law has one certain historical model, indeed, a model of monumental proportions. The Digest of Justinian, from the sixth century CE, one of the greatest achievements in the history of law, was just such a compilation. At that time, the writings of classical jurists from some three centuries earlier were cited in court as binding authority, which led to great confusion and inconvenience, since, on the one hand,

---

Ancient Near Eastern Law', *RB* 97 (1990), p. 550.

52. E.g., M. Noth, *Exodus* (Philadelphia: Westminster, 1962), p. 180; B. Childs, *The Book of Exodus* (Philadelphia: Westminster, 1974), p. 470.

much was no longer applicable to the conditions of the Byzantine empire and, on the other, they contained innumerable disputes and contradictions. Several committees were, therefore, charged with excerpting from those writings such material as could produce a relevant and coherent body of law. Under the guiding hand of a law professor, Tribonian, they completed the massive task in a mere three years but only at the cost of considerable tampering with their sources. Each excerpt was cited by author, work, chapter, and verse, but by editing, in particular by interpolation, the passage cited was brought into line with contemporary law. The process inevitably left inconsistencies in style and content which can be identified by modern scholars.

In the early years after the discovery of Codex Hammurabi, King Hammurabi was indeed regarded by some scholars as an early Justinian. An eminent legal historian schooled in Roman law, P. Koschaker, attempted to apply the techniques of that field to the cuneiform code. His approach lacked any historical justification, however; the peculiar circumstances of the late Roman Empire, its legal system and its intellectual climate that led to the compiling of the Digest could not be reproduced in the second millennium BCE. Instead, apparent inconsistencies in the provisions of the cuneiform codes are progressively being dissipated through our growing understanding of their linguistic, cultural, and social background, due not least to the continuous stream of newly discovered cuneiform documents.[53]

53. See Codex Hammurabi, para. 164, which Koschaker suggested was an interpolation because of its clumsy and over-elaborate discussion of a set-off mechanism (*Rechtsvergleichende Studien zur Gesetzgebung Hammurapis* [Leipzig: Hinrichs, 1917], pp. 87 n.6, 187-88). It was subsequently discovered, however, that the paragraph was in fact taking into consideration a certain marriage custom, in the light of which (and with a different interpretation of the syntax) the paragraph was well formulated and perfectly appropriate: for discussion and references, see Yaron, *Eshnunna*, pp. 176-79. The one case where Koschaker's approach is generally thought to have been vindicated is Codex Hammurabi, para. 125, where his postulated development of the law is said to have been confirmed by the subsequent discovery of Codex Eshnunna, paras. 36-37, containing an earlier, more 'primitive' rule (Koschaker, *Rechtsvergleichende Studien*, pp. 26-33; see also A. Goetze, *The Laws of Eshnunna* [AASOR, 31; New Haven: American Schools of Oriental Research, 1956], p. 104; Yaron, *Eshnunna*, pp. 250-251; E. Otto, 'Die rechtshistorische Entwicklung des Depositenrechts in altorientalischen und

By the same token, it is inappropriate and anachronistic to apply, consciously or unconsciously, the model of Justinian's Digest to the editing of the Covenant Code. The Bible has no background documentation like the cuneiform codes, but the Covenant Code has a ready substitute for such documentation in the cuneiform codes themselves, since it belongs to the same literary genre and the same intellectual tradition as the latter.

As we have seen, one of the cuneiform codes, HL, has at least two chronologically separate versions, and can therefore provide explicit evidence of the process of editing that may be expected in texts of this genre.[54] While the two versions were seen to differ but little in substance, the same is not so for their form, which presents many variants. A good proportion may be dismissed as deriving from the peculiarities of the cuneiform script (variant spellings, use of Sumerograms) or of the Hittite language (use of active instead of medio-passive),[55] but some changes in language are more radical, for example, the earliest version's 'strikes and wounds' (*hunikzi...istarninkzi*, 10) is replaced by 'injures the head' (SAG.DU *hapallasai*, IX). Of relevance here is Hoffner's discussion of a fragment of a version still earlier than the main text (164-66), written in the Old Ductus.[56] Although the two versions contain the same law, Hoffner points to considerable differences of language, which he ascribes to a desire by the later scribe to modernize archaic expressions. A more serious reason for change is provided by IV of the later version, which extends the circumstances discussed to cover a murder committed on land outside the city. Accordingly the expression 'in another city' (*takiya* URU-*ri*) in the earlier version (6) is changed to 'in another field and meadow' (*damedani* A.ŠÀ A.GÀR). Finally a

---

altisraelitischen Rechtskorpora', *Zeitschrift der Savigny Stiftung [Rom.Abt.]* 105 [1988], pp. 4-16). All such comparisons, however, rely on translations that disregard certain difficulties in the text. See my forthcoming study of the term *napṭaru* in *JCS*.

54. Among biblical scholars, only L. Schwienhorst-Schönberger has noticed this possibility. He employs it in a single, isolated instance, without considering the wider implications (*Bundesbuch*, p. 121).

55. 15, 16 = XIV, XV.

56. H. Hoffner, 'The Old Hittite Version of Laws 164-166', *JCS* 33 (1981), pp. 206-209.

most telling change of style occurs between 48 and XL—from apodictic to casuistic.

The important point about these changes, and the much more frequent additions and omissions in the later text, is that they are achieved without disrupting the logic of the provision or the thread of their discourse in any way. Were there no extant earlier version of the text, one would scarcely be aware from the later versions that it had ever existed, the presence of scattered archaisms in the language being the only indication. It would certainly be impossible to reconstruct anything of the earlier version. The assumption, therefore, that the process of editing the Covenant Code left tell-tale traces in the form of inconsistencies can only be justified by reference to a model far removed from it intellectually and culturally, while a model that stands in the same intellectual tradition supports no such conclusions. At most, the tendency that we have seen in the later version of the Hittite Laws, after the method of cuneiform science, to add new circumstances might justify concluding that in the Covenant Code as well certain rules subsidiary to a main problem, such as the distinction between a warned and unwarned ox in the case of ox goring ox, were secondary accretions.[57] Unless, however, they signify some change in the substantive law, it is an arid exercise to speculate as to which components of a legal problem are 'original' and which are a later accretion.

It could be argued that, the Hittite evidence notwithstanding, so special is the character of the biblical law and its role in the religious life of ancient Israel that its texts nonetheless acquired a canonicity that demanded more conservative editing. The Bible itself, however, attests to the contrary. There is a salient example within the Bible of the same law existing in an earlier and later version: the slave-release law of Exod. 21.2-6 and Deut. 15.12-18. The Deuteronomic version pays no respect to the earlier text, but changes the person of the verb and the identity of the slave and makes the transaction *ex latere venditoris* (from the seller's point of view) rather than *ex latere emptoris* (from the buyer's point of view).

Accordingly, the premise of a conservative process of editing is not supported by empirical evidence, external or internal. The present text must be presumed to be clear and coherent. At most, one might

---

57. Cf. Schwienhorst-Schönberger, *Bundesbuch*, p. 121.

argue for the minor editorial emendations and glosses that could be found in any genre of text.

Conclusions

Conventional wisdom regards the Covenant Code as an amalgam of provisions from different sources and periods, the fusion of which has left tell-tale marks in the form of various inconsistencies in the text. That view is based upon assumptions as to the history of the law and its expression which are unsupported by empirical evidence. At most, they can rely on inappropriate models from the classical and later periods.

Such models may have been acceptable in the last century, but since the discovery of massive quantities of cuneiform sources, they are no longer so. Interpreters of the Covenant Code need to come to terms with the fact that it is part of a widespread literary-legal tradition and can only be understood in terms of that tradition.[58] The starting point for interpretation must therefore be the presumption that the Covenant Code is a coherent text comprising clear and consistent laws, in the same manner as its cuneiform forbears. Apparent inconsistencies should be ascribed to the state of our ignorance concerning the social and cultural background to the laws, not necessarily to historical development and certainly not to an excess of either subtlety or incompetence on the part of their compiler.

---

58. See now M. Malul, *The Comparative Method in Ancient Near Eastern and Biblical Legal Studies* (AOAT, 227; Neukirchen–Vluyn: Neukirchener Verlag, 1990), pp. 140-43, arguing for a close literary dependence of the Covenant Code on the Mesopotamian law codes.

THE CASE FOR REVISION AND INTERPOLATION WITHIN THE BIBLICAL LEGAL CORPORA

Bernard M. Levinson

In 'What is the Covenant Code?', Raymond Westbrook brings to bear on a specific corpus of biblical law the entire range of critical insights that he has developed over the past decade and which culminated in his recent book, *Studies in Biblical and Cuneiform Law*.[1] Informed by that larger perspective, Westbrook here challenges the methodological and theoretical assumptions that govern rival approaches. Conventional literary and historical criticism bear the brunt of this critique. Westbrook contends that diachronic analysis, whether applied to the biblical or the cuneiform legal collections, is methodologically invalid and its assumptions illegitimate. Ostensible textual inconsistencies, redundancies or contradictions should not be diachronically resolved: they do not betray the work of later editors who revise or rework earlier material and do not represent additions or interpolations.

Westbrook argues that such assumptions about the composition and editing of biblical and cuneiform law lack empirical evidence. 'Empirical' is a key word in the essay: the thesis is that the compositional norms of the cuneiform legal collections mandate a different methodological stance than the diachronic one conventionally employed. The synchronic method is alone valid. The legal collections are 'coherent text[s] comprising clear and consistent laws'.[2] In other words, they possess original compositional unity, free of the imprint of secondary reworking. Moreover, the very assumption that such activity has taken place and that diachronic analysis is necessary to resolve the textual problems represents the imposition of an alien cultural paradigm. While diachronic analysis is entirely justified in the

---

1. CahRB, 26; Paris: Gabalda, 1988.
2. R. Westbrook, 'What is the Covenant Code?', in this volume, p. 36. Subsequent references to this article will be provided in parentheses.

context of Roman law (Justinian's *Digest*), its application to cuneiform and biblical law is invalid.

Although it is not explicit in this essay, Westbrook's approach entails an additional basic interpretive stance. In his book he extends the argument regarding the internal coherence of the individual legal collections to their external coherence relative to one another. Just as there are no inconsistencies or redundancies internal to the sundry collections—so too in absolute terms do the various legal corpora cohere in relation to one another. Each provides partial witness to a more systematic 'common law' that subsumes the specific cases selected for discussion by the drafters of a particular legal corpus.

Westbrook thus assumes a 'meta-coherence' of all the legal collections relative to one another. Indeed, this assumption motivates his overall interpretive project, which is to unify and systematize that which has only fragmentary expression in a given corpus: 'Our approach is a holistic one: to reconstruct the legal problem from all the sources available'.[3] In light of this larger system, ostensible difficulties—gaps, repetitions, inconsistencies—whether within or between the legal collections, provide evidence neither of legal-historical development nor of literary reformulation. Instead, they implicitly represent divergent legal cases whose difference from one another may be reconstructed with reference to the self-consistent, larger legal system, the existence altogether of which is Westbrook's most crucial postulate.

Few scholars have attempted such a systematic rethinking of the theory and the methodology for the study of biblical and cuneiform law. Westbrook attempts to provide an account of the constituent features of the legal corpus as a literary genre, including not only those collections found in southern, central and northern Mesopotamia, ancient Israel, and Anatolia, but also, aspects of Greek and Roman law.[4] Importantly, he emphasizes the academic origins of the genre and attempts to reconstruct the intellectual activity underlying it: how it functions as a form of legal thought. His work, synthesizing legal history, Assyriology, and biblical criticism, effectively clears the scholarly deck of a number of long-standing, inappropriate models and attempts to forge a more valid and culturally immanent model.

3.   Westbrook, *Studies*, p. 8.
4.   For an earlier attempt at such synthesis see M. Smith, 'East Mediterranean Law Codes of the Early Iron Age', *Eretz-Israel* 14 (1978), pp. 38*-43*.

All of this constitutes an immense contribution to the field which merits a considered response.

In such a comprehensive undertaking, some difficulties are inevitable. In this paper I wish to examine Westbrook's arguments for the coherence of the Covenant Code. I contend that Westbrook's synchronic approach doubly contradicts its own mandate. First, classical literary criticism is in effect smuggled in through the back door, as the text is redefined, transformed or reconstructed in order to accommodate the theory. Secondly, the claim that the 'empirical evidence' of cuneiform law requires compositional unity overlooks the extent to which that claim is itself an elaborate exegetical construction. Maintaining the claim requires specific techniques of harmonistic legal exegesis that are employed, when confronted with legal redundancy or inconsistency, ostensibly to solve the problem by arguing 'the cases are different'. In almost all such cases, the *textual* evidence to support these interpretations is at best ambiguous and thus the very claim of empirical verification is not based upon any clearly existing empirical evidence. The history of the discipline, moreover, problematizes the notion of what constitutes empirical evidence, a concept, after all, easier in the claiming than in the providing.[5] Both synchrony and diachrony, finally, are interpretive constructs. The only question is, which better explains the textual phenomena?

My position is that the compositional norms of cuneiform literature involve extensive redactional activity. That fact creates the logical expectation that Israelite literature, including the legal collections, should be consistent with such norms, and therefore involve revision and interpolation. Examination of selected cases within biblical law not only supports that expectation but shows diachronic analysis to provide a more powerful explanation of the details of given texts.

---

5. There have been previous attempts to reject diachronic analysis of biblical law as an unjustified construction by modern scholars who fail to understand the compositional norms of ancient legal texts. This is the position of H.M. Wiener, 'The Arrangement of Deuteronomy 12–26', *JPOS* 6 (1926), pp. 185-98, especially pp. 185-86. Wiener defends his claim by distinguishing biblical from cuneiform law on the basis of the religious component of the former.

The Transformation of the Text

Westbrook sharply rejects the diachronic analysis of biblical law, rejecting it as both obsolete and unjustified:

> Conventional wisdom regards the Covenant Code as an amalgam of provisions from different sources and periods, the fusion of which has left tell-tale marks in the form of various inconsistencies in the text. That view is based upon assumptions as to the history of the law and its expression which are unsupported by empirical evidence. At most they can rely on inappropriate models from the classical and later periods.
>
> Such models may have been acceptable in the last century, but since the discovery of massive quantities of cuneiform sources, they are no longer so (p. 36).

Two issues are here salient. The first is the dismissal of conventional methodology as empirically unjustified, with the implicit further claim that the analysis of cuneiform law self-evidently justifies Westbrook's synchronic alternative. Secondly is the problem that the position that Westbrook ascribes to the consensus—that the Covenant Code represents 'an amalgam of provisions from different sources and periods'—is in fact almost never held by classical literary or form critics. Westbrook defines 'the "Covenant Code" strictly so called' as *Exod. 20.22–22.16*.[6] The position that Westbrook rejects, however, more conventionally applies to the larger literary unit, the complex of material comprising the Covenant Code as a whole (Exod. 20.22–23.2). That larger unit combines third-person and second-person law, casuistic and apodictic law, the altar laws that precede the legal superscription of Exod. 21.1, parenesis alongside more normative legal forms, religious law alongside civil and criminal law, and so on. The Covenant Code thus conventionally comprises:

Exod.		
	20.22-26	redactional transition and altar law
	21.1–22.16	*mišpāṭîm*
	22.17–23.19	*dĕbārîm*
	23.20-33	parenetic conclusion

When classical biblical scholarship asserts the diversity of the Covenant Code, it is this larger heterogeneous complex whose (a) composition and structure, (b) relation to the surrounding Sinai

---

6. Westbrook is inclined also to include Exod. 22.17-19 (see p. 15). On the issue of the delimitation of the legal corpora, see further p. 53 below.

narrative (whether original or secondary), and (c) source-critical attribution (note the parallels between Exod. 23.10-19 and 34.18-26) it attempts to resolve. The position that Westbrook rejects—the assertion of internal inconsistency, needing to be diachronically resolved—has thus in fact been maintained, but for the whole of the Covenant Code (Exod. 20.22–23.33), whose legal-historical and literary-critical unity are not part of Westbrook's investigation. Conversely, concerning Exod. 21.1–22.16, to which Westbrook restricts his analysis, classical biblical scholars of previous generations displayed a remarkable unanimity that it is internally coherent— exactly the position that Westbrook maintains. Eissfeldt and Noth, in fact, elsewhere never slow to wield the text-critical scalpel, in different ways go even farther than Westbrook does, and maintain the coherence of the *entire* Covenant Code.[7]

Although Westbrook here presents his polemic as one directed against a century-old consensus within biblical scholarship, his critique is mislabeled. Here and elsewhere he asserts that he rejects 'the classic methods of biblical criticism'.[8] He considers classical literary criticism valid for narrative strata or for dating the legal

7. O. Eissfeldt, *The Old Testament: An Introduction* (New York: Harper & Row, 1965), p. 217 [German editions: 1934, 1955, 1964] emphasizes the integrity of Exod. 21.1–22.16. He also asserts that even despite its formal incongruity, the entirety of the Covenant Code (Exod. 20.22–23.33) is systematic and deliberate in its arrangement rather than arbitrary and thus displays redactional coherence. M. Noth, *Exodus* (OTL; Philadelphia: Westminster Press, 1962) is even more conservative, arguing that the entire Covenant Code (Exod. 21.1–23.19), minus the parenetic conclusion, (23.20-33) circulated 'as a self-contained unity' prior to and independent of the crystallization of the narrative sources (p. 173). The casuistic and apodictic material, while ultimately separate in origin, are fully coherent with one another within the Covenant Code (p. 175). Thus Noth views the Covenant Code as more of a uniform text than Westbrook does. Noth even retains as original the participial series Exod. 21.12 + 15-17 (elsewhere often excised as secondary). The only material Noth considers extrinsic is Exod. 21.13-14, the distinction between premeditated homicide and manslaughter added to 21.12 (p. 180). That conventional biblical scholarship generally agrees that Exod. 21.12–22.16 reveals a 'strictly uniform style' is also clear from B.S. Childs, *The Book of Exodus: A Critical, Theological Commentary* (Philadelphia: Westminster Press, 1974), p. 454. So pristine is this unit, Childs insists, that there are no signs even of redactional activity. The only interpolation he allows is the participially formulated unit 21.12-17, which he links with 22.18; otherwise it is free of secondary glosses (pp. 456-57).

8. Westbrook, *Studies*, p. 7.

collections relative to one another, but invalid when applied to 'a single code'.[9] In the present article, he aims his specific criticisms at the work of Albrecht Alt, Eckart Otto, David Daube, Bernard S. Jackson and Ludger Schwienhorst-Schönberger (pp. 16-19). None of these, however, is a classical literary critic. Alt is a form critic, as Westbrook here recognizes. Similarly, with regard to Otto and Schwienhorst-Schönberger, at issue is not conventional literary criticism, but more recent developments in German form criticism and in redaction historical analyses of biblical law. Westbrook challenges the potentially circular reasoning of form criticism that a specific literary form derives from a distinct oral life-setting (*Sitz im Leben*) which is then reconstructed by the critic.[10] Cuneiform literature does indeed help establish that many biblical genres and texts have no life-setting, technically understood, but are rather conscious *literary* creations from the beginning.[11]

The remaining two scholars whose work Westbrook challenges, Daube and Jackson, are not originally 'biblical scholars', but legal historians who turn to rabbinic, biblical and cuneiform law from the vantage point of classical and Roman law. In a sense, Westbrook's real critique is of the application of models that derive from an alien rather than an immanent cultural context (pp. 32-36). He valuably demonstrates here (p. 18) and elsewhere that such models leave some problems in the structure and sequence of Exod. 21.37–22.3 unexplained.[12]

As for Alt's classical study, in fairness, Westbrook's critique should

9. Westbrook, *Studies*, p. 7.

10. For a critique of the assumptions underlying earlier redaction-historical approaches to the legal corpus of Deuteronomy see B.M. Levinson, *The Hermeneutics of Innovation: The Impact of Centralization upon the Structure, Sequence, and Reformulation of Legal Material in Deuteronomy* (Ann Arbor: University Microfilms International, 1991), pp. 101-106.

11. On such a basis Moshe Weinfeld properly rejects earlier attempts to identify the origins of Deuteronomy's structure in levitical sermons. He argues, on the basis of cuneiform treaty literature, that Deuteronomy's sermons do not have a *Sitz im Leben* but rather represent the 'programmatic compositions drafted by scribes'. See his *Deuteronomy and the Deuteronomic School* (Oxford: Clarendon Press, 1972), pp. 8-9, 54-58.

12. Westbrook, *Studies*, p. 120. Elsewhere, however, Daube's 'coda' model does provide a valuable explanatory model. Such issues must be decided on a case by case basis.

be nuanced in two ways. The first is that Alt's point of departure in analyzing the Covenant Code—that 'it consists of passages of different origin set side by side with virtually no formal connection'—does not refer to Exod. 21.2–22.16, but rather to be larger complex of heterogeneous material in Exod. 20.22–23.22.[13] He actually deems the unit which Westbrook treats largely as Westbrook himself does, as unified and coherent in origin, although he does allow some secondary accretions.[14]

Secondly, Alt's emphasis on the range of formal divergence within the larger Covenant Code needs to be seen in its context within the history of scholarship. From the time of its emergence with Gunkel, form criticism was itself a reaction against literary criticism. Form critics attempted to move behind the late date assigned to each of the documentary sources of the Pentateuch. In working only with the final redaction, literary criticism relegates all biblical law 'to what could in no way be called creative periods in the history of the law'.[15] Alt emphasized the lack of form-critical cohesiveness within the larger Covenant Code so as to justify moving behind the late, redacted form of the text to the creative period, romantically conceived, of oral originality. He claimed that by analyzing the 'prehistory' of each form he would be able to gain access to reliable information about the earliest periods of Israelite history and history. Casuistic law provides a window to the earliest Settlement period; apodictic law, back even further, to the pristine desert experience.[16] Although I do not find these assumptions tenable, it is important to recognize the motivation for Alt's claims.

Having established that classical literary criticism already maintains the same basic position that Westbrook here urges, and in some respects actually goes farther in recognizing coherence, it is important to compare how each handles certain difficulties within the unit (Exod. 21.1–22.16). Two questions arise. (1) What interpretive

13. A. Alt, 'The Origins of Israelite Law' [1934], in his *Essays on Old Testament History and Religion* (Garden City, NY: Doubleday, 1967), pp. 101-71, at pp. 107, 104.

14. Alt, 'Origins', p. 112. The secondary material is principally the participial series of Exod. 21.12 + 15-17 (pp. 142-44).

15. Alt, 'Origins', p. 106.

16. Alt, 'Origins', pp. 132-34.

strategies does Westbrook employ to defend the unit's coherence? (2) What happens to the text when it is read synchronically?

Implications of the Denial of Development, Revision and Interpolation

Westbrook's system can only assert textual coherence by means of classic techniques of textual harmonization well known in postbiblical exegetical literature, both Rabbinic and early Christian. The magic key is the assertion: 'the cases are different'. In a system that promises epistemological certainty—diachronic analysis of cuneiform and biblical law is 'unsupported by empirical evidence' (p. 36; similarly, pp. 19, 24, 25)—it is best to put that claim to the test. I believe that Westbrook's technique for saving the synchronic coherence of the text exacts too high a toll. Importing legal, logical or grammatical references from other legal texts so as to provide a different application for a problematic passage frequently cuts against the grain of a given unit and substitutes a strained reading for a plain one.

The clearest example occurs in the final chapter of Westbrook's book in a discussion of one of the participial laws of the Covenant Code: וגנב איש ומכרו ונמצא בידו מות יומת (Exod. 21.16).[17] As Westbrook indicates, Daube exploits what he purports to be the literal meaning ('He that steals a man and sells him and he is found in his hand shall be put to death') to argue that the law does not make sense: once kidnapped and sold, how shall the man then be found in the possession of the kidnapper?[18] Daube argues that the law incorporates an addition that derives from the growth in evidential procedure. Theft and attempted sale of persons were thus, in his reconstruction of the law's original form, the necessary conditions for conviction for kidnapping: as such, 'He who steals a man and sells him shall be put to death'. The addition of the allegedly disruptive phrase ('and he is found in his hand') represents a new development in judicial procedure: now mere possession, even without sale, satisfies the requirements for sufficient evidence to convict.

The context for Daube's analysis is his chapter analyzing 'Codes and Codas' in biblical law, where he maintains that, whether due to 'laziness', 'undeveloped legal technique', 'writing on stone', 'oral

---

17. Westbrook, *Studies*, p. 119.

18. D. Daube, *Studies in Biblical Law* (Cambridge: Cambridge University Press, 1947), p. 95.

transmission of the law', or 'regard for tradition', there are 'several examples in the Pentateuch', as also in Roman law such as *lex Aquila*, 'of the method . . . of new provisions being joined to an existing code as an appendix instead of being worked in properly'.[19] Such claims about inept, primitive or conservative editing of the legal collections provide the warrant for Westbrook's repeatedly urging that we not attribute 'apparent inconsistencies . . . to historical development and certainly not to an excess of either subtlety or incompetence on the part of their compiler' (p. 36).

The difficulty is that Westbrook's alternative introduces new problems. He argues that there is no legal-historical development or interpolation in the verse. Instead, there is a concealed change of subject which extends the law to a third party not previously named, the person who purchases the kidnapped man. Thus he translates the verse: 'He that steals a man and sells him *and he in whose possession he is found* shall be put to death'.[20] This proposed English rendering of Exod. 21.16 simply cannot be derived from the original Hebrew. Such a 'translation' would require, at the very least, a crucial relative pronoun not present in the Hebrew: וְאֲשֶׁר נמצא בידו. The 'translation' thus in effect rewrites the text, revising it to support an interpretation of the text as coherent.

Notwithstanding this philological issue, Westbrook defends his solution on two counts. First, he cites Yaron's analysis of the *Laws of Eshnunna* to assert that unmarked changes of subject are not uncommon in cuneiform law.[21] Secondly, he argues that this law corresponds to CH §6, in mandating capital punishment for the recipient of stolen goods—the reference to whom *is* marked by the relative pronoun *ša*—as well as for the thief himself. In each case there is a difficulty. In the first instance, Westbrook's new translation requires not simply, as he suggests, 'a change of subject' but rather the introduction of an entirely new subject, a third party to the transaction who is unmentioned in the protasis. Despite Westbrook's citation, Yaron's point about the change of subject does not refer to that type of change but instead covers the situation that obtains here with the verse as conventionally translated. Sometimes the direct or (indirect) object of the protasis ('He who steals *a man*') may become a subject in

19. Daube, *Studies*, p. 77.
20. Westbrook, *Studies*, p. 119.
21. Westbrook, *Studies*, pp. 118-19.

the apodosis ('whether he sells him or *he* is found in his possession').[22]

In the second instance, Westbrook justifies his appeal to CH §6, despite its governing theft of property rather than kidnapping, on the basis of the common requirement for capital punishment. Given the broad range of cases in CH with this penalty, that provides insufficient rationale for claiming legal analogy. Further, although CH §6 indeed penalizes the recipient of stolen goods (who has not demanded that the sale be accompanied by witnesses and contract; see CH §7), this case has no obvious bearing on the specific legal problem at issue in Exod. 21.16. To the best of my knowledge, in none of the cases found within the cuneiform legal collections involving theft of persons, whether free or slave, is there any mention of third-party liability.[23]

Attempting to save the coherence of the text, Westbrook in fact creates a new text consistent neither with the original Hebrew verse in question (Exod. 21.16) nor with the terms of the cuneiform provisions that he considers analogous to it. The proposed synchronic interpretation, despite claiming to be empirically grounded in compositional norms, thus doubly undercuts its own claims. First, the new reading of Exod. 21.16 lacks clear empirical ground, both grammatically and legal-historically. Secondly, the very attempt to reject literary criticism nevertheless smuggles in text-critical restoration through the back door. A new, problem-free text is created by means of exegetical suppletion: details allegedly missing in one context are imported from another on the assumption of analogy.[24]

I agree with Westbrook's rejection of Daube's argument. I would defend the law's coherence philologically, however, in terms of syntax, rather than by means of harmonistic legal exegesis. There is no reason that conjunctive *waw* need mechanically mark simple consecution ('and'). In many instances in biblical law, or in quasi-legal authoritative pronouncements, *waw* functions to introduce alternatives

22. R. Yaron, *The Laws of Eshnunna* (Jerusalem: Magnes Press; Leiden: Brill, 2nd edn, 1988), pp. 95-96, discussing LE §§ 9, 22, 37. In none of these cases is a party not already explicitly mentioned in the protasis introduced as a new subject of the apodosis. (In Yaron's first edition, cited by Westbrook, the discussion occurs on pp. 58-59.)

23. CH §§ 14 (free), 17-20 (slave); HL 19 (free), 20-21 (slave).

24. On this tendency to harmonize, see the detailed review by R. Yaron of Westbrook's *Studies* in *Zeitschrift der Savigny-Stiftung für Rechtsgeschichte, Romanistische Abteilung* 107 (1990), pp. 417-33.

('either A *or* B') into a protasis or an apodosis: Gen. 26.11; Exod. 12.5; 20.4; 22.9a; Lev. 2.4b; 20.9; 25.47a; Deut. 22.2a; 24.7. The clearest proof may be found in Deuteronomy 13. Attempting to incite apostasy, a false prophet or oneiromancer may offer אות או מופת 'a sign *or* a wonder' (Deut. 13.2). Nevertheless, even ובא האות והמופת 'if the sign or the wonder come true' (Deut. 13.2), the prophet or oneiromancer must not be heeded. The reformulation with *waw*, employing a singular verb and immediately following the use of the conjunction או to express the same alternative, confirms that the two phrases are identical in meaning.

This understanding of the syntax also applies to the verse in question within the Covenant Code. That the *waw* on the second term of Exod. 21.16a is not cumulative or sequential but alternative in function is evident within the same distinctive series of participial formulations in the Covenant Code among which this law is found. In both Exod. 21.15 and 21.17, the meaning has to be: 'Whoever strikes his father *or* his mother'; 'Whoever curses his father *or* his mother'.[25] The confusion in the case of Exod. 21.14 is created by this *waw* which expresses the alternative (ונמצה בידו) being found after the conversive *waw* (ומכרו). The correct translation is: 'Whoever steals a man, whether he sell him or he is found in his hand, shall surely die'.[26]

Moreover, the law concerning theft of persons in Deut. 24.7

---

25. Gershon Brin makes the same analogy and also argues for the use of the copula to express 'or' at Exod. 21.16a in 'The Development of Some Laws in the Book of the Covenant', in H.G. Reventlow and Y. Hoffman (eds.), *Justice and Righteousness: Biblical Themes and their Influence* (JSOTSup, 137; Sheffield: JSOT Press, 1992), pp. 60-70 at pp. 62-63. As I have above, Brin demonstrates this usage as a broader syntactical possibility in his 'The Uses of או (= or) in the Biblical Legal Texts', *Shnaton* 5-6 (1982), pp. 25-26 (Hebrew). Interestingly, in 'Development', Brin attempts to retain Daube's diachronic reading of the law as the law's original form, whereby the phrase would mark a later legal amendment, while he also stresses the coherence of the law in its current form because of the 'or' function of the copula. This two-stage proposal seems problematic, however, in maintaining that the same law is simultaneously coherent and incoherent.

26. The medieval exegete Abraham Ibn Ezra implicitly recognized this fact. With his insight that simple possession, without sale, constituted sufficient grounds for capital punishment for kidnapping, Ibn Ezra established his independence of the entire thrust of classical and medieval Judaism's understanding of the law. See his *Commentary on the Pentateuch* (ed. A. Weizer; 3 vols.; Jerusalem: Mossad Harav Kook, 1977), II, p. 149 (Hebrew).

48   *Theory and Method in Biblical and Cuneiform Law*

confirms that, at least by the time of the composition of Deuteronomy, the word ונמצא was already in the text of the version of the Covenant Code that lay before Deuteronomy's authors.[27] Deuteronomy retains both the legal topos (man theft) and the key terminology (finding, stealing, selling). Deuteronomy restricts, however, the law's application to Israelite victims and moves the problematic clause with 'finding' into the beginning of the law, thereby eliminating the syntactical ambiguity:[28] כי ימצא איש גנב נפש מאחיו מבני ישראל והתעמר בו ומכרו ומת הגנב ההוא ובערת הרע מקרבך 'If a person is *found stealing* a person from among his fellow Israelites, whether he enslave him or *sell him*, that thief shall die; thus shall you remove evil from your midst' (Deut. 24.7).[29]

A similar issue, whether the synchronic analysis compromises the plain sense of the text, arises in relation to the long problematic series addressing (A) theft of animals (Exod. 21.37); (B) housebreaking (22.1-2a); (C) and requiring restitution if stolen cattle are still in the possession of the thief (Exod. 22.3). So problematic is the present

27. See M. Fishbane, *Biblical Interpretation in Ancient Israel* (Oxford: Clarendon Press, 1985), p. 189.

28. Strikingly, both the Palestinian exegetical tradition, reflected by *Targum Pseudo-Jonathan* (ed. E.G. Clarke *et al.*; Hoboken, NJ: Ktav, 1984; p. 92), and the Babylonian, reflected by *Targum Onqelos*, harmonize the original law with its reformulation—by introducing Deuteronomy's restriction of the law to Israelite victims into the text of Exod. 21.16, which was unqualified in its formulation.

29. In my translation of והתעמר as 'enslave', I follow the RSV, the *Tanach* (Philadelphia: Jewish Publication Society, 1988), and the *Einheitsübersetzung*. Nonetheless, the Targumic tradition understands the Hithpael verb, which is unique to Deuteronomy (see also 21.14), rather differently, as 'make a profit from'. Defending this rendering as the word's original meaning, see M. David, '*Hit'āmēr*' [*sic*], *VT* 1 (1951), pp. 219-22. The postbiblical tradition is not uniform, however. Legal exegesis in the Tannaitic period understood the violation in question to involve 'abducting the victim and forcing him to reside with the abductor, i.e., taking him into the abductor's possession'. For this analysis of *Sipre Deuteronomy, pisqa* 273 (ed. L. Finkelstein [New York: Jewish Theological Seminary, 1969], p. 293), with justification in the Aramaic dialects, see I.B. Gottlieb, 'Midrash as Biblical Philology', *JQR* 75 (1984), pp. 134-61, at pp. 148-49. If this notion of forcible possession is correct, it is possible that the *Sipre* preserves an ancient tradition of the word's meaning in Northwest Semitic. Note the recourse to Ugaritic by A. Alt, 'Zu *Hit'ammēr*', *VT* 2 (1952), pp. 153-59. For first drawing my attention to the Targum's rendering, I am thankful to Stephen A. Kaufman.

arrangement of the text that NEB, in its translation, imposes a text-critical solution, rearranging the sequence so that C precedes B, thereby joining the two provisions dealing with theft (A and C) and neatly separating off as a different topic the house owner's liability in case of burglary (B). The allegedly restored sequence is thus Exod. 21.37 + 22.3; 22.1-2.

Westbrook comprehensively challenges the legal-historical claims used by Daube and by Jackson to account for the present disorder. His detailed critique of their assumption that Exod. 22.3 is in effect a *coda*, added to the original text because of a later development in the laws of evidence, from primitive (the necessity of slaughter or sale to establish guilt, in Exod. 21.37) to more sophisticated (mere possession with intent) is entirely convincing. Here again the arbitrariness of legal-historical models which treat the texts as statutory law is confirmed.[30]

The difficulty arises with Westbrook's alternative solution. Once again, the attempt to preserve the original coherence of the text creates what is, in effect, a new text. The assumption, as with his explanation of Exod. 21.14, is that there has been a change of subject. Exod. 22.3, Westbrook argues, does not address the same case as Exod. 21.37, nor does it have that thief as its subject. Instead, the verse actually refers to a third party, the unwitting purchaser of stolen goods, a legal motif found in cuneiform law.[31] Consequently, Westbrook maintains, the case here is different from the one immediately preceding. In Exod. 22.2b the housebreaker (of 22.1-2) must either negotiate an unspecified price to purchase his freedom once he has been apprehended (שלם ישלם 'he shall surely pay') or else become indentured to the house owner on account of his attempted burglary (אם אין לו ונמכר בגנבתו 'if he lacks the means, he shall be sold for his theft').[32]

There are several difficulties involved in this attempt to defend the text's coherence. First, there is no evidence to support the notion that Exod. 21.37 addresses the liability of an innocent purchaser.[33]

---

30. Westbrook, *Studies*, pp. 111-13.
31. Westbrook, *Studies*, pp. 118-19.
32. Westbrook, *Studies*, pp. 118-19.
33. See also L. Schwienhorst-Schönberger, *Das Bundesbuch* (BZAW, 188; Berlin: de Gruyter, 1990), p. 184.

Granted, the liability of the purchaser who does not seek witnesses and a contract is a well known and explicit motif in the cuneiform legal collections (CH §§6-7, 9-13).[34] Nevertheless, biblical law, with less emphasis on such contractual transactions, never, to the best of my knowledge, addresses the question of third-party liability: the issue is not among the legal topics.

The second problem is that the interpretation of Exod. 22.2b as referring to the *housebreaker* apprehended in the act and 'sold for his *theft*' if he cannot afford 'the ransom for his freedom' involves two questions: (a) if ransom (כפר) were indeed imposed upon him (יושת עליו), why does none of the expected technical terminology appear, as it does elsewhere in this unit? (Exod. 21.30, cf. v. 23); (b) what is the meaning of בגנבתו 'his theft' in Exod. 22.2b when, as Westbrook concedes, in effect no theft has been committed since he has been apprehended?[35]

The attempt to maintain the compositional coherence of Exod. 21.37–22.3 requires rewriting the text by means of exegesis, importing antecedents or legal applications that are extrinsic to the given text's formulation, language and range of legal-literary problems. Finally, the synchronic reading fails to clarify how and why Exod. 22.1-2a enters the picture.[36] The unit, particularly v. 2a, remains intrusive in the context of theft or burglary laws because it addresses a different issue: the limits to the homeowner's right of legitimate self-defense.

If the synchronic reconstruction of the text compromises its meaning, I believe that the diachronic method allows the coherence of the text to emerge. The logically structured original law was composed of a paradigmatic case followed by two sub-cases:

---

34. R. Westbrook and C. Wilcke, 'The Liability of an Innocent Purchaser of Stolen Goods in Early Mesopotamian Law', *AfO* 25 (1974/1977), pp. 111-21. The 'three-cornered presentation' is also stressed at Westbrook, *Studies*, p. 115.

35. Westbrook, *Studies*, p. 126.

36. Neither the summary of the problematic sequence of the unit in 'What is the Covenant Code?', p. 18, nor of the solution to the problematic found in *Studies*, p. 128, directly addresses the house owner's liability for homicide should he kill a burglar by day (Exod. 22.2a).

general statement of legal principle:
multiple damages for slaughter or sale of stolen animals (21.37);
first contingency: indenture of the thief who is unable to pay
    multiple damages (22.2b);
second contingency: lesser damages for simple possession (22.3).[37]

The coherence of that original law was broken both syntactically and in terms of the legal topic with Exod. 22.1-2a. In Exod. 22.2, the difficult שלם ישלם 'he shall surely pay' lacks any clear antecedent: contextually it can refer neither to the homeowner nor to the housebreaker of 22.1-2a. The phrase also lacks any grammatical object or complement. Thus syntactically detached from its context, the phrase marks a *Wiederaufnahme* or repetitive resumption.[38] It repeats the key verb of the apodosis of 21.37b, ישלם 'he shall pay'.[39] In the context of a law otherwise concerned with liability for the theft of animals, the repetitive resumption frames a new law with an entirely different legal focus, whose concern is to distinguish legitimate versus illegitimate homicide in the case of housebreaking (22.1-2a).[40]

This is not the context to address the ethical, legal and religious issues implicit in the reader's disruption of this theft series with the

---

37. My presentation here draws on the helpful comments kindly offered by Stephen A. Kaufman who, however, analyzes Exod. 21.37–22.3 synchronically.

38. Eckart Otto, reviewing Westbook's *Studies* in *TRev* 86 (1990), pp. 283-87, provides a similar analysis (p. 287). For analysis of and bibliography on this editorial device, which brackets an interpolation by framing it with a repetition of material preceding the insertion (thus ABC X C'DEF), see Levinson, *Hermeneutics of Innovation*, pp. 142-50.

39. For the most detailed discussion of the syntactical and legal-historical issues, with extensive literature, see Schwienhorst-Schönberger, *Das Bundesbuch*, pp. 175-82. I disagree, however, with his conclusion that Exod. 22.2b represents part of the interpolation, rather than part of the original law. For solutions analogous to the one proposed here, although differing in some details, see also E. Otto, *Wandel der Rechtsbegründungen in der Gesellschaftsgeschichte des antiken Israel* (StudBib, 3; Leiden: Brill, 1988), pp. 19-21; *idem*, *Rechtsgeschichte der Redaktionen im Kodex Ešnunna und im <<Bundesbuch>>* (OBO, 85; Freiburg: Universitätsverlag, 1989), pp. 76-77; Y. Osumi, *Die Kompositionsgeschichte des Bundesbuches* (OBO, 105; Freiburg: Universitätsverlag, 1991), p. 128.

40. The interpolation, although not the technical device for including it, has long been recognized. Note L.B. Paton, 'The Original Form of the Book of the Covenant', *JBL* 12 (1893), p. 82; J. Hogg, 'Exod. 22.23 [*sic*] ("Nocturnal Thief" and "Restitution")', *AJSL* 44 (1927), pp. 58-61.

addition of Exod. 22.1-2a, which restricts the homeowner's right of self-protection. Finkelstein argued that the 'digression' represents the intentionality of an author concerned to establish fundamental moral categories and to distinguish between wrongs against the person and wrongs against property.[41] While his analysis is very illuminating, I believe he errs in considering the entire text to be the work of a single author. The disruptions of syntax and grammar, in conjunction with the total shift in legal topic, tip the balance decisively in favor of a diachronic analysis: the disruption represents an interpolation in which a redactor revises an original civil law to reflect upon the moral and ethical limits to self-help. The redactor uses the *Wiederaufnahme* as a literary device to bracket the interpolation, which thus serves as the elegant signature of his handiwork.[42]

Revision and Interpolation Elsewhere in Biblical Law

In attempting to compare how synchronic and diachronic readings work, I have thus far concentrated only on the casuistic section of the Covenant Code. I would like to submit a pair of examples from other legal corpora within the Bible, where I think the evidence for revision and interpolation is undeniable. Because Westbrook rejects both phenomena, it is crucial first to address a question of literary demarcation. It is well known that biblical law combines cultic, criminal and civil and ethical law; in general, the cuneiform collections, with the exception of the Middle Assyrian and Hittite Laws, rarely have such a mixture, and primarily include criminal and

---

41. J.J. Finkelstein, *The Ox that Gored* (Transactions of the American Philosophical Society, 71.2; Philadelphia: American Philosophical Society, 1981), pp. 38-39.

42. An interpolation should never be claimed merely on the basis of the device alone, but only when other, independent criteria also exist. I leave open here the question of whether the device, particularly in legal material, intrinsically marks interpolations, or whether it may also be used compositionally. Provisionally, I believe the former is the case. Nonetheless, especially in some narrative contexts, there is evidence that the repetitive resumption may be compositional rather than redactional in origin and thus not have diachronic significance; see S. Talmon, 'The Presentation of Synchroneity and Simultaneity in Biblical Narrative', in *Studies in Hebrew Narrative Art throughout the Ages* (ed. J. Heinemann and S. Werses; ScrHier, 27; Jerusalem: Magnes, 1978), pp. 9-26. The question can only be decided, of course, on a case by case basis.

civil law.[43] Given the reality of the profound transformations in Israelite religion to which the cultic laws in particular testify, they might logically be expected to provide sites where reformulation would occur.[44] Strikingly, however, Westbrook excludes them from consideration.

Westbrook contends that the biblical legal 'codes' are comprised of 'the legal corpus of the Covenant Code (*Ex 21,2–22,6* [*sic*; must be a typo for 22,*16*]) and of Deuteronomy (*Dt 21,1–25,11*)'.[45] I have already noted the more conventional demarcation of the Covenant Code as Exod. 20.22–23.33; that of the legal corpus of Deuteronomy is Deut. 12.1–26.19. Westbrook's attempt to exclude the Holiness Code of Lev. 17.1–26.46 as having 'a different subject-matter'[46] is unjustifiable because it employs a criterion—topical similarity to the cuneiform legal collections—that imposes an arbitrary, external standard upon the biblical material. Moreover, multiple points of topical overlap among the biblical corpora have long been noted.[47]

Whatever the criteria for these demarcations, they are not empirically grounded: the author does not justify them in relation to specific literary or editorial features of the biblical legal collections themselves. Such handy redefining of the corpus of biblical law constitutes *de facto* textual criticism without the accompanying controls. The price of imposing such a Procrustean theory is the excision of significant constituent parts of biblical law as functionally secondary. Moreover, the criterion for the redefinition, the attempt to create secular or civil 'codes' out of the corpus of biblical law, itself

43. See B. Landsberger, 'Die Babylonischen Termini für Gesetz und Recht', in *Symbolae ad Iura Orientis Antiqui* (ed. T. Folkers *et al.*; SD, 2; Leiden: Brill, 1939), pp. 219-34, especially pp. 221-23.

44. Elsewhere I demonstrate ongoing inner-biblical reformulation of the concept of divine justice as involving vicarious punishment; see B.M. Levinson, 'The Human Voice in Divine Revelation: The Problem of Authority in Biblical Law', in *Innovation in Religious Traditions: Essays in the Interpretation of Religious Change* (Religion and Society, 31; Berlin and New York: Mouton de Gruyter, 1992), pp. 35-71.

45. Westbrook, *Studies*, p. 2 n. 6 (my emphasis). Similarly, *idem*, 'Biblical and Cuneiform Legal Law Codes', *RB* 92 (1985), pp. 247-64, at pp. 247-48.

46. Westbrook, 'Biblical and Cuneiform Law Codes', p. 248 n. 3. In the current article, however, the Priestly code is mentioned on p. 28.

47. S.R. Driver, *Deuteronomy* (ICC; Edinburgh: T. & T. Clark, 3rd edn, 1901), pp. iv-vii.

imposes a foreign canon upon the Israelite material. This process of redefining the legal corpus thus contradicts the claim that synchronic interpretation is alone culturally immanent and that diachronic analysis is alien. Ironically, such demarcations hinder Westbrook from carrying out his overall goals, as two examples from Deuteronomy show. On the one hand, the single example of legal development in the Bible that Westbrook does allow (p. 35), the case of manumission law (Deut. 15.12 revising Exod. 21.2), now falls outside of the legal 'code' of Deuteronomy! On the other hand, the demarcation excludes the prohibition against removing boundary markers (Deut. 19.14). That provision would be important to Westbrook's own larger project to demonstrate cross-cultural legal continuity because similar divinely sanctioned prohibitions are common to cuneiform *kudurru* law, Israelite law, Egyptian wisdom and Roman law.[48]

Although in this context I focus on the biblical legal corpora, the same question of *de facto* textual criticism arises with respect to the cuneiform legal collections. Westbrook's analysis of 'the codes' concentrates on the legal paragraphs to the exclusion of the religious and literary frame in which they are found, a frame which is composed in a hymnic-epic dialect different from the language of the laws. That redactional association of frame and legal corpus itself raises a further series of questions that militate against a synchronic reading. First, it is not clear whether the combination of law and frame is original or secondary, since each has been found without the other; either answer, however, requires the recognition of redactional activity in the construction of the legal corpus. Secondly, the frame itself presupposes the revision and updating of literary models drawn both from prior legal collections (the Laws of Ur Nammu) and from the royal edicts (Uru-inim-gina).[49] Thirdly, there is strong evidence, controlled by philology, for revision and interpolation within the legal paragraphs themselves.[50]

---

48. See B.S. Jackson, 'From *Dharma* to Law', *American Journal of Comparative Law* 23 (1975), pp. 490-512 at pp. 507-508.

49. For analysis and bibliography see J.H. Tigay, 'The Stylistic-Criterion of Source-Criticism in the Light of Ancient Near Eastern and Postbiblical Literature', in *Empirical Models for Biblical Criticism* (ed. J.H. Tigay; Philadelphia: University of Pennsylvania Press, 1985), pp. 150-73, at pp. 159-67.

50. For important recent demonstrations see Westbrook and Wilcke, 'The

I have already suggested that the profound transformations within the history of Israelite religion, as reflected in the literary sources, provide ready contexts for observing textual reformulation. The religious calendar of ancient Israel offers one of the most striking examples of such ongoing development. The calendar's expansion, historicization and phenomenological transformation may be charted by comparing it in each of the literary strata; moreover, the calendar undergoes interpolation within the strata. For example, the authors of Deuteronomy radically transform the paschal slaughter, originally an apotropaic slaughter of sheep or goats in the doorway (Exod. 12.21-23, JE), into all but a normative sacrifice of cattle or sheep at the centralized altar (Deut. 16.1-8). Not only do they void the original blood ritual, they *textually* rework the older protocol as well, in effect fusing it with the quite dissimilar norms proper to Unleavened Bread as a pilgrimage festival.[51]

A pair of striking examples of the phenomenon of development, warranting detailed analysis, occurs within the festival calendar of the Holiness Code. The festivals are designated מועדי יהוה 'the fixed times of Yahweh' (Lev. 23.2, 4). Within such cultic calendars (see Exod. 23.14-17; Deut. 16.1-17), the focus is on the annual occurrences whose date must indeed be 'fixed'—thus, the root יעד 'to set, designate'. Anomalous in such a context is the weekly celebration of the Sabbath, which does not mark a calendrical phenomenon and needs no fixing.[52] Consequently, the colophon of this calendar explicitly emphasizes that the foregoing unit lists the 'fixed times of Yahweh . . . מלבד שבתת יהוה *apart from* the Sabbaths of Yahweh'

Liability of an Innocent Purchaser', pp. 111-21; T. Abusch, ' "He Should Continue to Bear the Penalty of that Case": An Interpretation of Codex Hammurabi Paragraphs 3-4', in *From Ancient Israel to Modern Judaism: Intellect in Quest of Understanding, Essays in Honor of Marvin Fox* (ed. J. Neusner, E.S. Frerichs and N.M. Sarna; BJS, 159; 4 vols.; Atlanta: Scholars Press, 1989), I, pp. 77-96; and B.L. Eichler, 'Literary Structure in the Laws of Eshnunna', in *Language, Literature, and History: Philological and Historical Studies Presented to Erica Reiner* (ed. F. Rochberg-Halton; AOS, 67; New Haven: American Oriental Society, 1987), pp. 71-84; and Samuel Greengus's and Eckart Otto's contributions to this volume.

51. See Levinson, *Hermeneutics of Innovation*, pp. 233-302.

52. As observed by B.A. Levine, *Leviticus* (JPS Torah Commentary; Philadelphia: Jewish Publication Society, 1989), p. 156. In the context of a commentary series aimed at a broader public, Levine does not pursue the implications of his analysis explicitly to argue that there is an interpolation here.

(Lev. 23.37-38). Despite the colophon's exclusion of the Sabbath, the Sabbath is nevertheless incongruously introduced into the unit, immediately following the superscription introducing the calendar of 'fixed times' (Lev. 23.3).

The literary context for the inclusion of the Sabbath law warrants further examination. Immediately after that anomalous inclusion, a second superscription occurs, closely overlapping with the first (Lev. 23.4, cf. v. 2). The contextually disruptive inclusion of the Sabbath law within the annual festival calendar, framed by the redundant repetition of the superscription and then explicitly asserted as extrinsic in the colophon, can most logically be explained as an interpolation. This interpolation marks an *ex post facto* tendency towards the programmatic incorporation of the Sabbath into the ritual calendar, even at the expense of the calendar's original coherence and specificity.[53] The editors responsible for the addition employ the conventional scribal technique of the repetitive resumption, framing the intrusive material (v. 3) with a repetition (v. 4) of the material preceding it (v. 2). The interpolation was added after the redaction of the original unit (Lev. 23.1-2 + 5-38). Strikingly, the colophon in vv. 37-38 was never itself revised in light of the addition and consequently provides a valuable window into the unit's redactional history.[54]

Whether the retention of the colophon intact, despite the interpolation, points to editorial conservatism, selective (in)attention, or non-concern with consistency given other priorities, I cannot say. Indeed, the issue, which arises in many contexts, merits a detailed examination. The results of the editorial activity, however, are undeniable. The attempt to make an originally specific calendar more systematic and comprehensive introduces contradiction into the legal corpus—and provides the textual evidence that gives rise to historical-critical scholarship.

This example is not alone, even within this unit devoted to the calendar. The final festival it lists is Tabernacles, whose observance is

---

53. For the most thorough analysis of the redactional issues involved see I. Knohl, 'The Priestly Torah Versus the Holiness School: Sabbath and Festivals', *HUCA* 58 (1987), pp. 72-76. More briefly, note also M.Z. Brettler, 'Jud 1,1-2,10: From Appendix to Prologue', *ZAW* 101 (1989), pp. 433-35 at p. 434.

54. On this approach, applying it to other texts, see M. Fishbane, 'On Colophons, Textual Criticism, and Legal Analogies', *CBQ* 42 (1980), pp. 438-39.

to be marked by seven days of sacrifices, a work stoppage on the first day, and an eighth day involving assembly, work stoppage and sacrifice (Lev. 23.33-36). The colophon of the festival calendar follows immediately (Lev. 23.37-38). That the colophon formally closes the calendrical unit is clear from its similarity in formulation to the opening superscription (note that Lev. 23.37a parallels 23.2aβ and thus forms an inclusio with it). After such a concluding summary, it is thus anomalous to find both a second presentation of the regulations for the Feast of Tabernacles (Lev. 23.39-43) and a second, if cursory, colophon (Lev. 23.44). This unit redundantly repeats the date formula (Lev. 23.39, parallel to v. 33) and adds provisions not mentioned in the preceding unit (celebration with various species of trees in Yahweh's presence for the entire duration of the Festival; dwelling in tabernacles; and a historical justification for the observance). It is difficult not to see the unit as an *ex post facto* addition to the calendar, again technically marked by the repetitive resumption, which incorporates into the text either a more popular form of observance than the original priestly one, or a newer form, or a form celebrated in a different region of Israel than the other. Whatever the specific explanation, the calendar is composed of inconsistent literary strata and underwent expansion. Importantly, the argument for revision is confirmed by two interlocking criteria: the presence both of substantive anomalies (the intrusiveness of Sabbath rules in a festival calendar and the redundancy of the Tabernacles codicil) and of scribal devices associated with redactional activity.

Once the power of diachronic analysis to explain the specifics of the text is recognized, instances of redactional activity, interpolation and development may frequently be detected. This is not the context to produce a list.[55] The key issue, it seems to me, is that Westbrook's real concern is that certain streams of analysis have indeed produced skewed results for lack of controls or appropriate models. At the same time, it is simply unjustified to claim that an immanent approach to biblical and cuneiform law mandates synchronic analysis. Such a claim overlooks the extent to which synchronic analysis is itself an interpretive construction that strives to explain the evidence. Synchronic harmonizations belie the 'empirical' evidence that is afforded by the

---

55. Fishbane's demonstration of the exegetical activity that occurs both within individual legal corpora and between them provides an extensive array of examples. See Fishbane, *Biblical Interpretation*, pp. 91-277.

text of redactional activity within it. All the major genres of cuneiform literature involve revision and interpolation.[56] This is alone the literary and intellectual context within which Israelite legal literature may properly be construed.[57]

Conclusions

When Rabbinic exegesis confronted the three separate legal collections of the Covenant Code, Deuteronomy and the Holiness Code, it had no choice but to construct a coherent system by means of harmonistic exegesis. That exegetical system entailed certain assumptions about the nature of the biblical text: that it is everywhere coherent and that it is free of redundancy. Of course, the facts of the redactional creation of the Pentateuch—the integration of three originally independent legal collections into a common narrative, the three equally asserted to be revelatory in origin—trigger such a response even as they ultimately belie it. Given that assumption of the meta-coherence of the system, Rabbinic interpretation found techniques to overcome the problem of redundancy, whether in separate contexts (as with the triple prohibition of boiling a kid in its mother's milk) or within a single, highly stratified text. For example, within Deuteronomy 12, the duplication of the concession allowing secular slaughter (vv. 15-16, 20-23) is harmonized by ancient Rabbinic exegesis as referring to two distinct cases: the first, to blemished sacrificial animals (see Deut. 15.21-23); the second, to profane slaughter of unblemished animals.[58] Similarly, the double prohibition of consuming the blood of animals (vv. 16, 23) equally is resolved through harmonistic exegesis: the first refers to the blood of slaughtered animals; the second, reading v. 23b literally ('You shall not eat the life with the flesh'), allegedly refers to

---

56. J.H. Tigay (ed.), *Empirical Models for Biblical Criticism* (Philadelphia: University of Pennsylvania Press, 1985).

57. The same issues apply equally to biblical narrative texts where synchronic analysis is increasingly championed. Nevertheless, the 'Bible as Literature' movement contradicts its own mandate, overlooking in its exclusive use of a synchronic method precisely the essential issues of authorship and creativity disclosed by means of diachronic analysis. See B.M. Levinson, ' "The Right Chorale": From the Poetics to the Hermeneutics of the Hebrew Bible', in *'Not in Heaven': Coherence and Complexity in Biblical Narrative* (ed. J. Rosenblatt and J. Sitterson; Bloomington: Indiana University Press, 1991), pp. 129-53.

58. *Sipre Deuteronomy, pisqa* 71 (ed. Finkelstein, p. 134).

the blood of flesh torn from a living body![59]

Clearly these resolutions of a highly stratified text into a synchronically coherent one illuminate neither the plain meaning of the text nor its compositional history.[60] The texts can be read that way but it is unlikely that they were written that way. Maintaining such a reading of enforced coherence entails specific hermeneutical moves, grounded less in the texts themselves than in hermeneutical need: the claim that the cases are different saves the coherence of the canon. What triggers such a reading is an external construct: the assumption, or the creation, of a meta-system of law whose origins are ultimately independent of the text yet which seek confirmation in it. Westbrook's 'common law', subsuming individual texts to a larger system that assumes coherence, has all the attributes of an exegetically harmonized scriptural canon. Diachronic analysis of biblical law is truer to the compositional norms of both cuneiform and Israelite literature and accounts for the specifics of the text more coherently.

---

59. *Sipre Deuteronomy, pisqa* 76 (ed. Finkelstein, pp. 141-42). In these two cases, I have used examples raised by Moshe Weinfeld in his review of G. Langer, *Von Gott erwählt—Jerusalem. Die Rezeption von Dtn 12 im frühen Judentum*, in *Bib* 72 (1991), pp. 111-12.

60. J.D. Levenson, 'The Hebrew Bible, the Old Testament, and Historical Criticism', in R.E. Friedman and H.G.M. Williamson (eds.), *The Future of Biblical Studies* (Atlanta: Scholars Press, 1987), pp. 19-59, at p. 21, analyzes the issue pointedly: 'By harmonizing inconcinnities, the tradition presents itself with a timeless document, one that appears to speak to the present only because the historical setting of the speaking voice or the writing hand has been suppressed, and all voices and all hands are absorbed into an eternal simultaneity'.

SOME ISSUES RELATING TO THE COMPARABILITY OF LAWS
AND THE COHERENCE OF THE LEGAL TRADITION[1]

Samuel Greengus

Biblical scholars have long been aware of similarities between the laws found in cuneiform sources and laws recorded in the Pentateuch; the similarities are, after all, obvious, particularly when one reads the casuistically formulated laws such as are found in the 'Covenant Code' (Exod. 21–23) and in the book of Deuteronomy (especially chs. 19–25). The problem has been, rather, how to describe the cultural and intellectual interconnections between ancient Israel and its pagan neighbors. The late J.J. Finkelstein fairly described the present state of the problem: 'There is, in short, no certain way at present of explaining the verbal identity between sources that are perhaps as much as five hundred years and as many miles apart. But the fact of this identity is incontrovertible and compels us to postulate an organic linkage between them even if this linkage cannot be reconstructed'.[2]

R. Westbrook, in this paper and in other recent writings, argues that we can solve the problem if we consider the ancient sources in a new and bold way. He asserts that both biblical and cuneiform laws must be seen as part of a single, coherent, 'common law' system based

1.   Before beginning my formal remarks, I want to express my appreciation to Raymond Westbrook for inviting me and the others to comment publicly on his paper as well as on his published works. His rich contributions are indeed worthy of special attention; they provide exciting new energy and stimulus to our study of law both in the ancient Near East and in the Hebrew Bible. He reminds us again of how important it is always to include consideration of cuneiform law when we speak of biblical law. Reading his work has given me many opportunities to learn and to grow; I offer my comments, therefore, in a spirit both of friendship and gratitude.

2.   J.J. Finkelstein, *The Ox that Gored* (Transactions of the American Philosophical Society, 71/2; Philadelphia: The American Philosophical Society, 1981), p. 20.

on traditions of scholarship that were transmitted and maintained by scribes writing in cuneiform, who lived and worked not only in Mesopotamia but also in Palestine, Syria, Anatolia, and beyond. The ancient collections of laws—like the Code of Hammurapi and the Covenant Code—were not legislation in a primary sense but 'scientific' treatises (in the limited character of pre-Hellenistic science)—textbooks as it were—created to instruct and teach the principles of law. Gaps and omissions in the various ancient law collections exist but need not be overemphasized. The ancient cultures all shared similar rules; related cases from the various collections can therefore be combined, in a process that Westbrook calls 'a positive argument from silence', to yield a coherent picture of legal practices both in ancient Israel as well as among its neighbors.[3]

Westbrook's theory of a shared coherent common law system inevitably raises questions about the ability or likelihood of even slow-moving ancient societies to maintain uniform views and practices over a span of no less than fifteen hundred years.[4] Westbrook's thesis will be weakened if one cannot reconstruct a 'common law' using materials taken from several if not all of the ancient law collections.[5] Westbrook anticipates and begins to answer such questions by arguing that the cuneiform legal materials emerge from essentially static social and legal systems. But at the same time, he must concede the existence of what appears to be social reform in ancient Israel. But he counters this by arguing that the Deuteronomic and Priestly Codes stand religiously and philosophically apart from the Covenant Code. Westbrook assigns the Deuteronomic and Priestly Codes to a later and different intellectual era; their rejection of earlier practices, such as

3. R. Westbrook, *Studies in Biblical and Cuneiform Law* (CahRB, 26; Paris: Gabalda, 1988), pp. 1-8 provides a fuller statement of his position. He does however also make many of these same points in his articles.

4. This span of time is minimally necessary in order to encompass the early Sumerian law collections beginning with Urnammu (Third Dynasty of Ur) c. 2100 BCE as well as the 'Deuteronomic' revisions and the Neo-Babylonian laws of the middle to late first millennium BCE. The entire cultural span is probably much longer.

5. In his review of Westbrook, *Studies*, M. Malul, writing in *Or* 59 (1990), p. 86, questions whether it is methodologically sound 'to treat as an integral whole more than 3000 years of law, spreading over the vast area of the ANE, including Asia Minor and Canaan, and view them as reflecting a unified and single law system so that any source from any period or era may be taken to explain, supplement and illuminate other sources from other periods and areas'.

vicarious liability[6] and ransom,[7] represents, for Westbrook, a departure from age-old customs, that were previously operative in the common law of the ancient Near East and in the Covenant Code.[8] Furthermore, says Westbrook, the differences in attitude between biblical codes are not simply the result of reforms or changes in Israel's religious, moral, and social ideology but rather reflect larger intellectual changes which embraced the entire ancient world, not just ancient Israel.[9]

I will take up only a few of the issues that Westbrook's thesis raises. I will offer comments that represent my own view of these issues, along with my suggestions for some modifications or alternative possibilities within the framework of the discussion. My comments do not come out of a philosophical opposition to his general hypothesis; but I believe it is possible—and for me, necessary—to refine or modify some of its attractive features.

1. *Legal Systems: Static or Dynamic?*

The first issue is his projection of an essentially unchanging and static ancient Near Eastern 'common law'. I have no argument with a general proposition recognizing the existence of cultural conservatism in pre-industrial and pre-scientific societies. The work of all modern

---

6.   Rejection of the earlier practice of extending responsibility to family members for crimes committed by an individual is stated in 2 Kgs 14.5-6; Deut. 24.16; Ezek. 18.

7.   Num. 35.31-34 strongly condemns the practice of giving ransom or compensation for intentional homicide.

8.   In *Studies*, pp. 134-35, Westbrook described the differences between the Covenant Code and the Priestly and Deuteronomic Codes in a less contrastive fashion: 'The real difference between biblical and cuneiform law lies in the fact the Bible . . . unlike the cuneiform texts. . . contains the voice of dissent as much, if not more, then that of the establishment. . . Of the biblical law codes, the Covenant Code is closest to the establishment and to presenting what might be regarded as the common law of Ancient Israel. . . What emerges. . . is that biblical law is neither a mass of internal contradictions nor a monolith, but reflects a single, coherent common law, upon which different opinions were expressed'.

9.   In his paper (p. 28) Westbrook states: 'The later biblical codes—the Deuteronomic and Priestly codes—share something of the intellectual ferment of contemporary Greek sources, and thus some taste also of their new legal conceptions'.

disciplines which use the comparative method after all incorporates recognition of such similarities. These disciplines include anthropology, linguistics, archaeology, sociology, and law. At the same time, we must also recognize that our methods of scientific analysis require that we, in a sense, must 'freeze' our objects of study in a moment of time or 'timelessness' in order to accomplish our comparison. The question for me is: despite conservatism and moments 'frozen in time', are there nevertheless evidences of dynamic forces and change within the horizons that we are comparing?

Westbrook maintains that for ancient Near Eastern law, such changes are limited in scope: temporary suspensions of otherwise valid laws, administrative reorganizations, or changes in prices and penalties. He proposes both to 'test' and 'prove' his hypothesis about the lack of change by examining the Hittite laws, a series of documents in which there are repeated references to what was done formerly alongside of the changes subsequently instituted by the newer laws. Westbrook points out that some of these changes relate to reductions in penalties.[10] Westbrook also makes fleeting reference to the fact that in HL §§ 9, 25, the reduction in penalty is made possible because the 'king has waived the share of the palace' (note 27). But he does not explore possible concomitant factors, for example, changes in Hittite society or polity, which might explain why such apparently permanent changes in the Hittite scheme of justice came about.

His discussion mentions the earlier 'Reform text' of Uru'inimgina which dates to the end of the third millennium BCE. But he calls it an 'Edict' and leaves the reader with the impression that all of the changes mentioned in it are 'of one piece' with the price changes, tariffs, temporary cancellation of debts that one finds in the Old Babylonian royal edicts. However, the prescriptions of Uru'inimgina include more than reductions in fees. They include measures which scholars generally interpret as restructuring the fundamental relationships between temple and palace as well as between these institutions and the population at large.[11] Moreover, the stated intent of these

10. HL §§ 9-13, 19, 25, 57-59, 67-69. For Hittite Laws (henceforth cited as HL), see J. Friedrich, *Die hethitischen Gesetze* (Documenta et Monumenta ad Iura Orientis Antiqui, 7; Leiden: Brill, 1971); see also the work of H. Hoffner cited in n. 15 below.

11. For a recent translation of the 'Reform texts' see J. Cooper, *Sumerian and Akkadian Royal Inscriptions: Presargonic Inscriptions* (The American Oriental

prescriptions conveys that these changes were instituted by a desire or need to rectify social injustices despite the fact that the 'conventions of former times' had been in place 'since time immemorial'.[12]

Moreover, while it is true that the social and economic relief measures given in the Old Babylonian edicts were temporary in nature, their purpose, as repeatedly stated, was also to 'establish justice [i.e. equity] in the land'.[13] So it is misleading, in my view, in any way to suggest that conservatism in law, which we recognize as being present, was in itself a factor or force limiting the range of what could be changed when reforms were enacted.

I am also reluctant to follow Westbrook when he says that the scope of ancient reforms is limited only to those areas actually covered in the Old Babylonian royal edicts.[14] The measures enacted in the edicts were, after all, responses to areas of abuse for which immediate relief was needed. A suffering populace would certainly wish for measures like cancellation of debts, administrative reorganization, setting the amounts of penalties, tariffs, and other economic benefits. The 'business of government' inevitably is weighted towards economic issues; is it any different today, in our own time, when we as citizens ask for relief from taxes, tariffs, high interest rates, and the abusive practices of government officials? In my view, therefore, there were dynamic forces operating in these ancient societies that did stimulate significant reforms and changes. If some of the laws remained

Society Translation Series, 1; New Haven: American Oriental Society, 1986), I, pp. 70-78 and literature cited there. For analysis see also C. Gadd's chapter 'Society and Social Problems', *CAH*, 3rd edn, I/2, pp. 139-142 and B. Foster, 'A New Look at the Sumerian Temple State', *JESHO* 24 (1981), pp. 225-41. Foster concludes (p. 237) 'In other words, Uruinimgina's acts were a reversal, based on divine authority, of customs established from earliest times'.

12. Cf. Cooper, *Sumerian and Akkadian Royal Inscriptions*, pp. 70-72, La 9.1. This text also includes statements such as 'administrators no longer plunder the orchards of the poor' and that 'Uru'inimgina solemnly promised Ningirsu [i.e. his god] that he would never subjugate the waif and the widow to the powerful'.

13. F.R. Kraus, *Königliche Verfügungen in altbabylonischer Zeit* (Studia et Documenta ad Iuris Orientis Antiqui Pertinentia, 11; Leiden: Brill, 1984), pp. 3-30.

14. On p. 25 Westbrook states: 'Any reforms, therefore, that are attributed to differences in the law codes, will only be credible if they fall within those three categories. . . .'. The categories he refers to are those found in the royal edicts, namely 'retrospective cancellation of debts, reorganization of royal administration and fixing of prices (which. . . also means pecuniary penalties)'.

conservatively the same, it was because they belonged to cultural areas in which there were no critical social policy issues.

We find evidence of 'reforms' or significant changes in social policy not only in the royal edicts but also in the law collections themselves. We turn again to the Hittite laws. Westbrook (note 28) in my opinion, minimizes the significance of the changes recorded in HL §§ 92, 101, 121 (which he omits), 166-67. They are all cases where formerly the corporal punishment was given but in the later laws only monetary payments or expiatory sacrifices were required. In § 92, a man who stole several beehives formerly was exposed to the stinging of bees; the new penalty was monetary. In § 101, one who stole certain vines or plants was subject to being struck with a spear in addition to monetary penalties; in the new law, the penalties appear to be increased but the corporal punishment is dropped. In §121 one who stole a plow was tied to what may have been part of a plow and his body trampled or sundered by oxen; the new penalties are monetary. In §§ 166-67, a man 'who sowed seed upon seed' had 'his neck put on a plow' attached to two teams of oxen who literally pulled his body apart; the oxen, too, were to be killed.[15] In the newer law, sheep were substituted for the man and the oxen along with a purification offering of bread and beer.

Leading Hittitologists have seen the removal or reduction of death penalties in these Hittite laws as part of a wider change in societal attitudes, rejecting talionic retribution in favor of compensation.[16] Westbrook's comment would have us believe, however, that the issue simply 'falls within the category of price-fixing'(on p. 25 and in note 28). He removes HL §§ 166-67 from the discussion by relegating it to 'the religious sphere'. Yet it does provide another illustration where capital punishment was rescinded.

The suggestion of a purposeful ancient Hittite social policy, rejecting

15. This offense has been compared with the prohibitions in Lev. 19.19; Deut. 22.9. But see the comments of H. Hoffner, *The Laws of the Hittites* (Ann Arbor: University Microfilms, 1963), p. 226.

16. See the comments and literature cited by R. Haase, 'Kapitaldelikte im Hethitischen Recht', *Hethitica* 7 (1987), pp. 93-107. Most of the passages cited are also treated by V. Korošec, 'Die Todesstrafe in der Entwicklung des hethitischen Rechtes', in B. Alster (ed.), *Death in Mesopotamia* (Compte Rendu Rencontre Assyriologique Internationale, XXVIe; Mesopotamia Copenhagen Studies in Assyriology, 8; Copenhagen: Akademisk Forlag, 1980), pp. 199-212.

the death penalty in talionic settings, is reinforced by the contents of a letter, KBo I 10, written by the Hittite king Hattusili III to the Babylonian king Kadashman-Enlil II (c. 1270 BCE) which responds to the latter's complaint about his merchants having been murdered in Amurru and in Ugarit, regions under the control of the Hittites. This letter describes the handling of murderers in the realm and seems to say, according to Klengel's restorations, that homicide is handled by compensation paid to the brothers of the deceased and a ceremony of purification at the site of his killing. But 'if the brothers of the deceased decline compensation, then they shall make the murderer...'. The passage (KBo I 10 rev. 21-22) is broken; Klengel suggests that the broken passage might have stated the enslavement of the murderer.[17] This suggestion is most plausible since the Hittite Laws, in a number of places, require slayers or persons otherwise held responsible for homicide to supply either themselves or members of their family or household to the family of the victim; this penalty appears in situations where compensation was not paid.[18] Otherwise, the payment of compensation for murdered merchants is in line with what we find in HL § 5, where the same rules apply.

Hattusili's overall policy is echoed in a series of contemporary documents from Ugarit, dealing with the murder of merchants and the payment of compensation.[19] Some are actual treaties dealing with this problem that were drawn up between the local rulers at Ugarit and

---

17. H. Klengel, 'Mord und Bussleistung im Spätbronzezeitlichen Syrien', in Alster (ed.), *Death in Mesopotamia*, pp. 189-97. The Akkadian states: (20) *ù šum-ma* ŠEŠ.MEŠ-*šú* (21) [KÙ.BABBAR *mu-ul-le]-e ú-ul i-mah-ha-ru da-i-ka-na ša na-pu-ul-ti* (22) [*l]i-pu-šu*. For Klengel's suggested restoration in line 22, cf. *ana ardūtim epēšu*, which is attested in the Boghazkoy text *KUB* III 19:4' cited by *CAD* E, p. 203. For Westbrook's reconstruction of this passage see below in connection with n. 21.

18. HL §§ 1-4, 43-44. The practice of giving over family members (as slaves) in cases of homicide is not limited to the Hittites but also occurs in early Sumer; see Falkenstein *NSG* II 40 and his discussion there. It is generally true, in antiquity, that persons who cannot pay their obligations are forced to become slaves.

19. These texts, cited by Klengel, 'Mord und Bussleistung' (n. 17), are RS 17.42, 17.145, 17.158, 17.234; these texts are treated in *PRU IV= MRS IX*, pp. 169-174. All of these record settlements ordered by the king of Ugarit for the murder of foreign merchants. Compensation is the only remedy considered for the murder of a merchant in RS 20.22, a letter written by the king of Carchemish; it is published in *MRS XVI = Ugaritica* 5, pp. 94-97.

Carchemish. These treaties consistently regulate that one who has murdered a merchant from the other ruler's country, if apprehended, must restore any lost goods with penalty as well as pay a heavy compensation to the family.[20]

Westbrook, writing elsewhere, has attempted to reinterpret the Hattusili letter in an effort to suggest that the murdered merchant's family also had an option to insist that the murderer be given the death penalty.[21] But this reconstruction would contradict everything else we know about contemporary Hittite practices in Anatolia and Syria.[22] It might be possible, however, to argue that in cases involving

20. The treaties are RS 17.146, 17.230, 18.115 which appear in *PRU IV* = *MRS IX*, pp. 153-160. The same level of compensation is paid for the loss of life whether the murderers are apprehended or whether they are not. The compensation payments are substantial; they are set at 3 minas in RS 17.146 and described as 'they shall pay the compensation of one person', *mullû ša ištēn amēlim umallûni*; cf. *CAD* M/2, p. 189b. 180 shekels (approximately equal to $3-3\frac{1}{2}$ minas) is likewise the amount of compensation paid for the life of a slain merchant in RS 17.42 and 17.158 (for references, see previous note). In 17.230 even higher payments are prescribed: 'they shall pay a three-fold compensation for a (loss of) life' (*napišta 3-šú umallû*).

21. R. Westbrook, *Studies*, pp. 51-52, proposes restoring something like [*damēšu l*]*ipušū* 'they may shed his blood' in *KBo* I 10 line 22 (see n. 17 above). Although the restoration is linguistically possible (cf. *CAD* E, p. 206a), it has no other support. It likewise seems pointless for Westbrook to have the Hittite king say (in line 16) 'they do not commit murder in the land of Hatti' when this very problem is dealt with in HL § 5 and is the reason for the Babylonian king writing to him in the first place. Klengel, 'Mord und Bussleistung', p. 190, translated 'in the land of Hatti they do not execute (for capital crimes)'. Moreover, in *KBo* I 10 lines 22-26, Hattusili goes on to say: 'If a man has committed a crime against the king and [flees (?)/ is sent away(?)] to another country, it is not the practice to kill him. My brother, ask others and they will tell you. . . now those who do not execute a political criminal should they execute a merchant (who has killed another merchant)?. . . . send the brothers of the slain merchants to me so that I may examine their case'. Klengel's translation and understanding of the passage is the same as that of Korošec, 'Die Todesstrafe', pp. 203-204 (n. 16) and R. Haase, *Texte zum hethitischen Recht* (Wiesbaden: Ludwig Reichert Verlag, 1984), pp. 52-53 (the passage is treated on p. 86). In his edict, an earlier Hittite king, Telepinu, reports how he determined not to execute a group of (royal?) conspirators, choosing instead punishments of mutilation and slavery (see further n. 27).

22. Westbrook, *Studies*, pp. 51-52, also mentions an important passage in the Edict of Telepinu where the family of the victim has the option of refusing compensation and insisting that the murderer receive the death penalty. But the Edict deals entirely with crimes done by members of the royal family to one another. The

the murder of merchants a fixed policy for compensation was instituted in response to problems inherent in trying cases involving foreigners or in arranging for the extradition of criminals between countries. These problems are still with us in modern times: countries are reluctant to try and impose death penalties on foreign citizens; and fellow countrymen of a murderer will certainly place pressure on their government to avoid extradition of their kinsman, even if he is a murderer. A fixed policy of compensation for such 'international' crimes might therefore be viewed as a more expeditious way of solving such situations.[23] This analysis may or may not be true. But in any case, we are still faced with explaining what otherwise appears to be a Hittite policy that reduces punitive measures both in the area of corporal punishment as well as in levels of compensation.

The Hittites, furthermore, appear to have revised their views on vicarious liability, eliminating it in ordinary cases but not necessarily in situations dealing with the king or with the royal family. There is a hint of vicarious liability in HL § 173: 'One who contests a judgement of the king's court—his house will be made into a ruin' (apparently with him in it).[24] More severity is seen in a document dealing with the care of the king and his household, where actions which put the pure

standards in such cases were apparently more severe than for commoners. See further below, in connection with n. 27.

23. A similar situation may be behind *ARM* 13 145:19-22, from the Old Babylonian period. Yawi-Ilâ, an ally of Zimri-Lim reports his discussion with a foreign king's representatives in which they told him: *šumma Bunuma-Addu dīn napištim id-di-[an] u napištam um-tal-al-[li] tasallimā* 'If PN will submit to a trial for the loss of life and (if) he will have paid (compensation for) the life (lost), then will you make a treaty (with us)'? We read here *umtalli*, G perfect, as *CAD* M/1, p. 182b rather than *umtalla*, Dt, as A. Finet, *ARMT* 13, pp. 152, 173; the phrase *napištam mullû* also occurs at Ras Shamra (see note 20 above, citing RS 17.23). One may also compare Middle Assyrian *napšāte mullû* ; for references, see *CAD* M/1, p. 183b.

24. The death penalty is implied because the paragraph goes on to say that if one contests the judgement of a noble, they shall cut off his head; and a rebellious slave will be 'put into a pot'(buried alive?). Cf. further the punishment threatened by Nebuchadnezzar in Dan. 2.5: 'you shall be torn limb from limb and your houses shall be laid in ruins.' Haase, 'Kapitaldelikte', p. 96, considers the 'ruin of the house' to imply that the death penalty was also applied to the offender's family. Many royal land grants contain a clause stating that anyone who contests the king's word will lose his head. For examples see Haase, *Texte zum hethitischen Recht*, pp. 69-72, who cites K.K. Riemschneider, 'Die hethitischen Land-schenkungsurkunden', *MIO* 6 (1958), pp. 354-55, 356-57, 360-61, 364-65.

state of the king in jeopardy are severely punished. A royal retainer who has done so or who knows of such action and conceals it will be punished along with his wives and children.[25] Vicarious liability remained an operative concept in Hittite vassal treaties, where kings who offend the gods by breaking the solemn oath of allegiance sworn by their names invoke punishment not only upon themselves but upon their families and possessions.[26]

The Edict of Telepinu, a Hittite king who ruled some two centuries earlier than Hattusili III (c. 1500 BCE), decreed a series of measures to diminish strife within the royal family by regulating succession to the throne as well as how members of the royal family should be treated when they commit serious (unspecified) crimes against one another. In such cases, when the perpetrators were of royal blood, even when capital punishment was warranted, only the offender was to be penalized, not his family, slaves, property, or livestock. This provision suggests that there was a changed attitude about the fairness of vicarious liability. The edict then goes on to state the regulation to be followed in case of homicide: when one member of the royal family murders another member, the family member closest to the victim may choose to accept compensation or may order the murderer to be executed.[27] This appears to have been a further attempt to avoid bloodshed between members of the royal family, offering compensation as an alternative to capital punishment.

We cannot say, on the basis of Telepinu's edict, whether a commoner

25. 'Instruction for Palace Personnel to Insure the King's Purity', translated by A. Goetze, *ANET*, 3rd edn, p. 207. Vicarious liability also appears in the ceremony of the military oath; see R. Haase, 'Die Kollektivhaftung bei den Hethitern, Ein Einblick', in *Studi in onore di Cesare Sanfilippo* (Pubblicazioni della facoltà di giurisprudenza Università di Catani, 96; Milan: Giuffrè, 1982), I, pp. 219-230. For a translation of the oath text see Haase, *Texte zum hethitischen Recht*, pp. 88-90.

26. Cf. V. Korosec, 'Die Kollektivhaftung im hethitischen Recht', *ArOr* 18/3 (1950), pp. 198-202. Mursilis II in his 'Plague Prayer' attributes the misfortunes visited upon his kingdom as punishment for his father having broken the treaty he swore with Egypt; see A. Goetze, *ANET*, 3rd edn, pp. 395-97.

27. The Edict of Telepinu has recently been translated by Haase, *Texte zum hethitischen Recht*, pp. 52-53. Haase used for his translation a 1970 Munich dissertation, *Der Telepinu Erlass* by W. Eisele. The Edict is sometimes cited by paragraphs; these divisions appear in an earlier treatment by E.H. Sturtevant and George Bechtel, *A Hittite Chrestomathy* (Philadelphia: University of Pennsylvania Press, 1935), pp. 175-200.

who murdered a member of the royal family would have escaped the death penalty. The severe regulations relating to the king discussed above suggest that royal blood was in some sense sacred. This is apparent, again, in Telepinu's edict, where he contemplated a case in which a relative of the king knew of sorcery commited by his own family member but did not come forward to disclose it. Telepinu promised to punish the entire family of that sorcerer. Hattusili III later recorded an actual case involving a relative who committed sorcery against him. Hattusili states that he did not exact a full measure of vicarious liability but contented himself with banishing the sorcerer and taking half of his lands away.[28] We may therefore view the edict of Telepinu as a 'forerunner' to the later Hittite social policies which worked to reduce vicarious liability and which also eliminated capital punishment in favor of compensation in cases of homicide.[29]

Westbrook argues elsewhere[30] that the division between talion and compensation has been overstated; in fact, both modes of settlement coexist at all times, in ancient Israel and in the ancient Near East. The inclusion of either compensation or talion in a given law formulation is the product of didactic selection; the laws should not be read in contrastive but in complementary fashion. I am not persuaded that this is the case for the Hittites in their dealing with homicide. I also see a number of problems in the other cuneiform law collections which, in

---

28. For a translation of this document, which has been called 'The Apology of Hattusili III', see Haase, *Texte zum hethitischen Recht*, pp. 54-55 and Haase's discussion in 'Die Kollektivhaftung', p. 226. The 'Apology' is also treated in Sturtevant and Bechtel, *A Hittite Chrestomathy*, pp. 42-99. In his treaty with Kupanta-^{d}KAL (Haase, *Texte zum hethitischen Recht*, pp. 82-83), Mursilis II, father of Hattusili III, describes a similar and, apparently by his time, customary penalty for treason: the son of the guilty party is spared but his property will be confiscated.

29. Hittite sentiment against capital punishment appears to draw upon deeply rooted beliefs and customs within their culture. A Middle Hittite document containing instructions for the government officials required that 'the commander of the border guards, the town commandant, and the elders shall judge and decide legal cases in accordance with the law. As it has been from olden days—in a town in which they have been accustomed to imposing the death penalty, they shall continue to do so. But in a town where they have been accustomed to imposing exile, they shall continue that (custom).' See A. Goetze, *ANET*, 3rd edn, pp. 210-211 (also in Haase, *Texte zum hethitischen Recht*, p. 59).

30. Westbrook, *Studies*, pp. 41-47.

my opinion, would make his hypothesis less 'sweeping'. Among them are (1) the need to reconstruct talionic reprisals in laws where they are absent, notably the law 'codes' of Urnammu and Eshnunna; (2) the need to insert compensation into cases which state only talion; (3) the apparently simultaneous practices of applying talion to injuries sustained by upper classes but requiring only compensation for injuries against lower social groups.[31] At the same time, however, one does find the coexistence of compensation and blood revenge in Assyria in all periods.[32]

The entire previous discussion relates to but one area of social and cultural change within the ancient Near East. There are in fact many such changes that have been observed; but scholars have not always looked for or been able to find the impact of these changes in the laws. Conversely, there are changes in the laws that have clearly occurred but which have not been linked with specific historical events. Some examples of the first category are: the disappearance of individual city political identities, typical of the earlier Old Babylonian period, into a

---

31. So, e.g. CH (Code of Hammurapi) §§ 196-205, 209-214, 218-20, 229-31. The laws of Ur-Nammu §§18-22 and LE (Laws of Eshnunna) §§42-48, which deal with similar injuries, require the perpetrators in such cases to pay only compensation; there is no mention of talionic reprisals. For Ur-Nammu laws see J.J. Finkelstein, 'The Laws of Ur-Nammu', *JCS* 22 (1969), pp. 66-82 (his paragraph numbers are §§15-19) and F. Yildiz, 'A Tablet of Codex Ur-Nammu from Sippar', *Or* 50 (1981), pp. 87-97. For the Laws of Eshnunna see A. Goetze, *The Laws of Eshnunna* (AASOR, 31; New Haven: American Schools of Oriental Research, 1956) and more recently, R. Yaron, *The Laws of Eshnunna* (Jerusalem: Magnes Press, 2nd edn, 1988). For the Code of Hammurapi, see G.R. Driver and J.C. Miles (eds.), *The Babylonian Laws* (2 vols.; Oxford: Clarendon Press, 1952–55).

32. MAL A §10, B §2. For these Middle Assyrian Laws see G.R. Driver and J.C. Miles, *The Assyrian Laws* (Oxford: Clarendon Press, 1935). See further M. Roth, 'Homicide in the Neo-Assyrian Period', in F. Rochberg-Halton (ed.), *Language, Literature and History: Philological Studies Presented to Erica Reiner* (AOS, 67; New Haven: American Oriental Society, 1987), pp. 351-365; and *CAD* D, p. 79 (*damu*). There is an oblique reference to compensation in *ARM* 8 1, an adoption contract from Mari written during the period of Assyrian rule. One of its provisions states that the one who breaks the agreement (lines 27-31) 'will have violated the taboos of (the gods) Shamash, Itur-Mer (as well as of the king) Shamshi-Addu and (his son, ruler of Mari) Yasmah-Addu and shall (also) pay $3\frac{1}{3}$ minas (an amount equivalent to) the silver of cases involving loss of life' (*kasap dīn napištim*). As we have already seen (n. 20 above), similar amounts were paid at Ras Shamra.

unified royal realm by the time of the Kassites; the rise and use of Aramaic and the eclipse of the Akkadian language. Some examples of the second category are: the disappearance of royal edicts establishing justice and equity after the Old Babylonian period; the disappearance of 'brideprice' (*tirhatu*) and the legal prominence of dowry (*nudunnû*) in the Neo-Babylonian period.[33]

Bible scholars, recognizing that the history of ancient Israel includes memory of a number of important social and cultural changes, have been more ready to create diachronic analyses. An earlier tribal, semi-nomadic phase was followed by a settled, agrarian phase; and during this development, the center of authority moved from elders and clan leaders to monarchy and, finally, to theocracy. There are also significant archaeological discontinuities, especially the one between the Late Bronze and Iron Ages, which suggest social change and upheaval. The question, of course, has always been: is it possible to correlate individual laws or collections of laws within the Bible with any of these identified historical changes? A great deal has been written in the attempt to answer this question. But clearly, scholars who have tried to do so face many difficulties because our received biblical texts are a diverse group of sources that, in addition, give evidence of later perspectives and advocacy positions superimposed upon older traditions and materials.

2. *Literary Editing in the Laws*

It is widely believed that the Covenant Code, which is the focus of Westbrook's paper, belongs to the oldest part of Israelite history because a large number of its casuistically formulated laws find their parallels in the ancient Near Eastern law collections.[34] Westbrook

---

33. E. Otto, 'Die Bedeutung der altorientalischen Rechtsgeschichte für das Verständnis des Alten Testaments', *ZTK* 88 (1991), pp. 139-168, citing examples of changes in cuneiform law, mentions (p.150) the phenomenon of the 'secularization' of the temples in Old Babylonian times discussed by R. Harris, 'On the Process of Secularization under Hammurapi', *JCS* 15 (1961), pp. 117-120, as well as the change from 'vom Streitbeendigungsvorschlag zum Streitentscheid' in the Old Babylonian period which was proposed by J.G. Lautner, *Die richterliche Enstscheidung und die Streitbeendigung im altbabylonischen Prozessrechte* (Leipziger rechtswissenschaftliche Studien, 3; Leipzig: Theodor Weicher, 1922). Both of these changes have been ascribed to the rising power of monarchy.

34. For a list of parallels see S. Greengus 'Law in the OT', *IDBSup*, pp. 533-34.

does not dispute the relative antiquity of the Covenant Code but would minimize or deny the effects of any literary or historical processes upon the drafting of its contents. He focuses on Alt's hypothesis of 'casuistic' and 'apodictic' laws, which is a 'capstone' placed upon a large edifice of scholarship that has sought to connect the forms of the laws with identified historical groups and processes.[35] Scholars have since found serious flaws in Alt's hypothesis, noting that all of the so-called 'apodictic' forms are also to be found in non-Israelite contexts.[36] I therefore believe that Westbrook is indeed correct when he says that 'the same rule may be drafted casuistically, apodictically, or in some other fashion' (p. 32). But, as I see the matter, accepting this conclusion does not automatically mean that one cannot look for or hope to discover other effects of literary or historical processes within the text of the Covenant Code.

I do not claim to be a literary specialist, so I will offer just a few comments on literary features in the Covenant Code. To begin with, we cannot escape recognition of the fact that the Covenant Code, as we have received it in the MT, is itself embedded in a larger framework

One should note, however, that not all laws in the Covenant Code find a parallel in the near Eastern legal collections.

35. For a useful, recent discussion of this scholarship see J.M. Sprinkle, *A Literary Approach to Biblical Law Exodus 20:22-23:19* (Ann Arbor: University Microfilms, 1990), pp. 1-34 (now published as *The 'Book of the Covenant': A Literary Approach* [JSOTSup, 174; Sheffield: JSOT Press, 1994]).

36. A few references are cited by Westbrook in n. 3 of his article in this volume. For others, see Sprinkle, *Literary Approach*, p. 27 n. 58. Some attention has been drawn to the presence of second person address in the Hittite vassal treaties. In this connection the recently published treaty from Ebla is especially interesting. It contains 'categorical' statements like 'The sons of Abarsal as well as the daughters of Abarsal shall be slaves of Ebla (lines 455-474)'. Many clauses in casuistic style, i.e. beginning in *šumma*, of course also occur as well as a number of quoted addresses, e.g. 'Thus the ruler of Ebla to Abarsal. . . ' The shift from third person to second person (and back) within the same document was not stylistically a problem of the same magnitude for the ancient Semitic drafters of the treaty as it has been for modern interpreters of the Covenant Code. For the text of the Ebla treaty, cf. E. Sollberger, 'The So-Called Treaty between Ebla and Assur', *SEb* 3 (1980), pp. 129-155 and the further remarks of B. Kienast, 'Der Vertrag Ebla - Assur in rechtshistorischer Sicht', in H. Hauptmann and H. Waetzoldt (eds.), *Wirtschaft und Gesellschaft von Ebla* (Heidelberger Studien zum Alten Orient, 2; Heidelberg: Heidelberger Verlag, 1988), pp. 231-43, who includes a list of other Akkadian treaties.

that is not a law code.[37] This feature is not fully unique because two of the oldest law collections, the 'codes' of Lipit-Ishtar and Hammurapi, are 'encased' in a prologue and epilogue of non-legal character. These non-legal frameworks of course have their own story to tell about political events and attitudes. But scholars have not been able to find many links between these frameworks and the laws themselves.

The case is certainly different for the Covenant Code. The arrangement of laws within Exod. 21.1–23.9 has been the subject of intense literary study since before medieval times; even pre-modern scholars, who were not motivated by any historical or apologetic considerations, saw patterns in these chapters which parallel the Decalogue in Exodus 20. Thus, for example Nachmanides, in his commentary to Exod. 21.1 states: 'The first *mishpat* begins with the [case of] the Hebrew slave because in the setting free of the slave in the seventh year there is a remembrance of the exodus from Egypt spoken of in the first [Decalogue] commandment... And after completing this *mishpat* dealing with [male and female] Hebrew slaves, [Exod. 21.1-11] the [next] *mishpat* [Exod. 21.12] takes up [Decalogue commandment of] "Thou shalt not murder"....'. Nachmanides also notes laws in the Covenant Code reflecting the commandments against theft (i.e. Exod. 21.37–22.3; 22.6-12) and reflecting honor of parents (i.e. Exod. 21.13-17).[38]

Finkelstein, in his noteworthy study comparing the 'goring ox' cases found in the Bible and in the Near Eastern law collections, saw what he believed was a meaningful disjunction between the case where the ox gored a human (Exod. 21.28-32) and the case where the ox gored another ox (Exod. 21.35-36). The close parallel cases in the Eshnunna Laws §§ 53-55, by contrast, are connected without any interruption between them. Finkelstein believed that the biblical writer consciously separated these cases. The first belongs to the grouping of laws dealing with damages to persons, the second to a group of laws dealing with damages to property or 'things'. Finkelstein was even ready to consider the possibility that the biblical writer was conscious of the

---

37. See the discussion by S. Paul, *Studies in the Book of the Covenant in the Light of Cuneiform and Biblical Law* (VTSup, 18; Leiden: Brill, 1970), pp. 27-42.

38. Paul, *Studies in the Book of the Covenant*, p. 107 gives other examples, ancient and modern, of commentators who have addressed these literary patterns.

traditional sequence of these laws in a non-Hebraic prototype available to him![39]

Are there any such traces of literary reworking in the cuneiform law collections? Westbrook, in his paper, takes Koschaker to task for having viewed the cuneiform law collections as if they were the products of intensive re-editing, emerging through a scholastic process similar to that which created the Digest of Justinian. This critique is part of his argument for a stable, coherent, and conservative text of the Covenant Code, that is, a text free from inconsistencies that are the result of editorial process. Koschaker's approach has not found many followers; but even some of his noted opponents believed in a 'layered' legal tradition evolving over time: 'It may be admitted that the laws are not all of the same date and that the author was working on existing material... No code is the original invention of its legislator; he must work on material provided by others, he may alter, amend, or extend it, but he does not create *de novo* a code of laws'.[40]

There is to my knowledge at least one instance where Koschaker's method of close reading produced indisputable results. This was his analysis of CH § 125, a case of deposit, where the bailee, whose house was broken into and who also suffered loss of his own property, was nevertheless required to pay for the lost property left in his keeping. The bailee's only redress was to search for the lost property and recover it from the thief if he could find him. When the Code speaks of the obligation of the bailee to pay for the loss, it describes him as 'the owner of that house who has been negligent'. Therefore, said Koschaker, it seems reasonable for the owner to pay for the loss. But what was puzzling to him, however, was the beginning of the paragraph where it says that the house was broken into and that goods of the bailee were also lost. Koschaker, adducing many examples from comparative law, observed that the rule usually found in many legal

39. Finkelstein, *The Ox That Gored*, pp. 36-39. More recently, M. Malul has argued that the exceptional use of the verb נגף (cognate to Akkadian *nakāpu*) for the action of the ox in place of the customary verb נגח is additional proof of a direct link between the Covenant Code and the Laws of Hammurapi; see *The Comparative Method in Ancient Near Eastern and Biblical Legal Studies* (AOAT, 227; Neukirchen–Vluyn: Butzon & Bercker Kevelaer, 1990), pp. 140-43.

40. This comes from an earlier critique of Koschaker's methodology: G.R. Driver and J. Miles, 'Koschaker's Theory of the Old Assyrian Laws', *Babyloniaca* 9 (1926), pp. 41-65.

traditions was to exonerate a bailee whose own goods were lost along with the deposited item. In some of these societies, the bailee would need to swear to the facts. Koschaker therefore suggested that the drafter of the Code had before him a *Vorlage* in which two cases were present: one where the bailee also suffered loss and another where the bailee did not. Koschaker believed that the drafter of the Code interpolated the case where both suffered loss into the case of single loss and negligence that was the basis of CH § 125.[41] Some thirty years later, Koschaker's surmise was confirmed by the discovery of two such laws side by side in the Laws of Eshnunna §§ 36-37. The first case is one of single loss and therefore the bailee must pay; in the second case there is double loss, along with signs of breaking and entering; the bailee has liability unless he swears that he did not steal or act in collusion with the thief.

In this light, Exod. 22.6-7 appears to go in a direction different from its cuneiform parallel cases. In Exodus, the bailee from whose house the deposited goods were stolen is allowed to clear himself from responsibility by coming 'near to God, [to swear] whether he had put his hand upon his neighbor's goods'. But Exod. 22.6-7 does not state whether goods of the bailee were stolen along with the deposited goods of the bailor nor does it tell us why an oath is necessary. S. Paul attributed the oath-taking, simply, to a 'lack of evidence or contradictory statements. . . '.[42] Goetze and, most recently, Otto have interpreted Exod. 22.6-7 as reflecting a more rigid, archaic outlook, assigning responsibility automatically and requiring 'coming near to God'—either for oath or ordeal—in order for the bailee to gain release from liability. The cases in the Laws of Eshnunna, for them, would represent, culturally, a further step and later development.[43] If they are correct, then we have an instance where legal change and development can be seen or, at the very least, a situation where the

41. P. Koschaker, *Rechtsvergleichende Studien zur Gesetzgebung Hammurapis* (Leipzig: Veit, 1917), pp. 26-33.

42. Paul, *Studies in the Book of the Covenant*, p. 6.

43. Goetze, *The Laws of Eshnunna*, pp. 103-105 (note 31 above); Otto, 'Die Bedeutung der altorientalischen Rechtsgeschichte', p. 162. For Otto this is further proof that the biblical laws of deposit could not have been taken over from cuneiform law. Their understanding of the oath is in line with the rabbinic view, *m. B. Meṣ.* 3.1, where the bailee, indeed, must either swear or pay the value of the lost deposit; concomitant loss of his personal goods is not a factor.

biblical laws are not fully congruent with cuneiform laws. It might be possible to 'explain' the incongruity by assuming that Exod. 22.6-7 is poorly drafted and that the case there actually involved loss of goods by the bailee, similar to what we have in LE § 37. But if this is so, then we have here another instance of textual editing and a faulty one at that!

3. *A Case for Oral Tradition*

The written law collections which we find in the Old Testament and in the ancient Near East do not encompass the complete range of laws operative in their societies. This point is obvious for the Bible but not so clear for Mesopotamian laws. My comments, therefore will focus on the cuneiform law collections. A good illustration of their incompleteness can be seen by comparing the Eshnunna Laws with the Laws of Hammurapi. Both collections were written within a century of one another and emanate from virtually the same cultural milieu in Babylonia. Legal areas mentioned in both collections, for example, are the hire of wagons and boats (LE §§ 3-5, CH §§ 236-39, 275-77). The Hammurapi Laws add a case (CH § 240) dealing with losses due to collision and sinking of a craft, whereas the Eshnunna Laws add another case, not covered at all in the Hammurapi Laws, dealing with loss caused by someone using a vessel without the owner's permission (LE § 6). Both additions seem to be valid cases that could have fairly been considered by either society in their respective law collections.

The collection of Eshnunna Laws, which is less than one-fourth the size of the Hammurapi Laws, includes many more provisions not found in that larger corpus.[44] Thus, for example, one finds: the hire of harvest workers (LE §§ 7-9); of a fuller (LE §14); a slave woman who covertly passed her child to a free family (LE §§ 33-35); a bailee falsely claiming the theft of bailed goods in his possession (LE § 36); sale of an inheritance share by one of two heirs (LE § 38); biting by a mad dog whose owner was previously publicly admonished (LE §§ 56-57); battery causing injury to a finger or collarbone (LE §§ 43, 46).

The incomplete nature of the Old Babylonian law collections is further demonstrated by other significant omissions. There are important legal areas which were, clearly, fully operative in

44. The CH, the largest and most coherent of the ancient Near Eastern law collections, contains some 282 'paragraphs' while the LE has approximately 60.

Babylonian society since they are abundantly reflected in the contemporary documents. Some of these areas are even mentioned in the 'codes' in a tangential or passing fashion but the activities themselves do not appear as the primary subject of a law paragraph or provision. So, for example, one finds no cases directly dealing with arson, treason, theft of livestock, surety, barter, murder, manumission, or sale. The omission of such common cultural areas in the law collections can hardly be the result of any design or plan, particularly when one considers that, in the Hittite Laws, some of these same areas are omitted while others like arson (HL §§ 98-100), murder (HL § 1-6), and livestock theft (HL §§ 57-70) are included.

There were certain cultural 'forces' operative in antiquity which made it difficult to achieve completeness. Westbrook reminds us that Mesopotamian legal tradition was expressed in casuistic fashion, a form which cannot express all variations of situation and circumstance. Their ancient mode of 'scientific thinking' did not generate statements of general categories or principles based on the norms implied in the individual cases. This mode favored cumulation of examples; accordingly, our law collections therefore only list individual cases and can never be complete.[45]

The use of casuistic style coupled with the fact that law collections, like the Code of Hammurapi, survived and were recopied by later generations of scribes, suggested to some scholars that the cuneiform law collections were primarily 'school texts' with little if any connection to legal practice.[46] This position is really too severely

45. See discussion of Westbrook cited in n. 3 above. Westbrook makes some of these points in this paper (pp. 27-28) and, in general, contrasts Mesopotamian and Greek science. This analysis goes back to observations made by B. Landsberger, 'Die Eigenbegrifflichkeit der babylonischen Welt', *Islamica* 2 (1926–27), pp. 355-72 (see especially pp. 370-71). This important article has been translated into English by T. Jacobsen, B. Foster, H. von Siebenthal and published as a separate publication under the title *The Conceptual Autonomy of the Babylonian World* (MANE 1/4; Malibu: Undena, 1976).

46. F.R. Kraus, 'Ein zentrales Problem des altmesopotamischen Rechtes: Was ist der Codex Hammurapi?', *Geneva* 8 (1960), pp. 283-96. See also J. Bottéro, 'Le "Code" de Hammurapi', *Annali della Scuola normale superiore di Pisa* 12 (1982), pp. 409-44. In a later study, *Königliche Verfügungen*, pp. 114-16 (n. 13 above), Kraus modified his earlier position in response to a critique by W. Preiser, 'Zur rechtliche Natur der altorientalischen Gesetze', in P. Bockelmann *et al.* (eds.), *Festschrift für Karl Engisch* (Frankfurt am Main: Vittorio Klostermann, 1969),

limiting because other academic 'school text' collections, such as are found in the vast omen literature, bear some relationship to the 'scientific' practice of their profession: diviners, physicians, and the like. There is also evidence that these collections were used and consulted.[47] Accordingly, Westbrook has argued, reasonably I think, that the law collections, in like fashion, related to the professional judiciary, especially the royal judges. Here, again, the Hittite Laws are instructive because they give evidence of 'legal life', preserving the new changes along with previous formulations.[48]

But how complete is the connection between writing and the tradition it represents? E. Leichty, who has worked extensively in the omen literature, observed that

> It is perhaps significant to note that this collection contains an unusually high percentage of historical omens. These historical omens often refer to periods long-antedating the first written omens. . . The historical omens and the disorganization of the first written collection seem to point to an oral tradition preceding our first written omens.[49]

The oral tradition of omens in fact continued even after the emergence and established use of 'canonical' or fixed written corpora. Writing did not render obsolete the use and continuity of oral tradition. One can find references to omens recalled from 'the oral tradition of the masters' in correspondence and records even as late as the period of Esarhaddon and Assurbanipal.[50]

---

pp. 17-36. Preiser notes the generally incomplete nature of ancient law codes along with their oft-stated general connection to government, justice, order, and societal concerns.

47. For references see Westbrook's article cited in the following note. One may add to them, E.K. Ritter , 'Magical Expert (*Ašipu*) and Physician (*Asû*)', in *Studies in Honor of Benno Landsberger* (AS, 16; Chicago: University of Chicago Press, 1966), pp. 317-21.

48. Westbrook states: 'In view of the association of most of the law codes with a king, it is reasonable to suppose that it was the king as judge, or at least the royal judges, that these lists were intended to serve'. See his article 'Biblical and Cuneiform Law Codes', *RB* 92 (1985), pp. 247-64 (citation from p. 254).

49. *The Omen Series Šumma Izbu* (TCS, 4; Locust Valley, New York: J.J. Augustin, 1968), p. 23. Westbrook, 'Biblical and Cuneiform Law Codes', p. 258, cites Leichty and agrees that the law collections probably 'began as an oral tradition and only gradually became a systematic written corpus'.

50. This oral 'stream' of tradition, *ša pî ummâni*, continued to operate alongside of two written ones, *iškaru*, 'canonical' or 'primary' and *ahû*, 'outside' or

The total mass of written materials relating to the conduct of legal life contained in the laws and in the edicts falls short of covering all of the areas known to have been regulated.[51] The incomplete and random character of the legal corpora suggests to me that we continue to deal with a legal tradition that is primarily oral rather than written. Moreover, there are reasons for this assumption that go beyond the simple tabulation of what is and is not preserved for us in written form. It is difficult to imagine that the 'professionals' who made use of the 'scientific tradition' were all literate. The difficulties involved in learning to read and write the complicated cuneiform scripts—let alone Sumerian, which was already long a dead language—remained a formidable barrier to literacy. Even scribes, themselves literate, could not have been trained as specialists in every art and field. Therefore, even though some parts of the tradition were written down and

'secondary'. For discussion, see F. Rochberg-Halton, 'Canonicity in Cuneiform Texts', *JCS* 36 (1984), pp. 127-44 (especially p. 130) and S.J. Lieberman, 'Canonical and Official Cuneiform Texts: Towards an Understanding of Assurbanipal's Personal Tablet Collection', in T. Abusch, J. Huehnergard and P. Steinkeller (eds.), *Lingering Over Words: Studies in Ancient Near Eastern Literature in Honor of William J. Moran* (Harvard Semitic Studies, 37; Atlanta: Scholars Press, 1990), pp. 305-36. Lieberman (p. 327) goes on to suggest that Assurbanipal's motive in collecting his great library was to remove power from the hands of experts and retain it himself. Assurbanipal was rare in being literate; therefore his ability to check their reports 'prevented advisors from choosing between variant traditions in order to affect royal decisions or willfully misrepresenting the scholarly tradition, and it therefore gave him independence from the whims and plots in the court'. This is an interesting idea that merits study. Similar motives may lie behind the writing down of laws, namely, to make the hidden revealed to all. Hammurapi in his epilogue to the laws (CH col. xxxb 59-xxxib 17) states: 'That the strong not oppress the weak (and) so to give justice to the orphan (and) the widow, I have inscribed my precious words on my monument. . . so to give justice to the oppressed. . . Let the oppressed man who has a cause. . . have the inscription on my stele read out and hear my precious words, that my stele may make clear (his) cause to him. . . ' A similar point has been made surrounding the publishing of the XII Tables in ancient Rome. H.F. Jolowicz, *Historical Introduction to the Study of Roman Law* (Cambridge: Cambridge University Press, 1954), p. 12 asserts: 'The compilation of the XII Tables was an episode in the struggle of the orders. . . Obviously the law had not only been administered by patrician magistrates but had been unknown in a large measure to the general public. The plebians wanted a code, so that, if a plebian was wronged by a patrician magistrate, he could point definitely to the provision in the code which the magistrate had broken.'

51. R. Haase, 'Gewohnheitsrecht', *RLA* 4 (1972–75), p. 323.

available in some scribal schools, it does not necessarily indicate that oral traditions were ever totally displaced by written ones.[52]

We know that the validity of the cuneiform legal traditions in no way depended upon their being written down. We find that even for royal edicts and treaties, there was significant oral activity connected with their execution and promulgation. Writing, after all, functioned primarily as a means of transmitting and remembering information. The act of writing was not necessarily an inherent part of legal process; documents were not written for all transactions but, apparently, mainly for cases arising out of complicated, potentially contestable life situations. Thus, for example, real estate sales, adoptions, and manumissions, more often than not, were recorded inasmuch as the new owners or freed slaves needed proof of the change in status. But many other transactions, including marriage, division of property, sale of immovables, and most criminal proceedings typically do not appear to have required regular use of written records.

Furthermore, there is some evidence showing detailed oral knowledge of Babylonian laws. TCL 18 153, an Old Babylonian letter, discusses the case of a man who adopted a slave but who already had a natural son. The writer says: 'There has never been a case like this in Larsa; the father of sons may not adopt his slave'.[53] Interestingly, the two Old Babylonian written law collections do not include a comparable case on the manumission or adoption of slaves except in the case (CH § 171) where a man legitimizes the children born to him from his own slave wife.

A second such statement appears in another OB letter, AbB 10 6, where one priestess (*nadītu*) of Shamash writes to another complaining that her brothers are neglecting to support her, despite the fact that they are holding and benefitting from the dowry that their father bequeathed to her. She declares: 'The matter is now clear to me: a

---

52. Interesting in this connection is the statement of Landsberger, 'Eigenbegrifflichkeit' (n. 45) that observation and experience 'erected the huge building of a science set forth in conditional sentences: the lore of omens, medicine, and law, among which the last is unfortunately least known to us, apparently because it was handed on by oral tradition'.

53. This text is treated by M. David, 'Kritik an einem Rechtsspruch aus Larsa (TCL 18 153)', in M.A. Beek *et al.* (eds.), *Symbolae Böhl* (Leiden: Brill, 1973), pp. 90-94.

nadītu whose brothers do not support her when she is in need may give away her inheritance to whomever she wishes'. Her statement conforms to CH § 178 which deals with the dowry of a *nadītu* and other priestesses. It states that her brothers shall take charge of her dowry property and supply her with food, oil, and clothing in proportion to the yield on her assets; if they fail to do so and do not satisfy her, she may give her producing assets to a cultivator of her own choosing. But there is a difference between the letter and the Code. CH § 178 specifically forbids a *nadītu* of Shamash, on her own, to sell or give away her inheritance. In the Code, this privilege was given only to a *nadītu* devoted to Marduk, the god of Babylon (CH § 182). We seem to have, here again, a divergence between living oral tradition and the written tradition of the Code.[54]

An important oral declaration is found in AbB 3 1, a brief letter written by Hammurapi's son and royal successor, Samsuiluna. After the address, the king writes: 'No person should purchase (as slave) any man or woman (originally) citizens of Idamaraṣ or Arrapha from the Suteans. A merchant who will purchase a citizen of Idamaraṣ or of Arrapha from the Suteans will forfeit his money'. This letter appears to be either 'instant law' or the king's recapitulation of a measure already promulgated but not being fully observed by the populace. F.R. Kraus noted that this measure was not like the other decrees that we find in the royal edicts, which generally focus on giving relief and temporarily suspending the operation of certain transactions.[55] It seems that this measure emanates from regulations of international relations between Babylonia and these outlying kingdoms.

Although writing was present and utilized, the conduct of business and government remained in the hands of officials who, like their kings, were mostly illiterate; this includes the judiciary. An Old Babylonian letter from Sippar, unaddressed but written to the king gives us a vivid illustration of how the royal edicts were introduced and administered.

---

54. This letter is discussed by C. Wilcke, 'Zwei spät-altbabylonische Kaufverträge aus Kish', in G. van Driel *et al.* (eds.), *Zikir Šumim: Assyriological Studies Presented to F.R. Kraus* (Leiden: Brill, 1982), pp. 447-48. Wilcke's interpretation (the same as the one given here) is accepted by R. Westbrook, *Old Babylonian Marriage Law* (AfO Beiheft, 23; Horn, Austria: Ferdinand Berger, 1988), p. 95.

55. Kraus, *Königliche Verfügungen*, pp. 72-73 (n. 13 above).

When my lord raised high the golden torch for Sippar instituting the Edict of Reform for Shamash who loves him and convened in Sippar Taribatum, commander of the army, the judges of Babylon, and the judges of Sippar—(at that time) they reviewed the cases of the citizens of Sippar, heard the tablets (i.e. read to them) dealing with purchases of fields, houses, and orchards (and) ordered broken (i.e. voided by physical destruction) those (tablets recording transactions on properties) which were affected by the Edict.

The writer of this letter goes on to present a petition, describing a situation where the judges had reviewed and affirmed the validity of his transactions but then another official later broke (and voided) them.[56]

Westbrook makes a great point about the presence of cuneiform scribal schools in places like Egypt, Palestine, Syria, and Anatolia. Although editions of cuneiform laws have not been discovered in these places, he is persuaded that 'Sumero-Akkadian tradition that produced this legal system spread throughout Western Asia through the medium of cuneiform writing' and that 'Akkadian was accepted in these societies as the language of lawyers'.[57]

In my mind, however, a number of questions must be asked. (1) Is this evidence sufficient to require us to assume the 'cultural dominance' of cuneiform law over indigenous or local law?[58]

---

56. J.J. Finkelstein, 'Some New *Misharum* Material and its Implications', *Studies in Honor of Benno Landsberger* (AS, 16; Chicago: University of Chicago Press, 1966), pp. 233-46. He thought that the 'raising of the torch' might have been the symbolic first act in a network of torches to signal the realm that the enactment was in force. This document, BM 80318, also appears in *AbB* 7 153. The 'raising of the golden torch' is also mentioned in another fragmentary letter, *AbB* 12 172. On the illiteracy of the judiciary, cf. the comments of R. Harris, *Ancient Sippar* (Uitgaven van het Nederlands Historisch-Archaeologisch Instituut te Istanbul, 36; Leiden: Nederlands Historisch-Archaeologisch Instituut, 1975), p. 116.

57. Westbrook, *Studies*, pp. 2-3 and in his paper (p. 21).

58. Malul, *The Comparative Method* (see n. 39 above), pp. 108-10, lists major examples of cuneiform tablets found in 'Canaan', including one legal document from Hazor. These are all from the second millennium BCE, i.e. Middle and Late Bronze Ages. Malul first cautions: 'However, when it comes to specific cases, such as comparing biblical laws with their Mesopotamian parallels, the claim could be made that the corroboration in this case is lacking; for, even though the array of epigraphic evidence discovered is quite impressive, there is no decisive evidence for the arrival into Canaan of the Mesopotamian tradition of law corpora'. Nevertheless, Malul is willing to say, on the basis of the Hazor legal document, that there is some evidence

(2) If we are dealing with an essentially oral-based law in Mesopotamia where Akkadian was the spoken language, what can we project for ancient Israel (and neighboring societies) where Akkadian was a foreign tongue? Can we demonstrate that the ancient Israelites enrolled themselves in the scribal schools of foreigners? And if they did so, was it for the purpose of learning anything more than the art of writing? (3) Would it not be more natural to assume that Israelite judges learned their own oral-based laws from other Israelite judges? Indeed, we must now doubt whether even Mesopotamian judges were trained in scribal schools. There is, moreover, evidence in ancient Israel that judicial duties were undertaken by elders, priests, as well as by civil and military officials (שׂרים).[59] This is not unexpected because, even in Mesopotamia, throughout the centuries, most cases were heard by lay judges![60]

Conclusions

My cautions to Raymond Westbrook can be summarized as follows. (1) I am reluctant to assume, with him, that we are dealing with static

'in Canaan of a legal tradition similar to the Babylonian model'. But then he further cautions (pp. 110-12) that, methodologically speaking, the presence of this tradition does not yet by itself automatically demonstrate connection or identical cultural experiences.

59. Cf. e.g. Isa. 3.11; 2 Kgs 23.1; 2 Chron. 19.4-11; Jer. 26.11, 16.

60. References from the Old Babylonian and Neo-Babylonian periods may be cited as illustrations of patterns persisting over time. For the OB period, Harris, *Ancient Sippar*, pp. 116-17, states: 'The Old Babylonian judge was, therefore, not necessarily a learned man—he might even be illiterate—but was one who knew what the community considered just and whose attitudes were respected by it and by the litigants. Thus qualifications for the office of judge would be a position of respect in the community, and wealth, to remove the suspicion of personal interest. . . The judges who appear in our texts. . . appear only once which suggests that they might have been appointed *ad hoc*, to serve as judges in a specific case only.' For the Neo-Babylonian period, M. Dandamaev, *Slavery in Babylonia* (trans. V.A. Powell; ed. M.A. Powell and D.B. Weisberg; DeKalb, IL: Northern Illinois University Press, 1984), pp. 46-47, describes the judicial system of that time. He states: 'Judicial authority belonged to the royal judges, the popular assembly of citizens with full rights, and the temple administration'. Dandamaev notes that the other 'courts were subordinate to the royal courts in the decision of important cases, received various instructions from them, and were obliged to furnish the latter with necessary information'.

and unchanging legal and social systems. The possibility of dynamic change does not prevent comparing biblical and cuneiform laws (or one cuneiform system with another) but it does allow for differences based on separate cultural experiences. (2) I do not see how we can totally avoid consideration of literary editing both in the Bible and in the cuneiform laws. While the phenomenon is less visible in the latter case, the possibility is present. It may be an inevitable feature of any tradition preserved in literary form over a long period of time. (3) Despite the ubiquity of writing, legal tradition and education appears to have remained orally preserved and transmitted. Written law collections are incomplete. They may have had an educational function but were not of central importance even for the training of judges.

As to (3), some scholars have gone even further. They suggest that we are dealing with informal, non-scholastic legal traditions of amorphous character that would make the possibility of interaction between the Mesopotamian and biblical legal traditions even more problematic than we have so far suggested. J. Bottéro was struck by the incomplete nature of Mesopotamian written legal corpora—even when taken in their totality. This led him to propose that Mesopotamian law was not only, largely, unwritten but also, largely, unformulated. The bulk of what we would look for as 'law' was not accessible in any formal way but emerged through the actions of judges expressing their own internalization and understanding of their society's values of fairness and equity (*kittum u mīšarum*). Judges relied on principles rather than upon specific rulings embodied in any set tradition.[61] D. Patrick has made a similar point for ancient Israel. Because of the obviously incomplete nature of biblical law corpora, he, too, has argued for an 'unwritten' (i.e. unformulated) law based on principles, concepts, and values which were manifested by judges who examined and decided the cases that came before them. For Patrick, the biblical laws we find recorded, were written down to provide judges with exercises in legal thinking as well as with appropriate, overarching moral values.[62]

My hypothesis about oral law does not go so far as Bottéro and Patrick. I would reconstruct, especially for Mesopotamia, an oral legal tradition composed of many specific cases. I imagine it to be a

---

61. Bottéro, 'Le Code de Hammurapi', pp. 438-43 (see n. 46 above).

62. D. Patrick, *Old Testament Law* (Atlanta: John Knox Press, 1985), pp. 190-204.

formal tradition that was known and transmittable. But writing, even in Mesopotamia, was incidental or even 'accidental' to this process. Legal principles were ideally taught by this tradition of illustrative cases.[63] If judges were confronted by situations that the tradition did not directly cover or address, I imagine that they would first try to extrapolate from similar, known cases. Only failing in this would the judges then address the new and unfamiliar situations, relying only upon general principles of equity and fairness.

In his discussion Westbrook criticizes earlier scholars like J. Morgenstern for denying any connection between the Covenant Code and the cuneiform law codes (p. 21). But this criticism is not quite accurate. Scholars like Morgenstern did not totally deny the existence of similar legal practices in the ancient Near East. Morgenstern, for example, was aware of many similarities; but at the same time, he also believed that these were long-lived common elements, utilized and reshaped by each one of the ancient Near Eastern cultures in order to fit in with their own needs and world-view.[64] Morgenstern recognized that there was extensive cultural influence from 'Assyro-Babylonian culture' upon that of ancient Israel

63. It may be instructive to note that we find evidence for oral citation of laws and legal tradition (e.g. in the OB letters cited above) but we have not found any references to written collections of laws *per se*. This could explain why we have so few, if any, citations referring back even to the great Code of Hammurapi. There are some references to laws and tariffs inscribed on steles. The Old Babylonian ones could perhaps refer to the stele(s) upon which the laws of Hammurapi were inscribed but this could hardly be the case for the Old Assyrian references. See *CAD* N/1, pp. 364-65 (*narû*). O.R. Gurney, *WZKM* 77 (1987), pp. 195-98, in his review of Kraus, *Königliche Verfügungen*, states that some of the frequent references to 'the king's regulations' (*ṣimdat šarrim*) actually also refer back to the Code of Hammurapi rather than to (other) royal edicts.

64. J. Morgenstern, 'The Book of the Covenant : Part II', *HUCA* 7 (1930), p. 93 n. 103, states the following: 'But while there are undoubtedly many points of close contact and obvious relationship between many of these *mišpātim*, and not only CH, but also CA [Assyrian Laws] and CHt [Hittite Laws] as both Jirku and Ring have shown conclusively, it is gradually developing in this paper that the points of contact and relationship with present day Bedouin practice are closer and more direct and indicate that, in the main at least, these points of similarity and relationship between CH, CA, C [Covenant Code], present day Bedouin practice, and even CHt also, must be explained primarily by the assumption of a common origin in and individual, cultural development out of primitive Semitic custom, and only secondarily and to a minor degree as the result of direct borrowing'.

beginning with the 8th and 7th centuries BCE but minimized its importance because he believed that the Covenant Code and the other laws in the Bible developed before this period.[65] All of this sounds familiar and the debate has continued to this day, despite the growth in cuneiform evidence. Was he and are the others who follow him in limiting the connection between ancient Israel and the ancient Near East all 'apologists' bent on separating ancient Israel from its pagan neighbors? I cannot say. But I myself would agree with them to the point of not yet being ready to accept Westbrook's hypothesis of an international 'common law' as an *a priori*, operating fact.

We must, of course, never abandon our demand that biblical scholars confront the irrefutable fact of similar laws occurring in neighboring societies who were in political and cultural contact with one another. But it would be my recommendation that we continue to follow the 'hard road' of taking up and examining each legal topic or group of laws individually, together with the data that apply, in order to determine the degree of similarity on a case by case basis. If there is then something approaching Westbrook's concept of an international 'common law', then we will have more securely proven its validity.

65. Morgenstern, 'Book of the Covenant', pp. 245-46.

LEGAL SCIENCE AND LEGISLATION

Martin J. Buss

A major legal distinction, which has a long history, recognizes a contrast between natural and positive law; the former expresses an intrinsic morality based on the presence of inner connections between participants in reality, while the latter expresses a lawgiver's free will, independent from others. Since natural law is grounded in the reality of things, it changes only insofar as the emergence of a new circumstance requires an adjustment; for instance, in an age of computers it may be necessary to clarify what constitutes a theft of intellectual property. In contrast, positive law can, in theory, be altered at any time upon a whim. It is important to note, however, that change, although it is typical of positive law, is not essential to it. One can hold, for instance, that God has decided upon a given rule and has not altered it.

Modern western society, at least since about 1700 CE, is marked by a consciousness of change. As a consequence, there are full-time legislators whose job it is to pass new laws and repeal old ones. The theoretical basis on which they do so is largely left open. Some legislators and voters accept a philosophy of personal positive law, which holds that one has the right to establish any law one wishes, although the exercise of this right is constrained by the fact that others have different desires so that in practice laws are formed by a compromise based on competing forces. The word 'force', just used, is deliberate, for the exercise of positive law is equivalent to the employment of power politics. (If God's law is 'positive', in this sense, it is based on divine power.) Differently, however, many legislators and voters are devoted to a notion of an intrinsic standard for right and wrong and do their best to put it into effect under present circumstances. Actually, most persons involved in the legislative process adhere to a mixture of the two perspectives outlined.

A sense of change was not to the same extent a part of ancient consciousness, so that R. Westbrook is probably right in saying that the Mesopotamian law codes were not 'legislation in the modern sense', that is, they did not have 'reforms as part of their. . . purpose' ('What is the Covenant Code', p. 24). This fact (if it is one), however, does not settle the question of whether the ancient codes presupposed a natural or positive view of law. That question is raised by Westbrook's characterizations of codes as 'academic documents' which describe law (p. 24).

What is meant by the phrase 'academic document'? Two possibilities come to mind. One possibility may be that an academic document describes law as it actually exists, without any indication of whether that legal tradition is approved or not by the writer of the document. The other may be that it analyzes a proper form of law. The first of these two alternatives can be in harmony with a positive view of law. Presupposing that law may be arbitrary, the document can tell the reader, 'This is how legal practice operates; keep this information in mind when you consider how you will act, so that you do not run afoul of the law as it is being decided'. The second alternative involves a theory of natural law. The code is then normative in the sense of saying, 'Here is a (or, the) good way to adjudicate legal issues'.

In his brief comments on this issue in the essay discussed, Westbrook does not make clear which of these two alternative interpretations he favors. He observes, however, that 'codes have a timeless quality, as perhaps befits an academic document' (p. 24). This observation links the codes with a theory of natural law, for natural law has a transtemporal character—although, as we have seen, it allows for adjustments to changing circumstances. A natural-law view of the codes may, in fact, help to explain why the codes are not cited in documents representing legal practice. If law is construed as positive, a court may need to cite the legislation upon which a decision is based. If law is considered to be natural, however, there is less need for such a citation, for the code is considered not a source but a formulation of proper law to which the court also has direct access in the social process.

It may indeed be the case that ancient codes, including those of Israel, were normative somewhat in the way a natural-law theory is; that is, they state what is useful for life. In contrast to this, positive law is not normative, in the sense of making a value judgment; it is, as has already been pointed out, an expression of force which others have to take into account when they act. (In modern law, admittedly, this is often called a 'norm', but a positivist promulgation is legal in a very narrow sense, without a moral character.)

It is thus good to see that Westbrook, in the essay being discussed, does not deny—as he did in an earlier one[1]—that the ancient codes were 'normative'. It is true, he also does not say that they expressed norms; it is likely, however, that at least those of the Bible did, in the sense that they presented something good for life.

One can ask whether the contrast between natural and positive law made in the present essay is one which the people of the ancient Near East, including Israelites, would themselves have made. It is indeed quite possible that a sharp contrast between the two types would have been foreign to their way of thinking. If so, Israelites and others did not distinguish sharply between reason and God's will or between legal science and divine legislation. They probably regarded order, with what can be called rationality, as an aspect of God.[2]

---

1. R. Westbrook, 'Cuneiform Codes and the Origins of Legislation', *Zeitschrift für Assyriologie und vorderasiatische Archäologie* 79 (1989), pp. 215, 222.

2. Evidence for believing that most laws, at least, were not viewed as arbitrary in the Bible is given e.g. in M. Buss, 'Logic and Israelite Law', *Semeia* 45 (1989), p. 52. In line with this, notable medieval Jewish philosophers (Saadia, Maimonides) held that the social laws of the Hebrew Bible were rational; they disagreed on whether the same was also true for ritual laws. (One can indeed argue that insofar as ritual is symbolic it can be largely arbitrary.) Roman Catholics and many (although not all) Protestants have also seen social laws as not arbitrary. (What the abandonment of natural law logically leads to has been seen in National Socialism and Stalinism.)

ANCIENT NEAR EASTERN LAWS: CONTINUITY AND PLURALISM

Sophie Lafont

The question of the literary and judicial coherence of the Covenant Code, and more widely of the existence of a general oriental law, is part of an old historical and judicial debate. Traditional exegesis admits that the Old Testament was formed from various sources during various epochs. Whether the Pentateuch is composed of distinct fragments which have been joined together, or, on the contrary, of an original narrative which was completed by later drafters, or of several overlapping frameworks, most scholars agree that the Bible has developed from many sources. The Torah has been consequently submitted to alterations reflecting the social and political changes which took place in the life of Israel.[1] There is a broad consensus that the Covenant Code was elaborated step by step by adding to, abridging, or adapting the content of the earliest provisions.[2]

It is precisely this evolutionist dogma that R. Westbrook is criticizing here, with respect to both the Covenant Code and, more generally, to the ancient Near Eastern laws. Against the almost unanimous acceptance of the diachronic interpretation, R. Westbrook puts forward a synchronic approach: the Covenant Code is homogeneous, stable and unchanged since the time of its composition, around the eighth century BC. According to him, the numerous contradictions and repetitions which have been identified by conventional scholarship should be explained on judicial grounds rather than in terms of modifications of the *Urgesetz*. The meaning of the laws of

---

1. H. Cazelles, 'Le Pentateuque comme Torah', in *Autour de l'Exode: Etudes* (Paris: Gabalda, 1987), pp. 9-52.
2. See lastly G. Brin, 'The Development of Some Laws in the Book of the Covenant', in H.G. Reventlow and Y. Hoffman (eds.), *Justice and Righteousness: Biblical Themes and their Influence* (JSOTSup, 137; Sheffield: JSOT Press, 1992), pp. 60-70.

the Covenant Code should then be searched for in the text itself, having recourse to literary and stylistic techniques. The stability of redaction and content would therefore be demonstrable in terms of internal criteria. In a wider sense, the whole judicial body of oriental sources would also be distinguished by fixity: law would have been laid down once and for all around the third millennium BC, and would have recurred from one century to another and from one civilization to another. The common basis of Near Eastern law would have been established in this manner, invariable and unalterable.[3]

Actually, Westbrook's innovation consists in replacing the diachronic approach, which has been in vogue until now, by the opposite view. He systematically postulates the complete unity of the sources, as their pure and original property. This theoretical construction leads to the rejection of any idea of change: development being an invention of our modern societies.[4]

This theory presupposes a global view of oriental history, which is denied by both the facts and the law. The main objection against Westbrook's interpretation is that it forces a very diverse historical reality into a rigid scheme. To be sure, the assumption of different steps in the redaction of the Covenant Code facilitates avoiding some scientific questions, instead of solving them: the slightest formal anomaly in a provision is cleared up in this way, thereby avoiding the necessity of looking for a possible judicial explanation. Nevertheless, if the diachronic method can lead to such misuse, the opposite one recommended by Westbrook also has its traps. As shown by B. Levinson for instance, the investigation's method of trying to explain the inconsistencies of the Covenant Code by internal evidence cannot always be applied, and sometimes even changes the grammatical and judicial meaning of a provision (for instance the statement concerning abduction in Exod. 21.16).[5]

The aim of the present article is twofold. Firstly, it appears that the broad discussion referred to here requires a preliminary consideration of definitions. Some of the terms used by Westbrook to uphold his opinion, and taken up elsewhere in orientalist works, need to be explained judicially. What is meant by 'laws' and 'codes of laws',

3. Cf. R. Westbrook, *Studies in Biblical and Cuneiform Laws* (CahRB, 26; Paris: Gabalda, 1988).
4. R. Westbrook, in this volume, pp. 21-24.
5. See his contribution in this volume.

'casuistic/apodictic formulation' and 'interpolation'? The answer of the jurist may guide the debate, or at least clarify its premises. Consequently, it will be necessary first to clear up some terminological misunderstandings.

Secondly, it seems convenient to stress the variety of ancient Near Eastern laws by means of several examples. There are of course recurring themes in the choice of the topics approached by the Mesopotamian, Hittite, or Hebrew legislators. Such affinities indeed reflect a common tradition, a kind of oriental judicial identity, which justifies the comparison of geographically and chronologically distant texts. Moreover, some of the subjects dealt with in the Near Eastern collections are common to other subsequent laws, especially in Western countries. The analogy does not establish any connection between those systems, but relates to the judicial patrimony of humankind: a great number of civilizations protect family and property in a more or less sophisticated way. These *lieux communs* of the universal or, more strictly, oriental law are compatible with pluralism, diversity, and development. The formulation of these topics shows interesting changes, emphasizing the persistency of cultural particularisms. The tension between the legislator's wish towards standardization and the strength of local practices is a constant feature of the history of law in the ancient Near East. The comparison also shows the different ways of dealing with the same matter. One of the favorite subjects in the collections of oriental laws is miscarriage. The study of this offense will demonstrate this diversity and the originality of some of the solutions which were developed with respect to it.

1. Defining a legal statement seems *a priori* futile, since everybody is supposed to know its content and its nature. In fact, the reading of recent works proves how necessary such a definition is, in order to rule out tenacious misunderstandings. This is not the place to sum up the whole question. We will just focus on Westbrook's opinion, according to which a legal text is a provision which introduces a reformation in the existing law.[6] Therefore, the only genuine legal documents would be the Old Babylonian *mīšarum* edicts, involving remission of debts, administrative reorganization, and tariff lists. These temporary and exceptional provisions, mostly economical, were

---

6. Westbrook, in this volume, p. 24.

designed to 'redress' abuses and to protect poor people against the consequences of recurrent financial crisis. In this context, the cuneiform codes would be merely 'academic treatises', that is, descriptive collections referring the judges to the appropriate sources of law. In a previous article, Westbrook expressed the same opinion, alleging as the sign of the legislative nature of a text its explicit use in the courts or in contracts.[7] Now, the provisions of the Mesopotamian codes are referred to neither in the decisions of the judges nor in contracts, whereas the application of the *mīšarum* edicts is attested in the documents contemporaneous with their promulgation. A rule would thus deserve the designation 'law' if it was cited. Therefore, the distinctive feature of a legal text would be its innovating scope or its demonstrably being implemented.

Such a conception is questionable for several reasons.[8] First, the author mistakes the effects and the nature of the law. A legal rule is not defined by its effect on judicial reality: other sources of law actually exercise a constraining effect even though they are not legal provisions. So does the common law, which is laid down by the repeated use of a group of people. Common law is a compulsory rule, which can be enforced against those who infringe it. But it is not a legal provision.[9]

Secondly, Westbrook's reasoning identifies legislation with innovation. The law must necessarily be reformatory. If this postulate were valid, then the whole French Civil Code would assume the appearance of a collection of 'academic' precepts, whose provisions would be merely indicative and deprived of any compulsory effect. As a matter of fact, Napoleon's masterpiece is primarily a synthesis of the adductions of Roman, Common, and Canon laws, as well as royal and revolutionary legislations. The choices carried out by the nineteenth century jurists ratify solutions which are sometimes much older. One cannot object that there is a geographic and chronological span between modern sources of French law and Near Eastern codes. A

7. R. Westbrook, 'Cuneiform Law Codes and the Origins of Legislation', *ZA* 79 (1989), pp. 201-22.

8. See lastly W. Leemans, 'Quelques considérations à propos d'une étude récente du droit du Proche-Orient ancien', *BO* 48 (1991), pp. 409-37.

9. About common law, see lastly the synthesis of G. Cardascia, 'La coutume dans les droits cunéiformes', *Recueils de la société Jean Bodin* 51 (1990), pp. 61-69.

definition has to be timeless and universal to be useful, especially in a comparative method. This is particularly true for the notion of a legal provision: it is necessary to agree once and for all on the content of this word, in order to bring an end to a sterile controversy. The lack of doctrine in the ancient Near Eastern laws precludes us from discerning their own conceptions on this matter. One has to look forward to later periods to discern the vocabulary and suitable definitions which can guide our research.

In modern hand-books, a legal provision is 'a rule of law set forth by the proper state institution'.[10] Consequently, the nature of a legal act depends on its institutional origin, and not on its influence on judicial or contractual life. Is this reference too modern? Classical antiquity supplies similar definitions. The word *lex* describes the texts proceeding from public authorities and expressing general compulsory rules. Capito states for instance that 'law is an order from the people or from the plebeians, given after the request of a magistrate'.[11] Here, the stress is once again on the institution invested with the power of working out the laws. Such reasoning may sound tautological: law is given by the one who has the power to do it. However, and contrary to all appearances, this analysis defines the limit and at the same time the peculiar nature of the legal provision as a source of law among others.

The idea of a timeless, general and impersonal rule is a further feature admitted unanimously by modern doctrine.[12] It helps to sharpen the definition of the law, to catch its technical distinctive aspect. *Stricto sensu*, positive law is general and legislates for the future; it is not a personal or temporary rule. Though these features are clear, simple, and easy to distinguish, the appellation 'law' has also been given to special texts restricted to a single individual, even

---

10. J. Carbonnier, *Droit civil 1: Introduction. Les personnes* (Paris: Presses Universitaires de France, 1974), p. 111; J. Mazeaud *et al.*, *Leçons de droit civil*, I (Paris: Montchrestien, 1991), p. 121: 'La loi est une règle qui émane de l'autorité publique'.

11. Definition quoted by J. Gaudemet, *Les institutions de l'Antiquité* (Paris: Montchrestien, 3rd edn, 1991), p. 219. See also Gaius's definition in his *Institutes*, 1,3: *Lex est quod populus jubet atque constituit*, 'Law is what the people commands and establishes'.

12. Mazeaud *et al.*, *Leçons*, pp. 129-30: 'La loi est une règle générale dans son application'; 'La loi est une règle permanente'.

during our century. If confusion exists in the language of the modern jurists themselves, one can understand that the point is more complicated when it comes to oriental antiquity, so indifferent to rationalization.

Finally, in the light of all these considerations, law appears as a text proceeding from an institution vested with legislative power, enforceable for everybody and for an unlimited time. Against this background, ancient Near Eastern law codes contain true legal rules, set forth by the king in accordance with the prerogatives he was given by the gods, valid for all his subjects[13] and designed to remain in force permanently, as is shown by the curses uttered in the epilogue of the codes.

Therefore, the timeless value of the oriental collections does not define academic documents, as Westbrook suggests, but points to real legal texts which, by nature, have to last. Similarly, the content of the rules only has a secondary importance in the search for a definition: regardless of whether a legal provision reforms or confirms a preexisting rule, or creates or abrogates law, its distinctive quality is that it is promulgated by the holder of the legislative power. The main consequence of the above observations is that the *mīšarum* edicts are not legal provisions, whereas another kind of source, the royal rescripts, are.

1.1. The *mīšarum* edicts are part of the royal activities, but they are not legal rules in the technical sense of the term. These documents contain temporary and retroactive provisions, which are limited in their subject. Incidentally, the reformative weight of these texts is in fact an illusion. Promulgation of these edicts denotes either an exceptional clemency of the king, or a calamitous economic situation. In the first case, if the *mīšarum* had a steady periodicity, it would be closely connected with the right of *joyeux avènement* of ancient France: at the beginning of his reign, the king confirms all the privileges which were given by his predecessors.[14] In the other case, remissions of debts are imposed for social and economic reasons: in a

---

13. This remains true even if social distinctions exist, modulating the punishment and the law according to the social status.

14. But this regularity is disputed. See lastly D. Charpin, 'L'application des édits de mîsharum: traces documentaires', *Nouvelles Assyriologiques Brèves et Utilitaires* (= *NABU*) 76 (1992), pp. 57-58.

context of crisis, and facing an extreme fiscal pressure, the state had no other choice than to cancel retrospectively promises which had no chance of being fulfilled. In both cases, the edicts are not real reforms. Instead they reflect either respect for a tradition or submission to external constraints. Both explanations are in fact compatible. Besides, it has recently been shown that the *mīšarum* edicts have been 'canonized', their content being copied out in full from one time to another.[15] This practice underlines the formal conservatism inherent in the written judicial tradition of the ancient Near East, and reduces or even deletes the reforming value of the edicts.

1.2. The legal provisions are not only to be found in the codes. They are also promulgated on the occasion of advice given by the king on special topics. These texts might be called rescripts, in the Roman sense of the word: they are answers given by the king to practical questions asked by jurists or individuals. The only oriental example known at the moment for this legislative application is a letter, kept in four copies and sent by Samsu-iluna to the judges of Sippar. It deals with two problems involving the *nadîtû*.[16] The main interest of this document is its exceptional testimony about the method whereby law was created. Old Babylonian royal letters known until now only showed the jurisdictional occupation of the kings, acting as judges in giving particular answers to specific litigations.[17] By contrast, no text has hitherto described the concrete method whereby a legal rule was created, broadening the specific matter into a general provision. The judges of Sippar submit two problems to the king: (1) the massive admissions to the Sippar cloister of priestesses without dowry, which requires the state to then support them; (2) the question of the lawfulness of the seizure of a *nadîtu*'s goods to pay her father's debt. Each case is presented in a detailed manner, including the names of the parties and of the places. On the other hand, the answer given by the king makes a sharp contrast because of its general and impersonal

---

15. D. Charpin, 'Les décrets royaux à l'époque paléo-babylonienne. A propos d'un ouvrage récent', *AfO* 34 (1987), p. 43.

16. C. Janssen, 'Samsu-iluna and the Hungry nadîtums', *Northern Akkad Project Reports* 5 (1991), pp. 3-40.

17. See on this question W. Leemans, 'King Hammurapi ad Judge', in J.A. Ankum, R. Feenstra and W.F. Leemans (eds.), *Symbolae Iuridicae et Historicae Martino David dedicatae*, II (Leiden: Brill, 1968), pp. 107-29.

drafting. Samsu-iluna first commands that admission to the cloister be reserved to *nadîtû* who possess property; in other words, the royal granaries cannot be used to feed the priestesses. Their support must be provided by their families and warranted by a tablet. This answer contradicts CH § 180, which allows admission of a *nadîtum* without dowry.[18] Abuses and difficulties arising from this allowance in Hammurabi's times may explain why the king rescinds the lenient rules of the Code. From now on, the support of an encloistered *nadîtum* is an exclusive duty of her family, the state refusing to care for them. Therefore, the rescript changes Hammurabian law.

The second question asked of the king is about joint responsibility of a *nadîtum* for the debts of her father: a creditor threatens his debtor with seizure of the slave-girl of his daughter, a priestess living in the cloister, if her father does not repay the money he owes to him. Samsu-iluna expressly rejects such a claim, which is illegal (ll. 54-55).[19] From this particular case, the king states a general rule valid for all the *nadîtû* of Shamash living in the cloister and possessing property. Debts and fulfillment of the *ilkum*-service are due solely by the debtor or the tenant of the land themselves. They are strictly personal obligations, which cannot be exacted from their heirs. The

---

18. *Contra* M. Stol, 'Kallatum als Klosterfrau', *RA* 73 (1979), p. 91 and A. Finet, *Le Code de Hammurapi* (Paris: Le Cerf, 1983), p. 105. M. Stol reads é-gi₄-a = *kallatum* instead of gá-gi₄-a. The code would then list three types of women, a *nadîtum*, a *kallatum* and a *zikrum*. This interpretation aims at harmonizing CH § 180 with the former rules on the same topic, which always includes three kinds of priestesses. However, the reading *é* is not certain, even if the sign *gá* is itself erased. Therefore, an epigraphical doubt remains. As for the meaning 'priestess' for the Akkadian *kallatum*, it does not seem to be sufficiently attested in the sources to be accepted. I.J. Gelb already suggested this interpretation (*RA* 66 [1972], p. 4), on the basis of several Old Babylonian texts from Eshnunna, Dilbat and Larsa, which mention the é-gi₄-a without children and gathered in a é-geme₂. Rather than a 'gynaeceum' occupied by 'betrothed/daughters-in-law', the latter term would denote a 'cloister' for real 'priestesses'. The translation of *kallatum* as 'nun', 'novice', or 'geistliche Dame' (M. Stol) is nevertheless hypothetical, for it lacks any consistent documentary basis. This might be the reason why M. Stol's proposal was not followed by the *CAD* (N, p. 63 b), nor by R. Borger in *Texte aus der Umwelt des Alten Testaments* (= *TUAT*), 1/1: *Rechtsbücher* (Gütersloh: Gütersloher Verlagshaus Gerd Mohn, 1982), p. 66.

19. ll. 54-55: *a-wi-lum šu-ú ia-a-bu ša* ᵈ*UTU*, 'such a man is the enemy of Shamash'.

royal answer has no parallel in CH, which talks only incidentally about the *ilkum*-service.[20]

In his advice, Samsu-iluna connects responsibility for debts and *ilkum*, whereas the judges of Sippar only mentioned the first point. The linking of the two notions has two possible explanations. First, in both cases, there is an obligation owed by someone: the debtor and the tenant respectively have to repay a debt or to perform a service (however vaguely defined). Secondly, the wish to set up a general provision extending the specific case may also justify the reference to the *ilkum*.

The determining fact, which seems to provide the clue in both cases, is the existence of goods belonging to the priestess and listed on a tablet. The written document is here necessary because of the official registration of the inheritance share given to the *nadîtum* when entering the cloister. If this formality is fulfilled, the nun becomes independent from a judicial and financial point of view. Therefore, she is not affected by the claims of a creditor of her parents, nor by the duties connected with the *ilkum*-service. This is not an exemption, but a new personal status. Contrary to the *nadîtum* of Marduk who is favored in CH § 182,[21] the one of Sippar can take advantage of her material independence to escape the obligations of her family. The establishment of her status as a priestess of Shamash, through the drafting of a tablet in front of the judges, has economic and judicial consequences: the *nadîtum* is now able to support herself (ll. 16-31) and to elude the joint responsibility for the family debts (ll. 43-55). Compared to the rules of the CH which have already been referred to, Samsu-iluna innovates: he completes the existing rough provisions in order to express clear principles. The resultant legislation is not so much a new creation as a formalization of a custom which was already in practice.

---

20. CH § 40 compels the *nadîtum* to perform the *ilkum*, while § 182 shows a special care for the priestess of Marduk of Babylon: she is exempted from that service if she receives in her inheritance share a plot of land burdened with this duty.

21. CH § 182: If a father has not bestowed a dowry on his daughter (who is) a priestess of Marduk of Babylon (and) has not written a sealed tablet for her, after the father goes to (his) fate she shall take one-third of her inheritance at the division with her brothers out of the property of the paternal estate but shall not render any service (therefor); the priestess of Marduk shall give (the charge of) her estate to whom she pleases. (Translation from G.R. Driver and J.C. Miles, *The Babylonian Laws*, II [Oxford: Clarendon Press, 1960], p. 73).

The main significance of this text is to show how a legal rule is built up: the king's response to the consultation which is addressed to him acquires a normative weight. This fact assumes an additional significance, considering that the law about the *nadîtû* was mainly provided in CH §§ 178-82. The echo of these provisions in the contemporaneous judicial practice has already been underlined.[22] Samsu-iluna therefore provides clarity on a matter which, although already ruled in the CH, is still unclear to the judges responsible for its enforcement. His successors certainly respected those provisions, since three copies were drafted under Ammi-ditana or perhaps Ammi-ṣaduqa. These copies are not scribal exercises, but had a practical scope: the law set up by Samsu-iluna was 'received' during the later reigns of the dynasty.[23]

1.3. A legal provision should therefore be understood as a bill which is promulgated by a public authority. One could object that this definition, valid for cuneiform law, is not applicable to the biblical sources. The Torah is in fact closely connected to religious life in Israel. The king has administrative, judicial, and military powers, but cannot publish laws under his own name. The whole civil, criminal, and cultural body of rules is said to be given by God to Moses, long before the Hebrew kingship. When this royal institution was created, it was first used as an intermediary between the divine will and the human community, reproducing the system of mediation which was inaugurated by Moses, the privileged intercessor and primary speaker of Yahweh on Sinai.

It is true that the religious aspect of biblical legislation is not specific to Israel. Mesopotamian collections are not merely secular works. Nevertheless, whereas Hammurabi, inspired by Shamash and elected by Marduk, asserts his own authorship for his code,[24] the Hebrew kings merely transmit the divine commandments by which they are themselves bound.[25] Therefore, the judicial texts of the Old

22. R. Harris, 'The naditu Laws of the Code of Hammurapi in Praxis', *Or* 30 (1961), pp. 163-69.

23. Cf. Janssen, 'Hungry nadîtums', p. 21.

24. Col. V, ll. 20-24: *ki-it-tam ù mi-ša-ra-am i-na* KA *ma-tim aš-ku-un*, 'I set forth justice and righteousness in the whole country'.

25. So Jehoshaphat is reforming justice at the beginning of the Judaean kingship in order to enforce the 'rule of God' (2 Chron. 19.5-7).

Testament are supposed to emanate from a single superior level, placed above human institutions and therefore imbued with sovereign authority. They are then truly laws. From such a perspective, the *mišpāṭîm* given by God to Moses on Sinai (Exod. 21.1) are not 'traditional customary laws'[26] but legal provisions: divine 'judgments'.

2. Westbrook again takes up the formal distinction which is usually drawn between two kinds of rules, apodictic and casuistic. The author sums up the various theories which have been developed to explain the coexistence of these two types of provisions. One has to conclude with him that the choice of one or another form has no judicial meaning: no firm explanation has been given to justify the origin and the value of apodictic and casuistic texts. However, two further observations may be made in the discussion.

2.1. In most of the works regarding this question, the terms 'apodictic' and 'casuistic' define a literary formulation. Of course, the stylistic difference is very clear between a laconic order on one hand, and the redaction of a protasis and then of an apodosis on the other hand. But regardless of the way it is expressed, Mesopotamian scientific thinking remains basically casuistic, not because of its conditional 'cloth', but because of its incomplete feature. Oriental codes do not aim at exhaustiveness; they rather clarify debated points or regulate topics thought to be interesting by their promulgators. By nature, written oriental law is lacunary: it is only designed to complete a mostly oral tradition. In this context, the question of the origin or of the judicial meaning of apodictic and casuistic forms is secondary. The redactor of a text builds his sentences according to subjective reasons, which have no legal relevance. The formal aspect of a legal document does not give any particular information about its content. Modern rules could be formulated in the 'casuistic' way, but they would still have a fundamentally different character from the Near Eastern laws. Even if one could write the whole French Civil Code in the manner of the CH, it would nevertheless remain a complete corpus, aiming at treating all matters of law and not only specific points. On the contrary, the apodictic form used in some rules

---

26. Cazelles, 'Le Pentateuque', p. 18: 'coutumes traditionnelles'.

of the LE, for instance, does not alter the fact that this collection is fundamentally casuistic.

In short, the opposition between two very distinct styles is a peculiarity of the oriental texts of law, but this should not hide their main characteristic: their supplementary nature.

2.2. The second observation concerns the opposition center/ periphery mentioned by Westbrook.[27] He summarizes the works of J. Muffs,[28] who assigns a 'provincial' or 'peripheral' origin to documents which mix apodictic and casuistic formulations, like the LE or the Covenant Code. By contrast, the more rigid literary tradition, using only the casuistic form, would be typical of the south, which is the 'center', the core of Mesopotamia. This stylistic difference would then cross an ethnic and cultural rift dividing the south with its Sumerian civilization on the one side, and the north with the surrounding areas (Nuzi, Susa, Ugarit, Alalakh) on the other side, where Akkadian elements grew and settled. A tradition of the 'center', with its roots in the judicial practice of Ur III, would then contrast with the 'peripheral' tradition, which blends various types of formulations drawn together by the common use of the Akkadian language. The casuistic form would then appear as properly Sumerian, as opposed to the other styles coming from cultural and linguistic areas more distant in time and space.

The problematic nature of the terminology 'center'/'periphery' is twofold.

2.2.1. First, the historical reality covered by these two words is today disputed. Of course, crucial techniques for the progress of humankind, like agriculture, urbanization, and writing, were invented in a well-defined area. But it seems dangerous to isolate this primitive core from the surrounding places. Such a procedure leads to an artificial contrast between a hypothetical 'mother' Sumer, and other derived or additional Semitic areas which only exist in comparison with the original Sumerian reference point. The whole body of Near Eastern history is then understood inside this binary framework: identity or difference in comparison with the essential core.

27. Westbrook, in this volume, p. 31.
28. J. Muffs, *Studies in Aramaic Legal Papyri from Elephantine* (Studia et Documenta ad Iura Orientis Antiqui pertinentia, 8; Leiden: Brill, 1969), pp. 90-95.

Following some recent historical works,[29] it seems better to abandon the words 'center' and 'periphery' and to talk about moving centers: from a narrow geographical area, source of the great discoveries, oriental history moves according to political events, enlightening very different peoples and cultures. The contested terminology is too static. It does not account for this constant movement of people, the continuous circulation that takes place in this part of the ancient world, nor for the influence of such exchanges on political and judicial life. Mesopotamia is, as is well known, a crossroads. Each period, each ethnic group leaves a more or less deep imprint and helps to build up, in a sedimentary manner, a heterogeneous whole which finds its unity in its belonging to the same oriental world. Therefore, there is not *one* but *several* centers, moving forward in time and space, and reflecting the temporary ascendancy of one region over the others.

In this respect, the case of the LE quoted by Westbrook is very interesting. The use of casuistic and apodictic forms would characterize this peripheral tradition, which should consequently be more flexible and open than the center's own tradition. In fact, the historical context surrounding the redaction of the LE shows how inappropriate the qualification 'peripheral' is. This collection was composed at the latest by Dadusha,[30] several years before the famous CH. At that time, Eshnunna was a great political entity, much more powerful than Babylon.[31] This hegemony stopped only with Hammurabi's victory in

29. See especially J.-M. Durand, 'Unité et diversités au Proche-Orient à l'époque amorrite', in D. Charpin and F. Joannès (eds.), *La circulation des biens, des personnes et des idées dans le Proche-Orient ancien, Actes de la XXXVIIIe Rencontre Assyriologique Internationale, Paris, 8-10 juillet 1991* (Paris: Editions Recherches sur les Civilisations, 1992), pp. 97-128; D. Charpin, 'Mari entre l'est et l'ouest: politique, culture, religion', *Akkadica* 78 (1992), pp. 1-10.

30. See most recently R. Yaron, *The Laws of Eshnunna* (Jerusalem: Magnes, 2nd edn, 1988), p. 20.

31. See recently D. Charpin, 'La suzeraineté de l'empereur (sukkalmah) d'Elam sur la Mésopotamie et le "nationalisme" amorrite', in L. De Meyer and H. Gasche (eds.), *Mésopotamie et Elam, Actes de la XXXVIe Rencontre Assyriologique Internationale, Gand, 10-14 juillet 1989* (Mesopotamian History and Environment: Occasional Publications, 1; Ghent: University of Ghent, 1991), pp. 59-66, especially p. 64; D. Charpin, 'Le traité entre Ibâl-pî-El II d'Eshnunna et Zimri-Lim de Mari', in D. Charpin and F. Joannès (eds.), *Marchands, Diplomates et Empereurs: Etudes sur la civilisation mésopotamienne offertes à Paul Garelli* (Paris: Editions Recherches sur les Civilisations, 1991), pp. 139-66.

1753. Therefore, the LE originated in the political 'center' of the turn of the eighteenth century. In the same manner, Samsu-iluna's rescript, which was commented on above, is written in an apodictic style, contrary to the casuistic tradition abundantly used in the CH and said to be typical of the Babylonian 'center'. These examples underline the uselessness of the word 'periphery' in this composite whole formed by the ancient Near East. Its history is a succession of shadows and lights, a city being prominent at one time and then disappearing from the political scene for a long time.

2.2.2. The terminology under discussion involves another disadvantage: it refers to a difference in the level of evolution of law. The law of the 'center' would be more sophisticated than the one of the 'periphery', which would be archaic. It seems useful to come to this point of the debate, although Westbrook does not allude to it,[32] to deal fully with this matter of historical vocabulary. The main idea is that the use of judicial symbolism, typical of the 'peripheral' documents, denotes a more primitive conception of the law, according to which the real efficiency of a transaction depends on precise rituals that are legally binding. By contrast, the sources coming from the 'center' progressively turn to writing, giving up the visual ceremonies in favor of a text which becomes the material evidence or the real basis of a right. This more modern view would dissociate itself from the less developed behavior of 'peripheral' Semitic peoples. Such reasoning is based on a misunderstanding.

The proposed evolutionary path stresses the progress symbolized by written proof, compared to a more archaic ritual. Now, the probative force given today to cuneiform contracts might be excessive. The tablets relating the content of a transaction and kept by the parties always include a list of witnesses at the end of the text. It is then highly possible that the writing of the contract was first motivated by the necessity of identifying these witnesses. In other words, the proof of a right or of a fact seems to rely mainly on testimony in the Orient.[33] For practical reasons, the oral and visual tradition remains

32. See on the other hand M. Malul, *Studies in Mesopotamian Legal Symbolism* (AOAT, 221; Kevelaer: Butzon & Bercker, 1988), p. 455.

33. From a private talk with G. Cardascia, who will develop this idea in an article to be published. This opinion is compatible with the frequent resort to the written text known at certain times. During the Old Babylonian period for instance, from Samsu-

in force, while the written text has a supplementary value. Therefore, the persistent resort to symbolism noticed in the contractual documents from the north, or the use of the oath in the south, have the same meaning: the ceremony helps the witnesses to remember the agreement of the parties. The form itself, ritual or sacramental, is less important and does not indicate an earlier or more developed level of the law.

3. The problem of the original coherence of the Covenant Code is treated by Westbrook from the point of view of the classical question of interpolations.[34] Are there, in the Bible, changes of the text comparable to those of Justinian when he collected Roman law? Westbrook rightly gives a negative answer. Nevertheless, contrary to what he seems to think, the lack of interpolations does not necessarily mean that the collection was not submitted to any alterations. In other words, a work might be taken up *a posteriori*, without any interpolations. It is then essential to clarify the discussion in order to define what an interpolation is.[35] It is a technique by which one author changes what another one wrote, pretending that his own ideas are in fact those of the other. So Justinian would for instance add to Ulpian's thinking by assigning an innovation of his own to Ulpian himself. The interpolator hides behind the identity of the one who signs the falsified document.

In the debate about the Covenant Code, it seems that the reverse

iluna on, there is an increasing number of sale tablets. In the reigns of the former kings, transactions for less valuable goods (such as building materials) took place without a written document. Under Hammurabi's successors, the judicial life becomes encumbered by a growing formalism (See on this matter C. Wilcke, 'Zu den spät-altbabylonischen Kaufverträgen aus Nordbabylonien', *WO* 8 [1975], pp. 254-85). But basically, the concern is the same: achieving the protection of the sale's wording by resorting firstly to the witnesses listed in the contract. The importance of the written tablet as a means of evidence still remains, at least for recent periods, as was shown by M.W. Stolper, 'Tobits in Reserve: More Babylonian in Ecbatana', *Archaeologische Mitteilungen aus Iran* 23 (1990), pp. 161-76: the redaction of the authentic copy of a debt receipt incurred in Iran but payable in Babylonia, is justified by the remoteness of the witnesses, who are hard to reach in case of litigation. The exhibition of the written text will make the proof of the claim easier.

34. Westbrook, in this volume, pp. 32-34.

35. Cf. G. Cardascia, 'La transmission des sources juridiques cunéiformes', *Revue Internationale des Droits de l'Antiquité* 7 (1960), pp. 32-35.

technique of plagiarism is alluded to. The collector ascribes to himself the thinking of his predecessors; in the above quoted example, Justinian indulges in plagiarism by signing Ulpian's work with his own name. This is the technique to which several scholars refer when talking about the Covenant Code, and which Westbrook criticizes. In interpreting some rules about theft, for instance, commentators like D. Daube stress the different levels of elaboration in the legal provisions, thereby describing the process of their historical evolution. The end result of this molding of the texts is a more or less coherent whole. In this kind of reasoning, the method consists in going back, across the stages of the formation of the legal rules, to the original core hidden by the compiler under modifications, revisions, and adjunctions.

The choice of the appropriate term is not merely a matter of vocabulary, but is determinative for the orientation of the discussion. Taking up the former law in order to alter it is a very well-known practice, as seen above. Talking of interpolations in this case is a technical mistake, for it implies a falsification of the text. On the contrary, employing the above definition of plagiarism allows one to accept an original source, and also to consider the process of its diachronic development.

The evolution of judicial rules by means of successive changes is highly probable, though this practice should not become a systematic postulate.[36] The Covenant Code remains an authentic source, or more precisely, a collection of authentic sources, which perhaps date from different periods and have been placed side by side by successive drafters. The same phenomenon can be observed in other Near Eastern codes, especially in the HL and the AL.[37]

This controversy is in essence the result of one basic element which is characteristic of the pre-classical Orient: oral culture.[38] Ancient Near Eastern civilizations developed (and still do) a tradition of speech. Writing is subsidiary, and furthermore distorting because it lessens the inherent pluralism of the word in favor of a more strict and fixed uniformity—a form of 'canonization'. This phenomenon can

36. Cf. Levinson, in this volume, pp. 52-59.

37. For the HL, both redactions explicitly mentioned in some provisions are sufficiently clear. For the AL, see G. Cardascia, *Les lois assyriennes* (Paris: Le Cerf, 1969), pp. 23-28.

38. See the articles by S. Greengus and E. Otto in this volume.

be observed in all the fields of science in Mesopotamia: omina or mythology, divination, weights and measures, and, of course, law.[39] The Old Babylonian *mīšarum* edicts examined above are a good example of this tendency. As soon as law is written, it changes, even formally, following a quite natural tendency towards normalization. In this sense, we will never be definitely sure of the complete authenticity of the legal rules: the influence of the judicial tradition, the necessary clarity required by a written provision, the convictions of the legislator are among the elements that might 'distance' the text from its original oral version. The Covenant Code is a typical illustration of this unavoidable alteration: each level of the Code's formation is guided by this tendency towards homogeneity and uniformity, which is imposed by the current formal conventions.

Paradoxically, this fervent respect for the tradition does not mean that Near Eastern laws are static. It is true that the Mesopotamian, Hittite, and Hebrew codes share a common tenor, which justifies their belonging to one and the same judicial and cultural entity. But behind this uniformity, particularisms, that is adaptations, appear in various judicial fields.

4. An initial indication of such adaptability is provided by the above quoted Old Babylonian rescript. The first case presented to Samsu-iluna shows how the law develops and improves, while still keeping the traditional formal patterns of the codes. If in its main principles, the legislation about the *nadîtû* is contained in the CH, it is not exhaustively and definitively set forth. The task of the later legislators is to adapt the existing rules to the problems that emerge. The cuneiform sale documents also reveal some divergences of form and content, testifying to the richness and the variety of oriental law on this topic.[40]

These examples show how Near Eastern, as well as other laws, are submitted to ideas of evolution, change, and alteration. By nature, law is in motion, because it belongs to the world of things. Law is an object,[41] a tool which adapts to the demands of a society. It is then

39. See B. Lafont, 'Normes, normativité, diversité dans le Proche-Orient ancien', *Cahiers du Centre G. Glotz* 5 (1994), pp. 1-25.

40. See Leemans, 'Quelques considérations', pp. 411-12.

41. This aspect is underlined in the Roman definition of law: law is an instrument of measure in order to 'give back everyone what he owes'. Cf. Ulpien, D. 1, 1, 11:

necessarily variable according to different areas and epochs. This diversity is especially striking in the field of criminal law.

4.1. One of the main classical topics of the judicial literature of the ancient Near East is miscarriage. Sources deal very often with this offence. While only one text punishes voluntary abortion,[42] nineteen texts allude to the loss of the foetus after blows are inflicted upon the mother.[43] The abundance of material is in contrast with the rarity of that kind of accident in everyday life. This observation has led several scholars, including Westbrook, to rank miscarriage among the 'scribal exercises', canonized by means of being copied by the scribes, but deprived of any judicial effect.[44]

Such an opinion is surely excessive. It has first to be stressed that the topic is dealt with later by the jurists in the medieval Occident.[45] If it is a stereotype, it is then one which is common to numerous societies. It is impossible that a mere scribal excursus became a true

---

Juris praecepta sunt haec: honeste vivere, alterum non laedere, suum cuique tribuere: 'The precepts of law are as follows: to live honestly, not to wrong others, to assign everyone what he owes'.

42. MAL § 53: If a woman has cast the fruit of her womb by her own act (and) charge (and) proof have been brought against her, she shall be impaled (and) shall not be buried. If she has died in casting the fruit of her womb, she shall be impaled (and) shall not be buried. If that woman was concealed (?) when she cast the fruit of her womb (and) it was [not] told [to the king]. . . (the end is lost). (Translation from G.R. Driver and J.C. Miles, *The Assyrian Laws* [Oxford: Clarendon Press, 2nd edn, 1975], p. 421).

43. Namely YOS I, 28 §§ 1-2 (Col. IV, ll. 1-10) and UM 55-21-71 (Col. III, ll. 2'-13'), as well as CH §§ 209-14; MAL §§ 21, 50-52; HL §§ 17-18 and XVI-XVII; and finally Exod. 21.22-25.

44. Westbrook, *Studies*, p. 61; M. Civil, 'New Sumerian Law Fragments', in H.G. Güterbock and T. Jacobsen (eds.), *Studies in Honor of Benno Landsberger* (Assyriological Studies, 16; Chicago: University of Chicago Press, 1965), p. 6; E. Otto, *Körperverletzungen in den Keilschriftrechten und im Alten Testament: Studien zum Rechtstransfer im Alten Testament* (AOAT, 226; Kevelaer: Butzon & Bercker, 1991), p. 23 and more generally the whole book, which is devoted to the process of reception of Mesopotamian law in Israel. See also J.J. Finkelstein for the goring ox, *The Ox that Gored* (Transactions of the American Philosophical Society, 71/2; Philadelphia: American Philosophical Society, 1981), p. 19 n. 11.

45. In ancient French law, miscarriage caused by blows (called *encis*), was punished from the very beginning of the Middle Ages, and later in the common law from the north of France. The offense was liable for the death penalty.

legal provision for western jurists. The later parallels support the real judicial scope of the rules concerning miscarriage in the ancient Near East.

Moreover, regardless of the frequency of the offense, this proliferation of oriental provisions denotes an essential preoccupation among the authorities and the people. Religious considerations might explain the concern for protection of pregnancy. In Mesopotamia, for instance, medical treaties and divination try to protect women from a premature birth or from the death of the foetus by wearing amulets that keep away the fearsome female devil Lamashtu. Moreover, brawls and other acts of violence were part of everyday life, and were perceived as a threat against the pregnant woman. Even if the medical danger was rather low, the risk of miscarriage arising from blows or from the charms of Lamashtu was enough to indicate the seriousness of the matter. For the men who wrote the laws and practiced divination and medical science, the pregnant woman was weakened because of her physical condition. Their fear, even if unjustified, finds expression in an abundant literature about the question.

More globally, the oriental world assigns a divine origin to the embryo, who represents a 'life to be born'. Though he is not assimilated to a human being, the foetus is considered as a rough sketch created by God or by the deities. It must therefore be protected, whether in the name of private, collective, or religious interests. The sacred aspect which lies behind all of these provisions thus justifies the rules promulgated by the various legislators in antiquity.

All the sources related to miscarriage follow the same pattern: a man hits a pregnant woman and causes the expulsion of the embryo. The offense is primarily directed against the woman, the loss of her foetus being an unexpected and unintentional consequence of the blows. In its main features, the offense is dealt with in the same manner by the Sumerians, the Semites, and the Hittites. Nevertheless, from this common general framework, significant particularisms appear, both judicially and culturally. On this point, the Covenant Code exhibits a highly original conception.

4.2. The study of the conditions in which the offence is perpetrated reveals a first series of differences.

4.2.1. In its older version, the Hittite collection attracts attention because it makes distinctions according to the stage of the pregnancy's development (tenth month; fifth month). This criterion, which disappears in the latest redaction of the HL,[46] is missing in the other collections. As a matter of fact, the word *ṣuhartu* in MAL § 50 (l. 80) does not qualify the 'small' embryo, not yet developed, but the female foetus.[47] In the same manner, the expression *lā murabita* in § 51 (l. 83) referring to the wife who suffered the blows, does not mean 'whose pregnancy is not advanced', but 'who does not rear her children', because of a physical inability to achieve a pregnancy.[48]

The Covenant Code does not allude to this distinction, in spite of the contrary view of the Septuagint. The phrases *lō' yihyeh 'āsôn* and *'āsôn yihyeh* (Exod. 21.22, 23) have been understood in the Greek version in reference to two steps in the evolution of the foetus. In the first case, the embryo would not be able to survive, whereas in the second case, the child would be viable, being near to the time of the birth.[49] This interpretation is based on the assimilation of the rare

46. HL § 17: If somebody causes a free woman to expel the fruit of her womb, if (it happens) on the tenth month, he shall give 10 shekels of silver; if (it happens) on the fifth month, he shall give 5 shekels of silver. For the fine, he (the husband of the woman) shall watch the house (of the culprit).

HL § 18: If somebody causes a slave girl to expel the fruit of her womb, if (it happens) on the tenth month, he shall give 5 (?) shekels of silver.

HL § XVI: If somebody causes a free woman to expel the fruit of her womb, he shall give 20 shekels of silver.

HL § XVII: If somebody causes a slave girl to expel the fruit of her womb, he shall give 10 shekels of silver.

47. MAL § 50: [If a man] has struck a married [woman] and caused her to lose [the fruit of her womb, the wife of the man] who [caused] the (other) married woman [to lose] the fruit of [her womb] shall be treated as [he has] treated her; [for the fruit of] her womb he pays a life (for a life). But, if that woman dies, the man shall be put to death; for the fruit of her womb, he pays a life (for a life). Or, if that woman's husband has no son (and) his wife has been struck and has cast the fruit of her womb, for the fruit of her womb the striker shall be put to death. If the fruit of her womb is a girl, he none the less pays a life (for a life). (Translation from Driver and Miles, *Assyrian Laws*, p. 419.)

48. MAL § 51: If a man has struck a married woman who does not rear her children and has caused her to cast the fruit of her womb, this punishment (shall be inflicted): he shall pay 2 talents of lead.

49. Exod. 21.22-25: If two men strive and hurt a pregnant woman, and her child comes out without being formed, the man shall be fined; he shall give as much as the husband of the woman will lay upon him, with a judicial sentence. If it was formed, he shall give life for life, eye for eye, tooth for tooth, hand for hand, foot for foot,

Hebrew word *'āsôn* to the Greek *asoma*, 'without any body', the meaning of the first being determined by the second through a process of 'homophonic contagion'. The Septuagint's choice of the translation *exeikonismeon*, literally 'created in the image' (vv. 22 and 23), would be justified in this manner. The suggested reading would be prompted by two texts in Genesis (Gen. 1.26 and 9.6): the one who causes the death of a foetus, created in God's image, or totally formed, is liable for the death penalty.

In addition, this topic is documented in several Egyptian papyri going back to the second century BC and to the first century AD.[50] Some petitions are addressed to the authorities so as to expose the attacks suffered by pregnant women who have lost their baby or are themselves in danger of death because of the blows they have received. These blows may certainly have been violent in order to cause, in at least one case, the death of the child.[51] Such examples are indeed later than the redaction of the Septuagint, but they document, nevertheless, the fatal danger of blows which are inflicted on a pregnant woman. So the homophony, and the existence of parallels in this matter, enlighten the Greek interpretation. Moreover, the philosophical context supports such an understanding of the Hebrew text. In particular, the theories worked out by Philo concerning the starting point of life underline the fact that the embryo is part of the body of the mother as long as it is 'not modelled and not differentiated' (*áplaston kaì adiatúpōton*). But the act of destroying an 'already formed' (*ēdē memorphōméon*) foetus is tantamount to homicide.[52] Aristotle had already distinguished an initial period after the

---

burning for burning, wound for wound, stripe for stripe. (Translation following M. Le Boulluec and P. Sandevoir, *La Bible d'Alexandrie II: l'Exode* [Paris: Le Cerf, 1989], pp. 218-21).

50. See S. Adam, 'La femme enceinte dans les papyrus', *Anagennesis: A Papyrological Journal* 3 (1983), pp. 9-19. See also V.A. Tcherikover, *Corpus Papyrorum Judaicarum* 1 (Cambridge, MA: Harvard University Press, 1957), pp. 246-47 n. 133; P.J. Sijpesteijn, 'Michigan Papyri (P. Mich. XV)', *Studia Amstelodamensia ad epigraphicam, ius antiquum et papyrologicam pertinentia* 19 (1982), pp. 8-10 n. 688. I wish to thank J. Mélèze-Modrzejewski who kindly drew my attention to these documents.

51. P. Mich. V 228, quoted by S. Adam, 'La femme', p. 18.

52. *De specialibus legibus*, III, 108-109.

conception during which the foetus is not 'animated'; only subsequently do 'sense and life' begin.[53]

All these philological, theological, and judicial elements explain therefore the translation chosen by the Septuagint for '*āson*. Consequently, it is not certain that this meaning reflects the original thinking of the redactors of the book of Exodus. Above all, this Hellenistic exegesis is debatable because it assimilates the second offence to homicide: the loss of the 'viable child' would be punishable by death. The foetus is then considered a human being. If this is the view of the Bible of Alexandria, as we have seen, nothing proves that the Hebrews adopted such a conception which is without parallel in other Near Eastern sources.[54] Here, doubt arises not only from the isolation of such an interpretation. To consider miscarriage as a homicide is especially debatable for a judicial reason: the statement of the rule of the talion in vv. 23-24, beginning with the words 'you shall compensate life for life', does not refer to the death penalty but to a substitution in nature or in money, in reparation for the damage.[55] The version of Alexandria seems therefore very far from the initial scope of the Hebrew rule. It is then better to reject the reading of the Septuagint. Consequently, the HL alone distinguishes according to the level of development of the pregnancy.

4.2.2. Contrary to all the cuneiform sources, which assume the intentional nature of the blows suffered by the woman, the Covenant Code postulates the lack of any malicious intent since the offense happens during a brawl (v. 22).[56] The blows exchanged by the men

53. *Politics*, VII, 16. Animation begins on the fortieth day for male embryos, according to *History of Animals* VII, 3. This doctrine was received in the Latin patristic, and then in canonical law, thanks to Augustine who places the point of vitality on the fortieth day.

54. Likewise in Rome, abortion was distinguished from homicide, since the foetus was considered as a part of the mother's body (Ulpien, D. 25,4,1,1).

55. See G. Cardascia, 'La place du talion dans l'histoire du droit pénal à la lumière des droits du Proche-Orient ancien', in *Mélanges offerts à Jean Dauvilliers* (Toulouse: Université des sciences sociales de Toulouse, 1979), pp. 169-83.

56. Exod. 21.22-25: 'If men fight and a pregnant woman is pushed and has a miscarriage, if there is no '*āsôn*, he (the perpetrator) shall suffer the punishment which the woman's husband shall impose upon him, and he shall pay alone. If there is a '*āsôn*, you shall give life for life, eye for eye, tooth for tooth, hand for hand, foot for foot, burn for burn, wound for wound, bruise for bruise'. A single

are of course voluntary, whereas those suffered by the pregnant woman are incidental. By contrast, the other codes of the ancient Near East postulate a deliberate attack against the victim, with the destruction of the embryo and the possible death of the woman being connected but involuntary. The hypothesis of the fight between several individuals pictured in Exodus seems to be an extenuating circumstance: the death penalty is a very heavy punishment against the one who intended neither to hurt the woman nor to cause her miscarriage.

4.2.3. In contrast to the other Near Eastern collections, the Covenant Code does not seem to deal with the manslaughter of the mother. The content of the biblical rule is nevertheless the subject of a debate. After having described the circumstances of the offense and the expulsion of the embryo, the redactor exhibits the following alternative: there is no '*āsôn* (v. 22) / there is an '*āsôn* (v. 23). In the light of the cuneiform provisions on this matter, '*āsôn* is usually understood in reference to a fatal accident suffered by the mother. The Old Testament would then deal successively with miscarriage (v. 22) and homicide of the mother (v. 23). However, such an assimilation of the biblical law to the Mesopotamian and Hittite sources is not plausible. Incrimination for two different offenses by means of a single, rarely used word, goes against the usual concern of the legislator for terminological precision. The Hebrew language knows several verbs or circumlocutions to qualify different criminal facts without ambiguity.

Two divergent explanations may be suggested. The first[57] understands the pericope in reference to premature birth on the one hand (v. 22), and then to abortion on the other hand (v. 23). In the first case, the premature childbirth (*w^eyāṣ^e'û y^elādêhā*, 'and her foetus comes out') is caused by the blows, but the new-born survives the accident (*lō' yihyeh 'āsôn*). In the second case, the embryo is destroyed ('*āsôn yihyeh*). The use of '*āsôn* would then be justified: the word would refer to the child. The root *mwt*, 'to die', expected to define the second case, would be inappropriate for the foetus. Westbrook gives a second

cuneiform provision contemplates the casual blows inflicted upon the woman: YOS I, §1. See n. 65 below.

57. B.S. Jackson, 'The Problem of Exod. XXI, 22-25 (jus talionis)', *VT* 23 (1973), pp. 273-304.

interpretation:[58] he assigns to the word *'āsôn* a judicial meaning by linking it to an idea of responsibility. The law in v. 22 deals with the case where the culprit is known. The one who struck the woman is identified. He is liable for a fine, the amount of which depends on the will of the husband. In v. 23, on the contrary, nobody knows who gave the blows to the pregnant woman. This is a case of 'perpetrator unknown'. It becomes necessary to enforce a principle of commutative justice through the compensation of 'life for life': the whole community, jointly responsible for the damage, has to give to the wronged pair the equivalent of a life. In both situations, the woman loses her baby; abortion is therefore the only offense considered here. The legislator only provides the suitable punishment, depending on whether the author of the blows is or is not identified. The initial circumstance of the brawl explains the alternative of the text: looking for the guilty person would be needless if the offense had been committed by a single man.

Westbrook's theory is very convincing. The other explanation is open to criticism because the opposition between premature birth and miscarriage leads to the assumption of a complex mechanism of later alterations of the *Urgesetz* in order to change the initial scope of the rule. The text would have been modified through the addition of vv. 24-25 in order to aim at the destruction of the foetus (v. 22) and then at the serious or fatal injuries suffered by the mother (vv. 23-25). Even if one cannot reject *a priori* some possible modifications of the original text of the Covenant Code, the technique of amendment would be especially unexpected and complicated in this occurrence.[59] Moreover, the purpose of the later alterations does not appear clearly: why did the later drafter change an obvious and certainly useful provision into an obscure one, where two different offenses are defined by the same rare word?

Therefore, the biblical law is here very distinct from the other Near Eastern sources on this topic in dealing with the difficult question of responsibility when the offence happens during a brawl.

4.3. The types of punishment described in the texts also present interesting peculiarities.

58. R. Westbrook, 'Lex Talionis and Exodus 21, 22-25', *RB* 93 (1986), pp. 52-69.

59. S. Loewenstamm, 'Exodus XXI, 22-25', *VT* 27 (1977), p. 355.

4.3.1. The texts first document several uses of talion. The Hammurabian and Assyrian laws prescribe talion through a third person for the manslaughter of a free man's daughter (CH § 210: the daughter of the culprit is killed) or for the miscarriage of a free man's wife (MAL § 50: the perpetrator will be deprived of the child that his wife bears[60]). Since the fulfillment of these punishments might sometimes raise problems, as when the guilty party has no daughter or no wife, it has to be assumed that these penalties were convertible into money. All of these examples are true applications of *lex talionis*, according to which the aggressor suffers a penalty strictly identical to the one he caused. The MAL also prescribe a partial talion by commanding that the culprit should be struck 'blow for blow' when the victim is a prostitute (MAL § 52, ll. 89-90: *mihṣi kî mihṣi išakkunuš*[61]). Finally, the capital punishment stated in the Sumerian and Assyrian sources against the man who lethally hit a pregnant woman (UM 55-21-71, ll. 7'-8';[62] MAL § 50, ll. 70-71[63]) is obviously a form of talion.

4.3.2. The AL also impose the death penalty in a specific case: the offender destroys a male embryo and wrongs a pair who had no sons. The severe punishment reflects the importance of male heirs in Assyrian society. Besides, it shows that the law indicts the culprit's *scientia*:[64] he struck the victim while knowing that she had no sons. The general law is restored if the woman was expecting a girl: the offense is redressed with compensation.

4.3.3. Miscarriage is mostly punished by the payment of financial compensation, legal or customary. The amount is determined by the social rank of the victim, the stage of development of the pregnancy (in the HL, cf. *supra*), or on whether this was voluntary or

---

60. See the translation *supra*, n. 47.

61. MAL § 52: If a man has struck a harlot and caused her to cast the fruit of her womb, blow for blow shall be laid upon him; he shall compensate life (for life).

62. UM 55-21-71: If a [. . .] has struck the daughter of a man and caused the fruit of her womb to fall, he shall pay half a mina of silver. If she dies, that man shall be killed. If a [. . .] has struck the slave-girl of a man and caused the fruit of her womb to fall, he shall pay 5 shekels of silver.

63. See the translation *supra*, n. 47.

64. P. Cruveilhier, 'Recueil de lois assyriennes (3e partie)', *Le Muséon* 41 (1929), p. 29.

involuntary behavior by the guilty man (YOS I, 28[65]).

The Covenant Code requires the payment of a customary indemnity. However, v. 22 seems to allow the husband the right to assess freely the rate of the penalty (*'ānôš yē'ānēš ka'ašer yāšît 'ālāyw ba'al hā'iššâ*). The risk of such an independence is perhaps moderated in the next sentence, *wᵉnātan biplilîm*, which is usually translated by 'he (the offender) will pay through the agency of assessors'. The intervention of third parties would then reduce possible exorbitant claims by the husband. Against this traditional view, Westbrook suggests the interpretation: 'he will pay alone', the word *pᵉlilîm* emphasizing that when the perpetrator is known, he alone is liable; the other men involved in the brawl are exonerated.[66] This suggestion fits v. 22, where the offense is attributed to a single individual. The legislator stresses that neither the culprit nor the victim have any resort against the third parties involved in the fight.

It remains to be understood why damage that is caused unintentionally is liable for a punishment chosen by the husband, without any legal control. According to Westbrook, the free assessment of the husband arises from the very nature of the penalty: the guilty party redeems his own life or that of his son by paying a ransom. He is in the same situation as the owner of the goring ox (Exod. 21.30). The sentence in v. 22, 'depending on what the husband of the woman will impose on him' (*'ānôš yē'ānēš ka'ašer yāšît 'ālāyw ba'al hā'iššâ*) would have the same meaning. The ransom will not be submitted to any legal limitation. The only restrictions accepted are the natural ones, based on the financial capacity of the pair and on the demand of the plaintiff, who cannot ask for more than the death of the offender.

If Westbrook's interpretation of the term *pᵉlilîm* is convincing, his justification for the lack of any legal limitation to the claim of the husband is open to discussion. First, the scope of vv. 22 and 30 is not exactly the same. Exod. 21.30 explicitly states the redemption of the life is a mitigation of the capital punishment as decreed in v. 29. On the contrary, Exod. 21.22 does not expressly allude to the death

65. YOS I, 28 §§ 1-2 (Col. IV, ll. 1-10): If (a man) has knocked the daughter of a man and caused the fruit of her womb to fall, he shall pay 10 shekels of silver. If (a man) has struck the daughter of a man and caused the fruit of her womb to fall, he shall pay one third mina of silver.

66. Westbrook, 'Lex Talionis', p. 61.

penalty being enforced. The severity of such a penalty rules out the possibility of an implicit reference. Moreover, the harshness of the biblical law for an unintentional offense would be incomprehensible. Finally, Westbrook's theory leads to the equation of the destruction of the foetus with a homicide. As we have seen before, it is not certain that Hebrew people adopted such a view. If the death of the guilty person seems unlikely, the resort to the talion through a third person is even more questionable. Among the attestations of such a practice in the codes (CH §§ 116, 210, and 230; MAL § 55), CH § 210 is the only provision connected with our topic. However, the execution of the culprit's daughter requites the death of the mother and not the loss of the embryo.

The silence of the legislator might be explained in another way: the law declares its inability to appraise the amount of the compensation and leaves this task to the common law. The offense and its punishment are withdrawn from the sphere of public law. Nevertheless, the husband is not totally independent. He decides himself the amount of the compensation following the usual practice which is in force. Instead of natural limitations, there would be a customary limitation, which protects equity.

Verses 23-25, dealing with the question of an unknown perpetrator, also prescribe the payment of a customary compensation. The expression 'life for life' (*nepeš taḥat nepeš*, v. 23) does not lay down the death of the culprit because such a penalty would be defined with the words *môt yûmāt*, 'he shall surely die'. The scope of the phrase 'life for life' is identical to the one in the Assyrian sentence *napšāte umallā* (MAL §§ 50 and 52): giving 'life for life' or 'replacing the life' consists of paying a sum of money reckoned according to the economic worth of the destroyed foetus.[67] Therefore, the rate is not set by the provision, which rather refers to the common law. The Assyrian and Hebrew sources are identical in this respect. The community will take up the payment.[68]

Verses 24-25, which refer to other corporal injuries, may not have

---

67. M.-H. Prévost, 'A propos du talion', in *Mélanges Jacques Teneur*, III (Lille: Université des sciences sociales de Lille, 1977), pp. 619-29; Cardascia, 'La place du talion', p. 172.

68. This kind of order appears elsewhere in the Covenant Code; see the examples quoted by Westbrook, 'Lex Talionis', p. 66; see also Deut. 25.12: 'you shall cut off her hand; your eye shall have no mercy'.

been added after the initial composition of the text, but instead point to a formula stemming from the oral tradition and quoted *in extenso*.[69] The phrase 'life for life' alone fits the offense contemplated here, that is miscarriage. The rest of the sentence does not concern the pregnant woman, and is designed to lay down in a written document the whole oral provision.

This brief picture of the Near Eastern sources about abortion shows that there is no definitive pattern fitting all of the texts. The diversity of the enforceable rules is an essential feature of these laws. The fact that they belong to the same cultural whole is nonetheless fundamental. The existence of immutable values common to all these texts seems hardly reconcilable with the diversity exhibited in the documents. It might then be hazardous to build up global and systematic judicial constructions. Part of the oriental judicial mechanisms still eludes us, because the lack of doctrine specifying the thought of the legislators prevents us from understanding their inner logic. We are then limited to the observance of the paradox of unity in diversity.

69. U. Cassuto, quoted by Jackson, 'Problem', p. 283.

THE ANTHROPOLOGY OF SLAVERY IN THE COVENANT CODE

Victor H. Matthews

The primary issue to be raised in this study regards the social purposes of law and of complex legal systems. Since legal systems or individual laws are never created in a social vacuum, one of the major questions to be raised about the law is its original intent within the community that formulated it. Specific events spark the need for restriction by or protection under the law. Recurring events (i.e., crimes or business transactions) require the setting down of legal precedents, which existed first as part of the culture's oral tradition, as well as the establishment of legal procedures—judges, witnesses, rules of evidence. Some evolution in these procedures would be necessary to meet the needs of a culture as it evolves from a village to an urban society. To be sure, such evolution in the ancient Near East was often quite slow, but the cultures in this region cannot be described as totally static. Thus laws would eventually have to be altered or augmented to respond to changes in economic and/or living conditions and to reflect more complex forms of political leadership.

These developments, which are designed to handle changing legal situations, raise the question of why formal legal codes are compiled and what purpose, if any, they serve within the society. Hamilton[1] summarizes some of the possibilities[2] by listing three groups of

---

1. J.M. Hamilton, *Social Justice and Deuteronomy: The Case of Deuteronomy 15* (SBLDS, 136; Atlanta: Scholars Press, 1992), pp. 56-58.

2. See also J.J. Finkelstein's discussion of the 'laws' in Hammurabi's Code in *The Ox that Gored* (Transactions of the American Philosophical Society, 71/2; Philadelphia: The American Philosophical Society, 1981), pp. 15-16. Here he defines them as 'a larger or smaller collection of posed hypothetical situations or actions involving one or several persons'. In his interpretation, enforcement is not an issue, only the 'conceptual framework and moral standards implied. . . in these law collections'.

theories: (1) the law code as addendum to common law, (2) the law codes as enumeration of case decisions around a series of themes with the purpose of serving as a guide to judges, and (3) the law codes as self-justification of the king to posterity concerning the just character of his reign.[3] It is my contention that the second of these theories best fits the case in the ancient Near East. It allows the law codes, which of course become technically out-of-date almost as soon as they are formulated, a useful function within society. They can provide direction in the courts, thereby creating a sense of continuity while not dictating the course of justice. They also function as the basis for a process of continual re-evaluation of the legal system, a social commentary, which does not discount previous legal statutes, but rather builds upon them. These practices do not, however, preclude the political use of law codes by monarchs who wish to enhance their status by proclaiming themselves to be 'law-givers'. They simply provide a larger social dimension for the codes than as simple propaganda or antiquarian curiosities.

There is also contained here the likelihood that the various biblical law codes have their own textual originality within their social context.[4] While they may not be totally dependent upon each other, or on cuneiform predecessors, certainly it is clear from formulaic and situational similarities that their authors were aware of the corpus of existing ancient Near Eastern legal materials.[5] This allows for borrowing and editing of original legal texts. In that sense, then, law is not restricted to one locale or culture. It is also not canonized until the society or the court system chooses to make it so.

In his discussion of the formulation of the Covenant Code, Westbrook notes only one example within the Bible of the same law existing in an earlier and later version (p. 35)—the slave release law of Exod. 21.2 and Deut. 15.12. He sees this as insufficient evidence for systematic editing of the legal corpus and holds to the premise that 'the Covenant Code is a coherent text comprising clear and consistent laws, in the

3.   A point which R. Westbrook, 'Biblical and Cuneiform Law Codes', *RB* 92 (1985), p. 253, also advocates.

4.   Hamilton, *Social Justice*, pp. 80-81.

5.   See E. Otto, 'Town and Rural Countryside in Ancient Israelite Law: Reception and Redaction in Cuneiform and Israelite Law', *JSOT* 57 (1993), pp. 3-22, for a convincing explanation of the rooting of Israelite legal drafting techniques in cuneiform legal tradition.

same manner as its cuneiform forbears' (p. 36). He further argues that it is our lack of understanding of the social and cultural background of the laws which prevents scholars from recognizing this fact. I will argue, using a social scientific evaluation of the institution of slavery and of the slavery laws in the biblical text, that the biblical law codes did not become static until the text was canonized. I suggest that there was, on occasion, a conscious attempt to modify legal texts found in the Covenant Code by later biblical writers. And this does not represent, as Westbrook asserts, a different intellectual path, but rather the natural social evolution of legal development in Israel.

Slavery as a Social Institution

Slaves provide the state with the laborers and children it needs.[6] Free citizens are encouraged 'to be fruitful and multiply' while slavery subsidizes childbirth by increasing the population available to serve as farmers, herders, childbearers or prostitutes.

Slavery exists in societies which have labor-intensive economies and a birth rate which cannot cope with the need for laborers. It is also found when labor service needs are coupled with a weak economy or marginal environment which drives households into debt which they cannot manage. The purpose of keeping chattel or slaves is to supplement the labor force and to provide additional workers through the birth of children. In the ancient Near East there was both permanent as well as temporary slavery. The former was due primarily to warfare and the latter to economic exigency. The Bible, as well as texts from the ancient Near East, contain both, although debt slavery is by far the more common factor in legal materials.

Prisoners of War as Slaves

Warfare was one factor in the development of the institution of slavery in the ancient Near East. Very often wars begin because the aggressors need additional laborers to enhance the infrastructure, expand agricultural production, or compensate for losses due to disease or some other calamity.[7] Prisoners taken in war and raids

6. G. Feeley-Harnik, 'Issues in Divine Kingship', *Annual Review of Anthropology* 14 (1985), p. 292.

7. R.B. Ferguson, 'Explaining War', in J. Haas (ed.), *The Anthropology of War* (Cambridge: Cambridge University Press, 1990), pp. 38, 48, 52.

became slaves (see Amos 1.6, 9). This may be a permanent condition, or may end with the ransoming of the prisoner by his tribe or his state.[8] For example, Lot is taken captive when Sodom is raided (Gen. 14.12). It may be presumed that if Abram had not rescued him from this form of slavery, Lot would have been sold as a slave.[9]

There is no conscious choice made by prisoners to become slaves except in the sense that they agree, not always freely, to serve in the military in the first place or to live within the boundaries of the victimized nation. Slavery as a result of warfare and raiding was most common in Mesopotamia where war between the city states was quite frequent throughout that region's history. Egypt, on the other hand, did not develop a large body of slaves during its early history. The state relied on its own households to do the bulk of the agricultural and construction work and on a smaller number of personal slaves which were devoted to domestic service.[10] This may have changed somewhat after the 15th century BCE when the expulsion of the Hyksos was followed by increased international interests and conflicts which sparked battles in Nubia and in Syria-Palestine.[11] The result was large numbers of prisoners of war who in many cases were assigned along with other booty to military commanders in Egypt.

Despite the increased numbers of persons taken in warfare, the idea of permanent chattel status, on the North American model (c. 17th–19th centuries CE), was unknown in the ancient Near East. Rather, those persons who survived the transition from freedom to slavery were generally returned to semi-free, serf status, a more productive condition since it included payment of taxes and was more conducive to establishing a family.[12]

In Syria-Palestine, large scale warfare was less common simply because the states were smaller. However, raiding for economic and

8.   V.H. Matthews, 'Legal Aspects of Military Service in Ancient Mesopotamia', *Military Law Review* 94 (1981), pp. 146-47; and I.J. Gelb, 'Prisoners of War in Early Mesopotamia', *JNES* 32 (1973), pp. 72-73.

9.   I.J. Gelb, 'From Freedom to Slavery', in D.O. Edzard (ed.), *XVIIIᵉ Recontre Assyriologique Internationale* (Paris: P. Geuthner, 1972), p. 84.

10.   I.J. Gelb, 'Quantitative Evaluation of Slavery and Serfdom', in B.L. Eichler (ed.), *Kramer Anniversary Volume: Cuneiform Studies in Honor of Samuel Noah Kramer* (AOAT, 25; Neukirchener–Vluyn: Neukirchener Verlag, 1976), p. 201.

11.   W.W. Hallo and W.K. Simpson, *The Ancient Near East: A History* (New York: Harcourt Brace Jovanovich, 1971), pp. 260, 265.

12.   Gelb, 'From Freedom to Slavery', pp. 86-87.

political reasons did occur, which resulted in the taking of animals as well as prisoners, both male and female (Deut. 20.14). For instance, there is a woman in the Stories of Elisha who advises her Syrian owner, Na'aman, to seek help from the prophet to cure his leprosy (2 Kgs 5.2-3). This woman came to be in the household of Na'aman as a result of a border raid on Israel by the Syrians.

In the stories of Jacob, Levi and Simeon take the women and children of Shechem as slaves (Gen. 34.29). In the book of Deuteronomy, some women captured as prisoners of war became house slaves.[13] Others, however, served as wives, providing an heir or simply increasing the fertility of the group. These women, however, enjoyed more rights than those taken simply as domestic slaves, and could actually be freed if not treated properly (Exod. 21.7-11; Deut. 21.10-14). The worth of slave women as potential concubines or wives required their persons to be protected by threat of fine (i.e., guilt offering—Lev. 19.20-22) in a similar fashion to laws protecting betrothed women (Deut. 22.23-27). In both instances, the principle of protection of property rights and values is safeguarded.

Slave Trade

The trade or purchase of slaves, evidenced in ancient legal texts, also contributed to the growth and mobility of the slave population.[14] Wars and raids generally provided slaves ethnically different from the slave owners. Racial differences allowed everyone quickly to identify who was a slave and who was free in a society. Few racially distinct (i.e., foreign) slaves were ever emancipated. Their only hope of liberation from the captive country was to escape or be repatriated to their country of origin with the payment of ransom (see CH 32).

This would most often involve persons of a nationality other than that of the seller and serves as another example of weaker population groups being preyed upon by more aggressive or advanced cultures.[15]

---

13. Gelb, 'From Freedom to Slavery', p. 83.

14. Gelb, 'Quantitative Evaluation', p. 197.

15. T. Gibson, 'Raiding, Trading, and Tribal Autonomy in Insular Southeast Asia', in Haas (ed.), *The Anthropology of War*, pp. 127-28. See also B.S. Jackson, 'Biblical Laws of Slavery: A Comparative Approach', in L.S. Archer (ed.), *Slavery and Other Forms of Unfree Labour* (London: Routledge, 1988), pp. 86-89, for a review of Greek and Roman sources on debt slavery and war captives.

These slaves would have most likely been sold into the service of temple communities, royal estates, or the estates of high ranking nobility rather than to the private households of average citizens.[16]

The story of the sale of Joseph by the Midianites to Potiphar in Egypt (Gen. 37.38) may serve as an example of the transfer of persons into new regions as slaves. Potiphar is described as a military commander, one whose estates required a foreman to manage its work force (Gen. 39.1-6).

Temporary Debt Slavery in Ancient Israel

At the heart of every economic situation are resources and labor. For example, the earth and the prevailing climate provide the resources for an agricultural economy, but human labor is needed to clear fields, build terraces, plant, cultivate, and harvest crops. In the marginal environment of Syria-Palestine, not every household could work its fields successfully. This could be due to a climactic catastrophe such as a drought, or to a labor shortage brought on by infertility, a plague which killed off a significant number of the able-bodied workers, or a war which took the men of the household away to fight for long periods of time.

Ancient Israel considered permanent slavery the most inhumane condition possible. Debt slavery, however, became a rich metaphor by which the Hebrews came to understand their own social development. The Hebrews were keenly aware of their own heritage as strangers without rights in a foreign land. In the beginning they were debt slaves temporarily without land and without children until Yahweh delivered them, and they became Hebrews—free people blessed with land and children (Gen. 12).

Although eventually any foreigner was accorded the honorable status of a 'stranger in the land' (Hebrew: *gēr*), originally this label was assigned to a debt slave temporarily living and working in a creditor's village.[17] Since debt slaves were members of the same culture as their creditors, the book of Deuteronomy is especially conscientious about allowing them to participate in the celebrations

16. Gelb, 'Quantitative Evaluation', p. 198.

17. See F.A. Spina, 'Israelites as *gērîm*, "Sojourner"', in C.L. Meyers and M. O'Connor (eds.), *The Word of the Lord Shall Go Forth* (Winona Lake, IN: Eisenbrauns, 1983), pp. 321-25.

and festivals of their creditors while they are paying off their debts (Deut. 16.11-14).

The biblical injunction for Israel as a state is to protect the weak, the helpless, and the poor. The book of Deuteronomy reinforces these statutes by reminding the people that 'you were a slave in Egypt' (Deut. 15.5; 24.18, 22). These laws reflect an understanding of the reasons for poverty and try to deal with its victims non-violently. The poor had the right to glean harvested fields (Ruth 2), and injunctions appear against oppressing the poor, such as by withholding their wages (Deut. 24.14-15). One sign of this concern may be seen in the practice which allows a household to pledge the work of its members as collateral when it borrowed goods or services from another household. To avoid confiscation of their land and children, the members of a household in default would work off their debt one day at a time. Each day the laborers of the household in default would take off the clothes or cloak which identified them as free, and work the day semi-naked as slaves. They would turn their outer garments over to their creditors for the day. These garments, however threadbare, tie them just as strongly as a sworn contract to the households of their creditors and require them, in what may be their last attempt to remain free, to carry out the agreed upon task. These laborers, who become slaves for a day, agree to become fully fledged slaves if they do not complete the tasks which their creditors set before them.

For instance, in the Yavne-Yam inscription, a slave indicts his creditor for confiscating his cloak for alleged failure to work as contracted. Should it not be returned, he would have no recourse but to sell himself into slavery since the one guard against that status, his garment, has been confiscated (Exod. 22.26-27; Deut. 24.12-13; Amos 2.8).

> Let my lord the governor pay heed to the words of his servant! Your servant was reaping in Hasar-asam. The work went as usual and your servant completed his reaping and hauling before the others. Despite the fact that your servant had completed his work, Hoshaiahu son of Shobai came and took your servant's garment. All my fellow workers will testify, all those who work in the heat of the day will surely certify that I am not guilty of any breach of contract. Please intercede for me so that my garment will be returned and I will (as always) do my share of the work. The governor should see to it that the garment of your servant is returned and that no revenge be taken against your servant, that he not be fired.[18]

18. V.H. Matthews and D.C. Benjamin, *Old Testament Parallels: Laws and*

For a similar reason, the book of Deuteronomy also prohibits using a millstone as collateral (Deut. 24.6). A creditor cannot deprive a household of the means of making a living and thus avoiding debt slavery.

The requirement that the garment be returned during the night as a guard against the evening chill speaks to a society which recognizes those citizens who are on the economic edge. It is also suggestive of a society which is not above violating its own social code[19] and needs to be reminded of its obligations to the community as a whole.

As a state, Israel tried to prevent debt from accumulating to the point where slavery was the only option.[20] Thus the laws against charging interest on loans worked in most cases to aid the poor (Exod. 22.24; Deut. 23.20; Lev. 25.35-37; Ezek. 18.13).

In these cases, a household could become destitute, and at the insistence of its creditors sell members of the household into slavery to pay debts (2 Kgs 4.1; Neh. 5.1-5). Slavery in this case is defined by the legal codes of the ancient Near East as temporary debt slavery since the law restricts the number of years a man may be held in slavery to six (Exod. 21.2-11; Deut. 15.12-18).

Regulations also restrict the sale or the enslavement of Israelites by other Israelites according to the laws in Lev. 25.35-42. In this case, the Israelite, who is in financial difficulties would be reduced to the status of a hired hand or indentured servant rather than a slave.[21] However, this is a late legal code and probably reflects a reaction against previous practice.[22] It should be noted that this statute is a further reflection of the fact that law is 'a category of social phenomena and, consequently, changes with time'.[23]

Both the book of Leviticus and the Code of Hammurabi (CH 1) place limitations on a debt slave's term. The most likely explanation

---

Stories from the Ancient Near East (Mahwah, NJ: Paulist, 1991), p. 133.

19. I. Mendelsohn, 'Slavery in the Ancient Near East', *BA* 9 (1946), pp. 85-91.

20. A. Phillips, 'The Laws of Slavery: Exodus 21.2-11', *JSOT* 30 (1984), p. 54.

21. B.A. Levine, *The JPS Torah Commentary: Leviticus* (Philadelphia: Jewish Publication Society, 1989), p. 179.

22. N.P. Lemche, 'The "Hebrew Slave": Comments on the Slave Law Ex. xxi 2-11', *VT* 25 (1975), p. 138.

23. L. Pospisil, *Anthropology of Law: A Comparative Theory* (New Haven: HRAF Press, 1974), p. 22.

for this is because the debt slaves and their owners both belong to the same race and culture. The interests shared by people of the same origin is so strong as to prevent creditors from permanently enslaving their own people.[24]

The book of Jeremiah indicts the slave owners in Jerusalem who swore during the siege of Jerusalem to free their male and female slaves.[25] After the siege was lifted, they returned them to slave status. The storyteller here draws a further connection between the failure of the people to keep their oath to the slaves and their failure to keep the covenant with Yahweh (Jer. 34.8-22). While this is an attempt to darken the character of those in power at that time, it very likely is indicative of actual abuse as well. Thus it can be seen that law codes, whether ancient or newly formulated, only provide guidance. The enforcement of the law must receive its primary impetus from the society itself.

A further reflection of this legal reality is found in the book of Leviticus, which only speaks of foreigners as permanent slaves (Lev. 25.44-46). This principal is based on an ideal which probably did not exist in the period before the exile. In any case, the law does not protect any Israelite, of any class or status, from being enslaved for debt should his economic circumstances justify it.[26]

In the Covenant Code slave statutes, which served as the legal foundation for both the Deuteronomic and Holiness Codes, the issue of citizenship is also raised. In this case members of a household might be temporarily sold into slavery to pay its debts (Exod. 21.2-11), based on the statement that after six years service (a period with the sabbath sequence in mind)[27] the man shall return to free status, 'without debt' (Exod. 21.2b; NRSV) or 'without payment' of additional fees.[28] However, there is a question of citizenship highlighted in this text by the use of the term Hebrew (*'ibrî*) in v. 2a. Lemche,[29] among others,[30]

24. Gelb, 'From Freedom to Slavery', p. 86.

25. R.P. Carroll, *Jeremiah* (Philadelphia: Westminster, 1986), pp. 648-49.

26. Phillips, 'Laws of Slavery', p. 64 n. 16.

27. S.R. Driver, *The Book of Exodus* (Cambridge: Cambridge University Press, 1911), p. 210; and Phillips, 'Laws of Slavery', p. 61.

28. J.I. Durham, *Exodus* (Waco, TX: Word Books, 1987), pp. 320-21.

29. Lemche, ' "Hebrew Slave" ', pp. 138-39.

30. A. Alt, 'The Origins of Israelite Law', in *Essays on Old Testament History and Religion* (Oxford: Oxford University Press, 1966), pp. 93-95; and M. Noth,

raises the question of whether Hebrew = Israelite in this social context. He defines the Hebrew as 'a person who sells himself as a slave for debt' and compares this contractual arrangement with those mentioned in documents from Nuzi involving the labor service of *'apirū*. Similarly, Na'aman[31] describes the *ḫābirū* as 'uprooted immigrants' who live as resident aliens on the margins of society, often band together, and are ultimately absorbed into the general population.

It may well be that originally Hebrew, like Habiru, was a generic term for land-less, state-less persons, who contracted themselves as mercenaries, laborers, and servants.[32] However, I am not convinced that this is necessarily a 'pejorative designation', as Childs suggests. There are some negative connotations present, since persons in the ancient world tended to identify themselves with a group or place. But considering the fact that the first 'Hebrew', Abram was a landless immigrant, it is doubtful that the term held stereotypical meaning such as the modern 'tramp' does today.

Certainly, by the time the Covenant Code was formulated, the Israelite villagers considered themselves to be *ḥopšî*, free landowners. To be termed an *'ibrî*, therefore, would mean a *ḥopš* who had become destitute (compare Jer. 34.9) or was living in foreign lands (Judg. 19.16).[33] The Hebrew had to work his full six year term in order to regain his mortgaged land and *ḥopš* status.[34] Thus the *'ibrî* in Exod. 21.2, Deut. 15.12, and Jer. 34.9 would be an Israelite,[35] who, unlike the non-Israelite, could not be sold into permanent slavery.[36] It was his right to release that distinguished him from the non-Israelite.[37]

Lemche suggests that the status change from *'ibrî* to *ḥopš*

Exodus (Philadelphia: Westminster, 1962), pp. 177-80.

31. N. Na'aman, 'Ḫābirū and Hebrews: The Transfer of a Social Term to the Literary Sphere', *JNES* 45 (1986), pp. 271-75.

32. B.S. Childs, *The Book of Exodus* (Philadelphia: Westminster, 1974), p. 468.

33. Na'aman, 'Ḫābirū and Hebrews', p. 286.

34. J.A. Thompson, *The Book of Jeremiah* (Grand Rapids, MI: Eerdmans, 1980), p. 610.

35. Hamilton, *Social Justice*, p. 84.

36. Phillips, 'Laws of Slavery', p. 64 n. 16. Jackson, 'Biblical Laws of Slavery', p. 93 also makes the argument that *'ibrî* in this passage relates to debt slavery.

37. Phillips, 'Laws of Slavery', p. 62.

(= Akkadian *ḫupšū*) really involves movement into a client, rather than a truly freedman condition.[38] However, having once contracted himself and proven his willingness to make good on his debts, it seems more likely that Israelite society would have restored the Hebrew slave to full citizen status as a *ḥopšî*. Clientage would only apply in the monarchy period when all citizens were subject to the state, paying taxes and serving in the corvée.[39]

Permanent Slavery as a Social Remedy

Further strengthening the argument that slavery provides both labor and children is the stipulation in Exod. 21.3-6 regarding permanent slavery. The text describes an option given to debt slaves when their six year term has been completed to remand themselves into permanent slavery to their owner. This option may be exercised through a ritual transformation of their status (Exod. 21.5-6). The ritual, similar to other status changing rituals in biblical law (Deut. 21.18-21), involves the following steps:

1. He makes a public declaration of love for his owner and his family, which he acquired while a slave. It is unlikely that this represents an emotional attachment to the master personally, but rather to his service.[40] By this statement he firmly designates his obligation and allegiance to persons other than himself.[41] The social significance of this statement, denying self and citizenship, is similar to that made by Ruth in transferring her allegiance to Naomi, the Israelites, and Yahweh (Ruth 1.16-17). There is no mention of family or love for owner in the public statement made in Deut. 15.16. Love for owner and his household are qualifiers here, but are not a portion of the oath he takes. This may be attributed to the removal of social barriers at the end of the six years of slavery, typical of the

38. Lemche, ' "Hebrew Slave" ', pp. 141-42. See also the argument of S.M. Paul, *Studies in the Book of the Covenant in the Light of Cuneiform and Biblical Law* (VTSup, 18; Leiden: Brill, 1970), pp. 45-46.

39. See on this N.K. Gottwald, *The Tribes of Yahweh: A Sociology of the Religion of Liberated Israel, 1250–1050 B.C.E.* (Maryknoll, NY: Orbis, 1979), p. 769 n. 412; Phillips, 'Laws of Slavery', p. 55; and E. Lipiński, 'L'Esclave Hebreu', *VT* 26 (1976), pp. 120-23.

40. Childs, *Exodus*, pp. 468-69.

41. This provision is not included in Deut. 15.12-18. It may reflect, as Lev. 25.39-42 appears to do, a growing distaste for debt servitude and its public rituals.

egalitarianism of the Deuteronomic Code. The freedman is thus a 'brother' (= equal) of his owner until he undergoes the ritual of permanent enslavement and is therefore free to make choices for himself.[42] The still later Holiness Code (Lev. 25.39), takes this a step further by removing the label of slave from an Israelite altogether, terming the debtor a 'hired or bound laborer'.[43]

2. He makes a public renunciation of the right 'to go out a free person'. In doing this, he gives up the fundamental right of all free citizens to own land, conduct business transactions, and pass freely back and forth through the city gate (see CH 15).

3. He is brought before God (i.e., in the presence of the judges/ elders) as witness. This aspect of the ritual is very similar to legal procedure in the Code of Hammurabi where an oath is taken 'before the god' (see CH 20, 103, 106, 120, 126). The participants would have probably gone to the temple to perform this oath.[44] Both human and divine witnesses are drawn in to certify this transaction and to determine that it is in fact a voluntary decision on the part of the slave. This provision is deleted from the Deut. 15.12-18 version. Phillips[45] suggests this may be the result of the Josianic reform which banned the use of household gods (2 Kgs 23.24), but it is more likely the Deuteronomic restriction on local temples and shrines which is at the heart of this omission in Deuteronomy 15.[46]

4. At the door of their owner's house, a nail is driven through their earlobe with an awl. This final step achieved two aims. It enhanced the significance of the ritual by adding place to action.[47] In addition, it,

42. M. Weinfeld, *Deuteronomy and the Deuteronomic School* (Oxford: Clarendon Press, 1972), p. 282.

43. See J. van der Ploeg, *Slavery in the Old Testament* (VTSup, 22; Leiden: Brill, 1972), p. 82; and Levine, *Leviticus*, p. 179.

44. F.C. Fensham, 'New Light on Exodus 21.6 and 22.7 from the Laws of Eshnunna', *JBL* 78 (1959), pp. 160-61; and O. Loretz, 'Exod. 21.6; 22.8 und angebliche Nuzi-Parallelen', *Bib* 41 (1960), pp. 167-70.

45. Phillips, 'Laws of Slavery', pp. 55-56.

46. B.M. Levinson, *The Hermeneutics of Innovation: The Impact of Centralization upon the Structure, Sequence, and Reformulation of Legal Material in Deuteronomy* (Ann Arbor, MI: University Microfilms, 1991), pp. 310, 359-60, notes that the phrase could also refer to a local temple and that 'before God' refers to a judicial oath in that temple.

47. V.H. Matthews, 'Entrance Ways and Threshing Floors: Legally Significant Sites in the Ancient near East', *Fides et historia* 19 (1987), p. 33.

like circumcision, distinctively scarred the individual.[48] A ring or tag of ownership, similar in purpose to the livery worn by Joseph while in Potiphar's service (Gen. 39.12-16), could then be inserted for easy identification of the person's status.[49]

The Exodus 21 text specifically notes that this action is taken because the slave does not wish to leave his wife and children. The wife, presumably also a slave, had been given to him by his owner and any children they had would remain the property of the owner. It would be difficult to make the decision to abandon them and it would probably have been nearly impossible for him to raise the funds to purchase their freedom. The practice of supplying a term-servant with a wife very likely had two intents:

1. It was done by the owner to keep a man as a slave rather than lose him after only six years service.[50] The Deuteronomic Code (15.12-18) addresses this issue by promising the owner that God would prosper him for aiding the slave to return to free status after the 'full six years' service' was completed.[51] Concern that the contract was fulfilled (both the period of slavery and granting of freedom) is therefore coupled with an awareness of economic loss and a benediction (Deut 15.18). Such a commentary on a previous statute suggests the ease felt by the biblical writers to put a new interpretation or enhancement on the law to fit their current understanding of covenant obligations.

2. Even if the man chose to leave his service, the owner retained the woman and any children she might produce, thereby materially increasing the strength of the household. Phillips[52] notes a reversal of intent in the Deuteronomic legislation. In this case there is a conscious promotion of the idea of the return to free status for the slave, resulting from the granting of a subsidy and the removal of marriage status as a legal or moral criterion. It seems unlikely, however, that the owner would be so altruistic that he would grant freedom to the former slave's family if they were born during the period of slavery.

---

48. Mendelsohn, 'Slavery in the Ancient Near East', p. 49, compares this scarring to tattooing.

49. Phillips, 'Laws of Slavery', p. 51.

50. Childs, *Exodus*, p. 468, contrasts this 'cruelty' to the concept of marriage in Gen. 2.24 and Mt. 19.6.

51. Phillips, 'Laws of Slavery', p. 58.

52. Phillips, 'Laws of Slavery', pp. 56-57.

That would have negated the slave's use as a propagator of additional slaves for the master.[53] The elimination of this section of the law in Deuteronomy seems to be only an attempt to simplify the choice made by the slave to return to freedom or to continue his/her slavery.

The other side of this drama is the opportunity afforded to the Hebrew slave who may not wish to leave the security of his owner's house. There is a distinct possibility that he would not be able to make a livelihood for himself as a free man and might slip back into the indigent condition which had caused him to be labeled a 'Hebrew' in the first place.[54] This might be due to the fact that the Covenant Code did not provide a subsidy to the newly freed slave by his former owner (a provision which is included in the revised form of the law in Deut. 15.13-14). Still, the 'easy' way, even with the possibility of subsidy in the later period, would have been to choose the certainty of his slavery to the uncertainty of a future in which he would have to manage for himself as a free man.

The decision to permanently reduce oneself to slave status, however, should also be recognized as a risk. The slave who becomes a permanent addition to the household faced the possibility that he could be sold to pay the debts of the owner (see CH 119) or transferred as part of an inheritance at the death of the owner.[55]

The Rights of Female Slaves

Unlike males, females do not have the option of selling themselves into slavery. They do find themselves in this condition, however, as a result of the action of their fathers or husbands[56]—either as a way of obtaining a marriage without a dowry or by joining their husbands as slaves to meet the debt obligations of the head of the household (Neh. 5.5).[57]

Legislation regarding female slaves changes from the time of the Covenant Code to the Deuteronomic Reform. In the Exod. 21.7-11 passage, the woman may or may not leave slavery at the end of six

53. Jackson, 'Biblical Laws of Slavery', p. 93.

54. T.J. Turnbaum, 'Male and Female Slaves in the Sabbath Year Laws of Exodus 21.1-11', in *SBL Seminar Papers* (Atlanta: Scholars Press, 1987), p. 548.

55. Phillips, 'Laws of Slavery', p. 51.

56. Turnbaum, 'Male and Female Slaves', p. 545.

57. Phillips, 'Laws of Slavery', p. 63 n. 15.

years. Her term may be shortened by the failure of the owner to treat her with due respect, provide for her needs, or uphold her legal rights (Exod. 21.9-11). These designated rights include food, clothing, and the marital rights of the first wife. If they are not provided, even when the owner takes another wife, then the slave woman has the right to leave that household a free woman without the payment of the debt which had led to her original enslavement (Exod. 21.11).[58] No such provisions are included in the Deuteronomic Code since both men and women are extended equal rights under the law[59]—both able to go out free at the end of six years or to chose permanent slavery (Deut. 15.12, 17).

However, there is a humanitarian provision in Deut. 21.10-14 which is similar to the injunctions in Exod. 21.9-11, which protects the rights of a slave woman taken in war. If preparations have been made to marry this woman, including a physical transformation involving shaving the head,[60] and then she is rejected, then she can go free and cannot be sold. This relates to breach of contract and a dishonoring of person when such a breach occurs (see Deut. 22.18-19). She therefore cannot be used, as the male slave is in Exod 21.4, as a sexual breeder without changing her status.[61]

If a man sells his non-betrothed daughter as a slave (Exod. 21.7-8), this gives her owner first claim on assigning her to himself or his son as a wife.[62] If she does not please her owner, who has taken her as a wife, then she can be 'redeemed' (i.e., have her contract voided for a price), but not sold 'to a foreign people'. Apparently, the right to sell her or other slaves outside the household was possible or the stipulation against such a sale would have no meaning. The restriction on such a sale may reflect an attempt to improve the basic conditions of

58. Compare Deut. 21.10-14 for the rights of captive women.

59. Phillips, 'Laws of Slavery', pp. 56 and 60.

60. Shaving the head, paring the nails, discarding of garments, and a month of mourning are all associated with a change of social condition. See for example Tamar's transformation in Gen. 38.14, Joseph's new condition defined by a change of clothing in Gen. 41.37-43, and the other Tamar's shame reflected in the tearing of her 'virgin's robe' in 2 Sam. 13.19.

61. Jackson, 'Biblical Laws of Slavery', p. 94.

62. B.J. Schwartz, 'A Literary Study of the Slave-Girl Pericope: Leviticus 19.20-22', in S. Japhet (ed.), *Studies in Bible* (Scripta Hierosolymitana, 31; Jerusalem: Magnes Press, 1986), p. 245.

slavery, thereby insuring better service during the period of slavery,[63] or it may be a further example of humanitarian legislation.

A similar piece of humanitarian law appears in the Holiness Code in Lev. 19.20-22, in which a slave girl, betrothed as a wife to one man but not yet 'redeemed' (i.e., had the bride price paid and freedom granted), has sexual relations with another man. This may imply concubinage[64] or perhaps may simply imply that steps which ordinarily would be taken to give her her freedom had not yet been completed. The couple, however, cannot be executed for adultery since she is not officially married until she has been redeemed.[65] Because her status is still technically that of a slave, intercourse with her does not require the same penalty (stoning) that would otherwise be the result of rape of a betrothed woman (Deut. 22.23-27). Interestingly, in this way both property rights and the rights of persons are protected.

Conclusion

Slavery as an institution in ancient Israel, unlike that in ancient Greece and Rome, probably did not account for a large percentage of the labor force.[66] However, indenture, tenant farming, and temporary debt slavery (for a day or six years) were common enough to require legal definition and constraints. The general force of these laws is to protect the rights of both the owner and slave so that neither party would be physically or economically abused.

Slavery is an institution which best serves the interests of the state, with its monumental construction projects and needs for a ready surplus labor supply. In the village setting, however, its primary function is to provide an option for debtors and for those who fail to maintain the economic viability of their households. The upshot of the above legislative survey is to show that the principal influence on the formulation and evolution of law in ancient Israel was the social context. The movement from village to state culture is the prime determinant here in requiring changes and additions to the law.

63. Gelb, 'From Freedom to Slavery', p. 86.
64. See Exod. 21.8-10 which suggests a sexual relationship and a legal obligation greater than that due to a slave.
65. Schwartz, 'Slave-Girl Pericope', p. 248.
66. Van der Ploeg, *Slavery in the Old Testament*, p. 83.

While the Covenant Code may have originated, at least in part, as a coherent set of statutes, as Westbrook suggests, it was not set in stone throughout its existence. Changes in the social world of ancient Israel required this code, as well as the Deuteronomic and Holiness Codes, to take into account ethical as well as economic considerations which were not a part of the village culture prior to the establishment of the monarchy. Thus the practice of continuously reshaping or redefining the laws, including the law codes, is a clearly acceptable one throughout Israelite history. While this study has concentrated on the slavery statutes, it seems clear that additional evidence for this process can be found through philological and literary examination of the other legal materials.

A GENERIC DISCREPANCY IN THE COVENANT CODE

William Morrow

Raymond Westbrook concludes his essay 'What is the Covenant Code?' with the statement that the present text of the Covenant Code (Exod. 21.1–22.19) must be presumed to be clear and coherent. The view that the Covenant Code can be an amalgam of provisions from different sources and periods is based upon premises which are unsupported by empirical evidence. Such premises rely on inappropriate models from the classical and later periods.[1] The purpose of this paper is to challenge Westbrook's conclusion. It will focus on the sporadic use of second-person references in the Covenant Code as one feature which likely has source critical implications.

According to Westbrook, the Covenant Code can be characterized as a provincial reflection of the cuneiform legal tradition. It is probably to be dated to the early monarchic period (10th century).[2] As such, it belongs to the same scribal tradition which produced works such as the Sumerian Codex Urnammu and Codex Lipit-Ishtar and the Akkadian Codex Eshnunna, Codex Hammurapi, the Middle Assyrian laws and the Neo-Babylonian laws. Given the widespread influence and diffusion of Mesopotamian culture into the Levant in the Bronze Age, it would be no surprise to find similar codes compiled from local law by Hittite (e.g., the Hittite Laws) or Canaanite scribes who were inspired by contact with this tradition. In fact, Westbrook suggests that Codex Eshnunna (which became a school text) must have reached the Israelite cultural sphere in some form because of the proximity of Exod. 21.35 and Codex Eshnunna § 53.[3]

---

1. R. Westbrook, 'What is the Covenant Code?' in this volume.
2. R. Westbrook, 'Cuneiform Law Codes and the Origins of Legislation', *ZA* 79 (1989), p. 219.
3. R. Westbrook, 'Biblical and Cuneiform Law Codes', *RB* 92 (1986), pp. 253, 256-57.

The scribal schools in the Mesopotamian tradition were centers of 'scientific' research where lists of omens, medical texts, etc. were compiled and refined. As a scientific subject, law would give rise to the same research and expect to enjoy the same pattern of diffusion. In the case of the law codes, their purpose was to act as reference works for royal judges in deciding difficult cases.[4] Therefore, when Westbrook states his conclusions, he is indicating that the formulations of the Covenant Code are homogeneous to the point that they all can be considered to be the products of a single genre of jurisprudence: judicial reference works produced by scribal schools patronized by royal authority.

It is my thesis that the sporadic second-person references in the largely third-person context of the Covenant Code are generic discrepancies which belie the homogeneity which Westbrook's model of composition presupposes. The possibility of more than one jurisdictional context arises if linguistic or contextual discrepancies are too great to be explained with respect to only one model.[5]

The Covenant Code contains the following second-person contexts: Exod. 21.2, 14, 24; 22.17. These references use second-person singular imperfect verb forms in the following syntactic conditions:

a. protasis of a conditionally introduced instruction: Exod. 21.2 ('If you buy . . . ').

b. apodosis of a conditionally introduced instruction: Exod. 21.14 (' . . . you shall take him . . . '), 24 ('then you shall give . . . ').

c. negated predicate of an unconditionally introduced instruction: Exod. 22.17 (' . . . you shall not let live').

Westbrook's explanation for the use of second-person forms in Exod. 21.14, 24; 22.17 is that the second-person singular directs a law to the community as a whole or its representatives.[6] I do not dispute this interpretation. What is to be questioned is whether such usage is compatible with the model of juridical practice he posits for the composition of the Covenant Code.

---

4. R. Westbrook, 'The Nature and Origin of the Twelve Tables', *Zeitschrift der Savigny-Stiftung für Rechtsgeschichte (Romanistische Abteilung)* 105 (1988), p. 89.

5. For a discussion of this methodological principle see R. Knierim, 'The Problem of Ancient Israel's Prescriptive Traditions', *Semeia* 45 (1989), p. 14.

6. R. Westbrook, 'Lex Talionis and Exod 21, 22-25', *RB* 93 (1986), p. 66.

I intend to point out that second-person instructional language was widespread in the same scribal schools which presumably both produced and transmitted the Akkadian Codex Eshnunna, Codex Hammurapi, the Middle Assyrian Laws, the Neo-Babylonian Laws and the Hittite Laws.[7] But a survey of these various law codes, which Westbrook points to as exemplars of the genre of judicial references and to which he claims the genre of the Covenant Code belongs, shows a complete absence of second-person references in their legal formulae.[8] To be sure there are isolated incidents of second-person references in quoted speech (e.g., Codex Eshnunna § 22; Codex Hammurapi § 192), but second-person references are not part of the formulations of the laws *per se*. This fact makes the absence of second-person language in the legal formulae of the law codes of generic significance. It suggests that the content of the Covenant Code owes its present form to some sort of conflationary activity.

The incidence of second-person instructions in the compositions of the scribal schools falls into several different categories. In some, the imperative (and its negation) predominate (e.g., collections of proverbs). Imperative expressions are derived from the Akkadian preterite tense. The imperative itself is expressed by *purus* forms (*purus* = 'decide'). A related form in the third-person form uses the particle *lū* with *iprus* (third-person preterite) forms (*liprus* = 'let him decide').[9]

The discussion which follows will focus on the use of second-person present indicative forms in instructional contexts. These instructions have both formal (because indicative) and semantic (because they connote incomplete time) parallels to the use of second-person imperfects attested in the Covenant Code. Conditionally introduced formulae are common in Akkadian instructions predicated by the second-person present, but instructions may also be unconditionally introduced. The examples below prove that scribes schooled in the

---

7.　Translations used: '*Rechtsbücher*', in R. Borger *et al.* (eds.), *Texte aus der Umwelt des Alten Testaments* (Gütersloh: Mohn, 1982), 1:1.

8.　The Sumerian Codex Urnammu and Codex Lipit-Ishtar also use only third-person language in their legal formulations. Presumably, the situation in the Sumerian scribal schools is generally analogous to that described for the Akkadian context, but no Sumerian evidence is given herein.

9.　W. von Soden, *Grundriss der Akkadischen Grammatik* (AnOr, 33; Rome: Pontifical Institute, 1952), § 81a, c.

Mesopotamian tradition were well acquainted with instructional uses of second-person indicative language and that such a mode of composition was widespread. These examples are sufficiently representative for the purposes of my argument, but no claim is made that the lists below are exhaustive.

As a positive command form, von Soden distinguishes three translation values for the Akkadian present tense: (a) *feststellendes Futur* ('you will do *x...*'); (b) *extratemporale Feststellung* ('you do *x...*'); (c) *heischendes Präsens* ('you shall do *x...*').[10] Nevertheless, as Richter points out, these uses are formally not distinguishable and, as instructional forms, they are related.[11] Consequently, the texts in which they are found will not be distinguished by the translation value assigned. It is important to recognize that the Akkadian present can express commands in either the third person or second person just as the biblical Hebrew imperfect. In the discussion that follows, the term 'prescription' normally indicates the incidence of the Akkadian second-person present. This use of the present tense is attested in various dialects of Akkadian.

The terms 'vetitive' and 'prohibitive' were coined by von Soden to identify two negative instructional paradigms which may be distinguished in the Akkadian dialect known as 'standard Babylonian'. Corresponding to the vetitive ('don't do *x...*') pattern is the pattern *ai* / *ē* negating the second-person preterite. This pattern is distinct from the Akkadian paradigm *lā* with the second-person present which von Soden calls the prohibitive ('you shall not do *x...*') and which he distinguishes from the incidence of the vetitive because of its stronger nature. Generally speaking, in standard Babylonian the negative particle *ul* negates the present when it is used indicatively, whereas the use of the particle *lā* indicates a volitive connotation.[12] In other dialects, the vetitive tends to disappear. In Assyrian, for example, the prohibitive form serves for both the normal negated present and negated imperative and a strong prohibition form is created by the particle combination *lū lā* negating the second-person

10. Von Soden, *Akkadischen Grammatik*, § 78dα-ε.

11. W. Richter, *Recht und Ethos* (München: Kösel, 1966), p. 77. See also W. Mayer, *Untersuchungen zur Grammatik des Mittelassyrischen* (Neukirchen–Vluyn: Neukirchener Verlag, 1971), § 63.1.

12. Von Soden, *Akkadischen Grammatik*, §§ 78d, f; 151c.

present.[13] In the material from Mari (a peripheral dialect of Akkadian) cited below, a prohibition is expressed by *ul* with the present.

To summarize: As in Hebrew, so in Akkadian one finds two command paradigms in the second person. Both can be negated. In the table below they are listed by terms used in this article and with a description of the conditions in which they may be encountered. Paradigm I is the 'imperative' paradigm; Paradigm II is the 'prescriptive' paradigm:

	Positive	Negative
I.	Imperative: Do *x*	Vetitive: Don't do *x*
	Hebrew: imperative	*'al* + (short) imperfect
	qᵉtol (kill)	*'al tiqtol* (don't kill)
	Akkadian: imperative	*ai / ē*+ preterite
	purus (decide)	*ai taprus* (don't decide)
		lā + present
		lā taparras (don't decide, e.g., Assyrian)
II.	Prescription: You shall do *x*	Prohibitive: You shall not do *x*
	Hebrew: imperfect	*lo'* + imperfect
	tiqtol (you shall kill)	*lo' tiqtol* (you shall not kill)
	Akkadian: present	*lā* + present
	taparras (you shall decide)	*lā taparras* (you shall not decide)
		lū lā + present
		lū lā taparras (you shall not decide, e.g., Assyrian)
		ul + present
		ul taparras (you shall not decide, e.g., Mari)

In the texts below, the prohibitive is normally used to negate both prescriptive and imperative contexts.

Treaties. The Vassal Treaty of Esarhaddon is an example of an extensive piece of conditionally introduced second-person address. As a rule, Akkadian treaties are not a typical locus for unconditionally introduced prescriptions; but a row of four prescriptions occurs in the Akkadian version of the Aziru treaty in KUB (*Keilschrifturkunden*

13. Von Soden, *Akkadischen Grammatik,* § 81h, i.

aus Boğazköi) III, 19:6ˋ-9ˋ.[14] There are also a number of unconditionally introduced prohibition forms in Esarhaddon's vassal treaty with the King of Tyre (verso col. 3:12-13).[15] Treaties may combine third-person and second-person references. See, for example, W1 and W2 from *Boğazköi*.[16] Treaties may also combine prescription and imperative forms. See, e.g., PRU IV § 17.338 where one finds the unconditional present form *tu-na-aṣ-ṣa-ar* ('you shall protect') in l. 5 but the imperative form *al-ka* ('go') in ll. 10-11.[17]

Prescriptive Ritual Texts. Prescriptive rituals are directions for cultic actions. Such texts are to be distinguished from other ritual texts described by Levine as 'descriptive ritual texts'. An example may be helpful. Exod. 25.10–27.19 is a prescriptive text which has to do with the construction of the tabernacle. It is framed as a series of commands in the second person. The parallel narrative in Exodus 35–39 is a descriptive document in the third-person dealing with many of the same details but belonging to a different genre.[18] This is not to say that all texts with third-person speech forms are necessarily descriptive. As opposed to prescriptive ritual texts, the descriptive form is written after the event and is not intended as a manual or code of ritual procedure but as a record of cultic expenditures and related procedures.[19] The examples listed below belong to the category of prescriptive ritual text because they are manuals for procedure which often use second-person address.

The second-person present is the major instructional verb form in the late Babylonian rituals published by Thureau-Dangin.[20] Most of

14. H. Klengel, 'Neue Fragmente zur akkadischen Fassung des Aziru-Vertrags', *OLZ* 59 (1964), p. 437.

15. See R. Borger, 'Die Inschriften Asarhaddons Königs von Assyrien', *AfO* 9 (1956), pp. 107-109 (§ 69).

16. See E.F. Weidner, 'Politische Dokumente aus Kleinasien', *Boghazköi-Studien* 8 (1923). The abbreviation W1 will signify the first treaty Weidner published; W2 the second, etc.

17. J. Nougayrol, *Le palais royal d'Ugarit*, IV (Paris: Klincksieck, 1956), pp. 84-85.

18. B.A. Levine, 'The Descriptive Tabernacle Texts of the Pentateuch', *JAOS* 85 (1965), pp. 307-309.

19. B.A. Levine and W.W. Hallo, 'Offerings to the Temple Gates at Ur', *HUCA* 38 (1967), pp. 17-18.

20. F. Thureau-Dangin, *Rituels accadiens* (Paris: Leroux, 1921). Levine

these ritual texts are translated in English in *ANET*.[21] There are also many examples in the rituals published by Zimmern.[22]

It might be objected that these examples have little comparative value for this paper because they are relatively rare and late in Mesopotamian literature.[23] The charge of lateness merits further consideration; the charge of rarity cannot be sustained. Although complex ritual instructions such as those published by Thureau-Dangin and Zimmern are uncommon, there are numerous other prescriptive ritual texts in Akkadian literature.

An important class of these is to be found in the Namburbi texts. These texts are written in the Standard Babylonian of the first millennium and can be dated between the late 8th–late 6th centuries BCE. It appears that the Namburbi rituals are essentially apotropaic rites meant to ward off or undo the threat of a bad omen. In fact, some Namburbis are found transmitted along with omen literature.[24] The Namburbi texts are important for comparison since their ritual prescriptions often contain directions both in the second person and in the third person. In most cases the liturgist is addressed in the second-person present with directions given for the suppliant in the third-person present. In a few cases, it appears that directions to the liturgist are given both in the second-person present and in the third-person present.[25]

Despite the fact that many examples of prescriptive ritual texts

('Descriptive Tabernacle Texts', p. 313) explicitly identifies the rituals published by Thureau-Dangin as examples of the prescriptive ritual genre.

21. Among major rituals published in *Rituels accadiens* where prescriptive present forms dominate see *Le rituel du Kalû* (= *ANET*, 3rd edn, pp. 334-38); *Le rituel du temple d'Anu à Uruk* (= *ANET*, 3rd edn, pp. 343-45); *Une cérémonie nocturne dans le temple d'Anu* (= *ANET*, 3rd edn, pp. 338-39).

22. H. Zimmern, *Beiträge zur Kenntnis der babylonischen Religion* (Leipzig: Hinrich, 1912). E.g., *Ritualtafeln für den Wahrsager* ## 1-20, 84-85; *Ritualtafeln für den Beschwörer* # 26; *Ritualtafeln für den Sänger* ## 60-61. Often these instructions consist of conditionally introduced prescriptions. In some cases, however, it is possible to discover rows of unconditionally formulated prescriptions. See, e.g., *Ritualtafeln für den Wahrsager*, pp. 100-101 (ll. 56-58); pp. 106-107 (ll. 157-163).

23. Levine and Hallo, 'Offerings to the Temple Gates', p. 17.

24. R. Caplice, *The Akkadian Namburbi Texts. An Introduction* (Los Angeles: Undena, 1974), pp. 7-8.

25. For discussion and references see R. Caplice, 'Namburbi Texts in the British Museum II', *Or* 36 (1967), p. 37.

come from fairly late cuneiform sources, this language use is an old one. For instance, the fact that the late (Seleucid) rituals published by Thureau-Dangin go back to earlier exemplars can be established from their colophons.[26] In the case of Assyrian rituals, their transmission can be traced back to the Middle Assyrian era. For example, prescriptive rituals from Boğazköi with second-person referents have been published by Meier.[27] Remnants of similar ritual instructions from the Old Babylonian period have also been published.[28]

Another important group of texts which contain prescriptive ritual texts are incantation texts. Prescriptive present verb forms often occur in instructions for cultic actions meant to be performed in conjunction with the incantations.[29]

Recipes and Training Texts. There are other kinds of prescriptions from the Middle Assyrian period which also confirm the antiquity and prevalence of the second-person prescriptive speech form in Akkadian literature.

Ebeling has published a group of perfume recipes belonging to the Aššur Temple which can be dated to the time of Tukulti–Ninurta I (13th cent. BCE).[30] These perfume recipes for the temple of Aššur contain lists of positive prescriptions and conditionally introduced prescriptions, and also have positive and negative commands occurring side by side in the course of the recipe.

A more common kind of recipe text is found in the Akkadian medical texts.[31] Mention can also be made of the Yale culinary tablets.

26. J. van Dijk, 'VAT 8382: Ein zweisprachiges Königsritual', in *Heidelberger Studien zum alten Orient* (Wiesbaden: Harrassowitz, 1976), p. 234.

27. G. Meier, 'Ein akkadisches Heilungsritual aus Bogazköy', ZA 45 (1939), pp. 195-215 (e.g., I:2-30).

28. J. van Dijk, A. Goetze and M.I. Hussey, *Early Mesopotamian Incantations and Rituals* (New Haven: Yale University Press, 1985), §§ 4, 12.

29. See, e.g., *Lamaštu* 1.I,10; 1.II,23-37; and III verso published in D.W. Myhrman, 'Die Labartu–Texte: Babylonische Beschwörungsformeln nebst Zauberverfahren gegen die Dämonin Labartu', ZA 16 (1902), pp. 141-95. Subsequent to Myhrman's publication, the reading *Lamaštu* has been established instead of *Labartu*.

30. E.R.F. Ebeling, *Parfümrezepte und kultische Texte aus Assur* (Rome: Pontifical Biblical Institute, 1950), p. 15.

31. See, e.g., R. Labat, 'Le premier chapitre d'un précis médical assyrien', RA 53 (1959), pp. 4-7; R. Labat and J. Tournay, 'Un texte médical inédit', RA 40 (1945–1946), pp. 114-15.

According to their editor, the orthography and style of these tablets points to the Old Babylonian period (c. 1700 BCE) as the time of their composition. The recipes in Tablet A typically begin in an unconditional fashion with the instructions, 'There is (i.e., one needs) meat. You set water. You throw (in it) fat'.[32] Related instructions in the third person also appear. Similar recipes in the second person are conditionally introduced in Tablet B.

The horse training texts are documents which have no overt cultic interests. They can be dated to the 13th century BCE.[33] As Ebeling notes, in the Akkadian text the instructions to the trainers and helpers are uniformly in the second person.[34]

Royal Decree. Marzal has studied a class of decrees found in the cuneiform archives of the kingdom of Mari known as the *šiptum* ('decree') for analogues to biblical 'apodictic' (unconditional prescriptive) formulations. The *šiptum* is a strong command found typically in an authoritative decree or edict given by the king or his representative. They affect the army (the army officers directly), have religious connotations, and imply a threat of punishment.[35] Normally the *šiptum* is cast in the third person and uses *liprus* forms.

There is, however, one example in the second person using what appears to be a prescription form followed by a prohibitive. The prohibitive expression uses the particle *ul* with the present.[36] This *šiptum* was issued by Kibri-Dagan, the governor of Terqa, to tribal leaders and was aimed at preventing the soldiers of tribal contingents from escaping. Evidently, it was issued with the express knowledge and permission of the king. The text is *ARM* II 92.14-19:[37]

32. J. Bottéro, 'The Culinary Tablets at Yale', *JAOS* 107 (1987), pp. 11-12.

33. E.R.F. Ebeling, *Bruchstücke einer mittelassyrischen Vorschriftensammlung für die Akklimatisierung und Trainierung von Wagenpferden* (Berlin: Akademie, 1951), p. 6.

34. Ebeling, *Vorschriftensammlung*, p. 47. These texts often contain rows of similarly formulated instructions, both conditionally (e.g., B) and unconditionally introduced (e.g., G).

35. A. Marzal, 'Mari Clauses in "Casuistic" and "Apodictic" Styles (Part I)', *CBQ* 33 (1971), p. 335.

36. A. Marzal, 'Mari Clauses in "Casuistic" and "Apodictic" Styles (Part II)', *CBQ* 33 (1971), pp. 498-99.

37. Marzal, 'Mari Clauses (Part I)', pp. 338-39.

14   ma-an-nu-um at-ta
15   ša 1 LÚ i-na a-li-ka e-li-iš
16   it-ta-al-la-ku-ma
17   ù la ta-ṣa-ab-ba-ta-šu-m[a]
18   a-na ṣe-ri-ia la te-re-de-[e]-šu
19   [ta-m]a-at ú-ul ta-ba-lu-u[ṭ]

(14) Whoever you are, (15-16) (you) from whose settlement a single man shall depart to the Upper Country (17) and you shall not apprehend him (18) and bring him to me (19) [you shall d]ie, you shall not live.

The text reflects the third-person *šipṭum* form beginning with a relative clause which appears in Mari.[38] Moreover the categorical death sentence in *ARM* II 92:19 is elsewhere found in the third person in Akkadian law codes.[39] It appears, therefore, that the forms *tamât* ('you shall die') and *ul taballuṭ* ('you shall not live') cannot be considered as commands to a specific addressee. The evidence suggests that the decree of *ARM* II 92:14-19 is derived from third-person legal language. It probably owes its second-person address to the fact that imperative decrees on an *ad hoc* basis were also used in issuing military instructions at Mari.[40]

The vast amount of Hittite material available makes any generalizations about usage always open to further investigation. Nevertheless, the examples below combined with the accounts available from Hittite grammars seem fairly normative. Hittite is capable of issuing positive instructions in both the present indicative and the imperative. Unlike Akkadian or Hebrew, Hittite does not appear to have two negative command forms. The ordinary form of a negated command is *lē* with the present indicative.[41]

---

38. Marzal, 'Mari Clauses (Part I)', pp. 349-50. Third-person laws of the form *awīlum ša* are well attested in Akkadian: see, e.g., Laws of Eshnunna §§ 12, 13, 19, 51, 52; Middle Assyrian Laws §§ 3, 40, 41, 47; and the Edict of Ammi-ṣaduqa §§ 12-20. See G. Liedke, *Gestalt und Bezeichnung alttestamentlicher Rechtssätze* (Neukirchen-Vluyn: Neukirchener Verlag, 1971), p. 115.

39. According to Marzal ('Mari Clauses [Part I]', p. 338) the virtually identical expression *i-ma-(a)-at ú-ul i-ba-(al)-lu-uṭ* ('he shall die, he shall not live') is found in the Laws of Eshnunna § 12:40 (of a thief) and § 13:7 (of a thief). Cf. Laws of Eshnunna § 28:36-37 (of an adulteress).

40. Marzal, 'Mari Clauses (Part I)', p. 349.

41. J. Friedrich, *Hethitisches Elementarbuch 1. Kurzgefasste Grammatik* (Heidelberg: Winter, 2nd edn, 1960), § 280b. In a few cases one finds the form *lē*

The Hittite Laws are formulated throughout in the third person. But the royal scribes obviously were familiar with second-person formulations. Many examples can be found in treaties and loyalty oaths. As McCarthy notes, Hittite treaties overwhelmingly favour the imperative for positive command forms.[42] In fact, the Hittite preference for the imperative and not the indicative in positive treaty stipulations is a linguistic feature which even McCarthy's discussions do not always make as clear as the situation deserves.[43]

Weinfeld argues that laws such as those in the social (Exod. 22.17–23.9) and cultic sections (Exod. 23.10-19) of the Covenant Code overlap formally with a genre found in Hittite literature known as 'instructions'. These instructions were addressed to military personnel, court officials, border commanders, temple officials, and even to the whole people. There are striking analogues to biblical presentations of 'apodictic law'. Like the Hittite instructions, biblical law contains commandments formulated in the second person, imposed by covenant and oath, and accepted by a pledge of the people addressed. Likewise, individual Hittite instruction documents will contain ordinances affecting different spheres of life including cultic, social, and military.[44] Where positive second-person address occurs in the Hittite instructions, the paradigm is that of the imperative as it is in the Treaties. See, for example, *Bēl Madgalti* 3A: 21-37,[45] and

with the imperative but this usage seems to be simply an archaic variant of the common negated command.

42. D.J. McCarthy, *Treaty and Covenant* (AnBib, 21A; Rome: Pontifical Institute, 2nd edn, 1978), pp. 82-83. There is a typographical error in McCarthy's citation of F3 § 22, F 25-27. The correct reference is F3 § 22, E 25-27

43. Cf. McCarthy, *Treaty and Covenant*, p. 63 where it is implied that it is acceptable to translate the Hittite imperative as a prescription. In this regard one might compare the Aziru treaty in its Hittite and Akkadian versions. In the Hittite version col. 1:9' attests the imperative form *pa-ah-ši* ('protect') where KUB III, 19:6f. has the Akkadian prescription form *tu-na-aṣ-ṣa-ar* ('you shall protect'). See H. Freydank, 'Eine hethitische Fassung des Vertrags zwischen dem Hethiterkönig Suppiluliuma und Aziru von Amurru', *Mitteilungen des Instituts für Orientforschung* (1959/60), p. 359.

44. M. Weinfeld, 'The Origin of the Apodictic Law. An Overlooked Source', *VT* 23 (1973), pp. 64-66.

45. E. von Schuler, *Hethitische Dienstanweisungen für höhere Hof- und Staatsbeamte* (Osnabrück: Biblio-Verlag, 1957), pp. 41-52. The same phenomenon can also be seen in the military instructions published by S. Alp in 'Military Instructions of the Hittite King Tuthaliya IV (?)', *Belleten* 11 (1947), pp. 388-97. In

'Instructions for Temple Officials' § 18 (col. 4:34-53).[46]

Hittite can express a positive command using the present. In the Hittite Laws, the third-person present functions in a prescriptive fashion.[47] Nevertheless, prescriptive uses of the second-person present are not unknown. For example, the use of the second-person prescriptive present occurs in the Soldiers' Oath verso III:36, 38, 46. The majority of the ritual instructions in this text, however, are expressed in the third-person.[48]

It ought to be evident from the examples given above that the absence of second-person language from the law codes has important formal significance. Scribes schooled in the Mesopotamian tradition were obviously well acquainted with the use of various second-person prescriptive genres. They were at home in using such language in both conditional and unconditional forms. They also do not appear to have minded mixing third- and second-person references in instructional contexts. Yet, for all this, they did not employ second-person prescriptive language in the composition of the protases or apodoses of the law codes. The appearance of second person instructions as part of the legal formulation of materials in the Covenant Code, therefore, is an unexpected and significant generic discrepancy given Westbrook's thesis. How is it to be explained?

A likely model of explanation is indicated on the basis of the *šiptum* decree discussed above. The *šiptum* is usually predicated in the third person. The unusual second-person example which has been cited seems to have been influenced by the fact that *ad hoc* military orders are often given in the imperative. So, the form of *ARM* II 92:14-19 can be explained as a generic hybrid in which the cultural functions of royal decree and military order have merged. The text, however, remains a product of the scribal tradition in the service of the royal court.

---

this text, third-person instructions are found in A:1-25; second-person instructions in A:28-37; and more third-person instructions in E:2-15 and the final fragments. All the second-person instructions are in the imperative mood.

46. See E.H. Sturtevant and G. Bechtel, *A Hittite Chrestomathy* (Philadelphia: Linguistic Society of America, 1935), pp. 164-65 (translated in *ANET*, 3rd edn, p. 210).

47. E.H. Sturtevant, *A Comparative Grammar of the Hittite Language* (Philadelphia: Linguistic Society of America, 2nd edn, 1951), p. 251.

48. See N. Oettinger, *Die militärischen Eide der Hethither* (Wiesbaden: Harrassowitz, 1976), pp. 12-13; it is translated in *ANET*, 3rd edn, pp. 353-54.

The second-person references in the Covenant Code, a text which has many affinities to the genre of judicial references identified by Westbrook, also suggest some sort of generic hybrid. What other genre has influenced the composition of the Covenant Code? As stated above, I accept Westbrook's thesis that the second-person references in the Covenant Code are references to the community as a legally bound body. But where references to the community are present in the Mesopotamian law codes, they appear in the third person as Westbrook's own examples (Codex Hammurapi §§ 22-24, RS 17.230) show.[49] Moreover, the scribal schools do not generally seem to have had in mind a community when they employed second-person references. Recipe, training and prescriptive ritual texts functioned as manuals of procedure for specialists. The exception to this rule appears to be treaty and loyalty oath texts.

It might be surmised, therefore, that it is the treaty (covenantal) paradigm which has influenced the sporadic appearance of second-person references in the Covenant Code. In fact, this text now appears in a context in which its stipulations are regarded as the objects of a loyalty oath ceremony described in Exod. 24.1-8.[50] Such a model could have existed under royal patronage, since the treaty/loyalty oath is a typical form of speech for Mesopotamian kingship. But if so, why was it only in Israel that this tradition interfered with the genre of judicial references?

A difficulty with an appeal to the treaty/loyalty oath tradition is that the contents of the second-person references in the Covenant Code are common concerns of the same kind of law which is described by the Mesopotamian law codes.[51] They do not touch on the usual themes of loyalty oath stipulations.[52] In other words, while one may be able to make some kind of formal correlation between the use of occasional second-person references in a third-person context and treaty language, there is little correlation on the level of topic.

This argument leads to the supposition that there existed in Israel legal traditions which were not composed under royal patronage. Scholars of biblical law often posit a stratum of customary law which

49. Westbrook, 'Lex Talionis', pp. 62-65.

50. M. Weinfeld, 'The Loyalty Oath in the Ancient Near East', *UF* 8 (1976), p. 392.

51. Westbrook, 'Nature and Origin of the Twelve Tables', pp. 85-86.

52. These are listed in Weinfeld, 'Loyalty Oath', pp. 383-92.

was only later codified by scribal circles.[53] The fact that the scribes who composed the Covenant Code were obliged to break the genre boundaries of the law code form suggests the powerful influence of a source of law other than the judicial reference model.

Besides the fact of generic inconsistency, what gives force to the supposition of a non-royal stratum of second-person law or ethics in the Covenant Code is the history of the monarchy in Israel. It is well known that the Israelite monarchy as an institution had to overcome prior divisions in Israel of various kinds of ethnic affiliations. It was resisted at times by these groups for both political and religious reasons. Moreover, the accoutrements of royal power had to be largely imported from outside Israel itself (e.g., Phoenicia). Consequently, one might expect that legal traditions reflecting a different mode of organization could influence a tradition reflecting direct royal patronage on the judicial reference model.

Where should the composition and transmission of such prescriptive traditions be located? The parallels listed in this article implicate two institutions in Mesopotamia which made significant use of the prescriptive paradigm: the palace and the cult. Both are connected through the scribal schools. By the same token, the search for early (or 'original') settings for the formulation of Israelite apodictic law ought to take into consideration the scribal context of the prescriptive paradigm. In the absence of a centralized monarchy, composition by scribes attached to some kind of cultic institution is probably indicated.[54]

But a statement about the possible identity of those who actually composed apodictic formulations leaves open the question of the number of social groups in ancient Israel for whom they were composed. Past researches, for example, have emphasized

53. See, e.g., B.S. Jackson, 'Ideas of Law and Legal Administration. A Semiotic Approach', in R.E. Clements (ed.), *The World of Ancient Israel* (Cambridge: Cambridge University Press, 1989), p. 199.

54. S. Greengus ('Law', *Anchor Bible Dictionary* 4 [1992], p. 425) has also noted analogues between second-person instruction in biblical Hebrew and Akkadian cultic formulations. Even Gerstenberger, who favoured the proclamation of obligations in the clan as the original cultural function of the second-person prescriptive genre (the so-called 'apodictic' speech form), observed that a surprising number of the prohibitions he identified in biblical Hebrew impinge on cultic responsibilities; see E. Gerstenberger, *Wesen und Herkunft des 'Apodiktischen Rechts'* (Neukirchen–Vluyn: Neukirchener Verlag, 1965), p. 62.

correspondences between second-person addressed commands and treaty language (e.g., Mendenhall), loyalty oaths on the model of the Hittite instructions (Weinfeld) or wisdom, whether originally located in patriarchal instruction of the clan (e.g., Gerstenberger, Fohrer) or in the educated circles of the royal court and temple (Richter).[55]

In fact, the assumption that there is a one-to-one equation between generic formulae and their *Sitze im Leben* is to be resisted. It is now generally admitted that such a position contains a methodological error. Many genres of ancient speech cannot be assigned to only one cultural setting. Also, the number of cultural settings appropriate for a specific genre may have varied through the course of history. Consequently, it is often difficult to establish clear connexions between a stereotypical pattern of speech and one particular situation.[56]

There is reason to believe, therefore, that at the inception of the Israelite monarchy prescriptive language could have had a number of different cultural functions in the biblical Hebrew *Sprachraum*. Judging from the comparative evidence, the use of prescriptions and prohibitions to give directions to cultic and military functionaries was well established by the Late Bronze Age. How much older this form of instruction is, one cannot know. Many of the Late Bronze Age functions are connected with highly organized (i.e., royal) bureaucratic institutions. But it is probable that communities more loosely organized could also have used the same forms to hand on recipes, issue binding instructions, and give instruction for cultic rites.[57]

The hypothesis of a tradition of proclamation of law and/or ethics in prescriptive genres combined with material belonging to the

55. See G. Mendenhall, 'Covenant Forms in Israelite Tradition', *BA* 17 (1954), pp. 50-76; Weinfeld, 'The Origin of the Apodictic Law'; Gerstenberger, *Wesen und Herkunft des 'Apodiktischen Rechts'*; G. Fohrer, 'Das sogennante apodiktisch formulierte Recht und der Dekalog', *KD* 11 (1965), pp. 49-74; Richter, *Recht und Ethos*, p. 190. For a general survey of past scholarship on this question see W.M. Clark, *'Law'*, in *Old Testament Form Criticism* (San Antonio: Trinity, 1974), pp. 107-13.

56. V. Wagner, 'Rechtssätze in gebundener Sprache und Rechtssatzreihen im israelitischen Recht', *BZAW* 127 (1972), p. 56; Clark, 'Law', p. 110; W. Richter, *Exegese als Literaturwissenschaft* (Göttingen: Vandenhoeck & Ruprecht, 1971), pp. 145-48.

57. The position I take here was earlier articulated for conditionally introduced prescriptive speech in H. W. Gilmer, *The If-You Form in Israelite Law* (SBLDS, 15; Missoula, MT: Scholars Press, 1975).

judicial reference genre would satisfy the conditions of composition the text of the Covenant Code requires. A likely source for the composition of the Covenant Code's prescriptive materials would be scribally trained functionaries situated in the Israelite cult. The language of their prescriptive genres was probably adapted to various purposes including the transmission of juridical lore belonging to Israel's traditional ethnic (i.e., premonarchic) and religious affiliations. If this hypothesis is feasible, then it should also be borne in mind that third-person and second-person prescriptive language can be observed combined in a number of genres in Mesopotamia. Therefore, it is possible that some of the third-person formulations now found in the Covenant Code also appear there under the influence of Israelite legal traditions which are not connected to the judicial reference model.

Dale Patrick

When one confronts such a comprehensive interpretive scheme as the one offered by Raymond Westbrook, its sheer magnitude is intimidating. If one is uneasy or dissatisfied with this or that detail, the whole weight of the system threatens to squash the demur. To raise a question, it seems that the scholar must be competent in all ancient Near Eastern law and jurisprudence and be willing to contest readings of a broad array of documents. I am not prepared to contest Westbrook's specific arguments, but I am willing to raise objections against an interpretive scheme requiring that sort of argumentation, and to defend a scholarly method that he dismisses.

I

Westbrook's interpretive scheme appears to be constructed on a developmental model of ancient law and jurisprudence. It is his contention that there is negligible conceptual development of law in the Near East between c. 2200 and 700 BCE. The reason is a combination of intellectual and sociopolitical factors:

> Intellectual expression was dominated by Mesopotamian 'science', a form of logic severely handicapped by the inability to define terms, create general categories or reason vertically from general to particular. A legal system cannot be more advanced than its social and intellectual environment, and the social environment was hostile to change, while the intellectual environment lacked the tools to give legal expression to anything more than superficial reforms (p. 28).

It was the 'intellectual revolution' evidenced in Greek literature which introduced 'change' into ancient law and jurisprudence (p. 28).

In effect, Westbrook is replacing one type of evolutionary model with another. He is convinced that it is mistaken to characterize

biblical or ancient Near Eastern law as 'primitive' or to reconstruct
layers within legal texts according to an evolutionary scheme (pp. 19-
24). All the ancient Near Eastern legal documents at the scholar's
disposal represent the same relatively advanced stage of development.
To account for this uniformity, Westbrook offers the evolutionary
concept of arrested development; in other words, the culture experi-
enced sociopolitical and intellectual stagnation. Further advances took
place on the periphery of the ancient Near East, in Greece and Israel
(pp. 24-28). Thus, despite Westbrook's rejection of evolution within
codes and between them, he in fact is working with an evolutionary
scheme.[1]

For Westbrook's interpretation of the Book of the Covenant,
however, it is the stagnation that counts. If he can maintain that the
entire Fertile Crescent was politically and culturally homogeneous and
static, he can interpret legal texts from various times and places as
representative of the same way of thinking with much the same legal
doctrine. Moreover, he can discount all attempts to reconstruct stages
in the growth of Exod. 21.1–22.16.[2]

Such comprehensive schemes of cultural evolution have been out of
fashion in this century, and for good reason. They curtail the freedom
of the interpreter to discover the truth the text has to divulge; the text
is reduced to grist for the conceptual mill. When a theory dictates
what a particular culture is capable of thinking, every expression of
that culture is allowed to yield only a variation on the culture's
intellectual horizon. In the case of ancient Near Eastern law,
Westbrook denies a cultural capacity of legal texts (a) to embody a
general conceptual scheme, that is, a system of concepts and
principles, or (b) to evidence any significant conceptual change.

I propose to dispute his position on these two subjects. First,
whether or not ancient Near Eastern codes embody a comprehensive
scheme of concepts and principles is as much a decision of the

---

1. His scheme resembles, at least superficially, Hegel's dialectical movement of
history. Each era works out its idea or principle, then stagnates, leaving it to another
culture to introduce a new idea into the progress of history. See G.W.F. Hegel,
Reason in History: A General Introduction to the Philosophy of History (trans. R.S.
Hartman; The Library of Liberal Arts, 35; New York: The Liberal Arts Press, 1953),
particularly pp. 68-95.

2. Although Westbrook speaks of the Book of the Covenant, he in fact restricts
the term to this portion of Exod. 20.22–23.19 (p. 15).

interpreter as it is a matter of evidence. If the interpreter is convinced that ancient Near Eastern jurists could not 'define terms, create general categories or reason from general to particular', each ruling will be construed as a discrete tradition. If, on the other hand, one is convinced that the legal mind seeks consistency and comprehensiveness, interpretation will work out the principles and concepts which would fit a set of specific rulings. J.J. Finkelstein's *The Ox that Gored* is an exemplary study of the latter sort.[3]

The choice of interpretive standpoint cannot be argued in the same way as a disagreement over how to construe an Akkadian sentence. Rather, it is a decision regarding what kind of explanation is appropriate to human creations[4] and what kind of relationship the interpreter desires to establish with a text. If scientific explanation is appropriate, then Westbrook is asking the right questions; if a humanistic explanation—an explanation in terms of intention and design—is appropriate, then the interpreter should seek to understand the conceptual scheme that is being applied to specific cases. According to the latter model, the interpreter seeks instruction and enlightenment from the text being interpreted rather than evidence for the stage of cultural development it represents.

Secondly, as for the possibility of conceptual change in ancient Near Eastern law and jurisprudence, it seems to me that Samuel Greengus makes a strong case for it in his response (pp. 63-66). The Hittite evidence he cites seems to be best interpreted as a legal reform dictated by a changing sense of what is a just proportionality between a class of acts and their punishment. Rather than force this evidence to conform to the mental horizon of 'Mesopotamian science', we should look for evidence of social or political upheavals behind the Hittite reforms.

Perhaps Mesopotamian political society and legal culture were less amenable to conceptual change, but one should not rule it out in principle. A regime based upon a religious world-view in which power is justified by its defeat of chaos would be reticent to undercut its own legitimacy by exhibiting 'human invention' behind the law, so

---

3.   Transactions of the American Philosophical Society, 71, Pt. 2 (Philadelphia: American Philosophical Society, 1981).

4.   See R.J. Bernstein, *Praxis and Action: Contemporary Philosophies of Human Activity* (Philadelphia: University of Pennsylvania, 1971).

most changes will be subtle and virtually invisible to the members of the community. Such changes would be virtually invisible to modern scholarship as well.

Certainly Westbrook's characterization of the Book of the Covenant is open to dispute. He believes that the numerous parallels between it and the ancient Near Eastern codes demonstrate that it belongs to the common ancient Near Eastern legal culture (p. 21). This means, evidently, that its provisions should be interpreted as representative of the same legal doctrine, hampered by the same limits on vertical reasoning, and equally impervious to change. He does not mention the comparative studies of J.J. Finkelstein and Shalom Paul,[5] but one must assume that he rejects their argument that biblical law, beginning with the Book of the Covenant, embodies a different scheme of values and legal principles than the ancient Near Eastern codes.[6]

If one is convinced by their argument, as I am,[7] one will be inclined to look for a political, economic, and religious upheaval behind its conceptual departures. While Norman Gottwald's theory of the Israelite 'conquest'[8] may not survive the severe criticism it has been subject to, he nevertheless is on the right track: Yahwism came into being as a 'revolutionary' religious and political movement which changed not only Canaanite theology but also its concepts of person and society. This revolution, however, is not a part of some grand cultural and intellectual evolution, but the emergence of a integral conception of reality which makes its own claims to truth.

II

In the course of our discussion of Westbrook's paper, the question arose as to why the ancient Near Eastern and biblical 'codes' were

5. *Studies in the Book of the Covenant in the Light of Cuneiform and Biblical Law* (VTSup, 18; Leiden: Brill, 1970).

6. He does dispute their position in *Studies in Biblical and Cuneiform Law* (CahRB, 26; Paris: Gabalda, 1988), pp. 41-7.

7. Of course, a person of religious conviction is attracted to arguments for the uniqueness of biblical religion, and that may impair our judgment. The issue, however, is only partly religious, for Finkelstein approaches it in the spirit of Feuerbach.

8. *The Tribes of Yahweh: A Sociology of the Religion of Liberated Israel, 1250-1050 BCE* (Maryknoll, NY: Orbis, 1979).

drawn up. This has been a conundrum which Assyriologists have puzzled over for decades. It is not surprising that it came up for discussion, but I was discouraged by the absence of any coherent strategy for addressing it. All the discussants seem to have dismissed the methodological tool best designed to answer that question, *viz.,* form criticism. Westbrook contested the use of form criticism to provide any insight into the genesis of the Book of the Covenant, the respondents concurred, and no one else raised an objection. There seems to be a consensus that the way a law is formulated is irrelevant to its use in a document.

There is an irony in this, for the Biblical Law Group of the Society of Biblical Literature originated in the 1970s as a subunit of the Form Critical project. Since that time, form criticism has been eclipsed in the scholarly discussion of biblical and ancient Near Eastern literature. I am convinced, however, that it was on to something and can be revived in conjunction with rhetoric. That is to say, form criticism is concerned with the social exchange involved in communication and how a speaker or author seeks to manage that exchange to achieve a particular end.[9]

A misunderstanding has arisen among biblical law scholars about form critical method and its potential. Frequently it is reduced to a kind of style criticism. That is, form criticism is considered to be a study of the style of linguistic formulations, in this case, legal statements. The best form critics, however, simply used style as an indication of the 'logic' of the speech-act and the sort of institutional setting in which this speech-act would carry its fullest force.

With respect to legal formulations, Alt attempted to discern the logic of several distinct types of statements found in series and collections of law, and from the logic or rhetoric postulated the kind of institutional setting in which such language would be used.[10] He was able to subsume most of the styles of law under two categories. Style was a criterion, but it is noteworthy that he included at least three different styles of formulation under 'apodictic' law. Despite their stylistic differences, Alt observed that all three were categorical and

9. See D. Patrick and A. Scult, *Rhetoric and Biblical Interpretation* (Sheffield: Almond Press, 1990), pp. 12-27.

10. 'The Origins of Israelite Law', in *Essays on Old Testament History and Religion* (trans. R.A. Wilson; Oxford: Basil Blackwell, 1967), pp. 79-132.

unconditional. To put this rhetorically, they would engender a different sort of transaction with an audience than would those carefully calibrated conditional statements Alt termed 'casuistic', and therefore must belong to a different oral setting.[11]

Alt belonged to an era of form criticism which was fixed on uncovering the original, 'pure' form. He even expected original series of apodictic laws that were stylistically uniform and of relative brevity. His student, K. Rabast, wrote a dissertation identifying short and long series of commandments and other types of apodictic law.[12] This line of scholarship simply dismissed the extant biblical codes as haphazard collections because they were a mixture of forms and styles.

In retrospect, these assumptions about the original form, homogeneous series, and the secondary nature of corpora of mixed forms are by no means self-evident. There is no intrinsic reason to surmise that a document like the Book of the Covenant is a mere collection of older documents. It can just as well be regarded as the product of intentional design. That would certainly be the postulate of an exegete seeking to interpret the text as the best text it can be.

Why was the Book of the Covenant composed? That question can be answered by a scholar who takes the code to be a speech form in its own right.[13] This would mean a careful consideration of the way the

11. Alt's synthesis was soon disputed by form critics who tended to fuse style and genre, e.g., E. Gerstenberger, *Wesen und Herkunft des 'Apodiktischen Rechts'* (WMANT, 20; Neukirchen–Vluyn: Neukirchener Verlag, 1965); G. Liedke, *Gestalt und Bezeichnung alttestamentlicher Rechtssätze* (WMANT, 39; Neukirchen–Vluyn: Neukirchener Verlag, 1971).

12. *Das apodiktische Recht im Deuteronomium und im Heiligkeitsgesetz* (Berlin: Heimatdienstverlag, 1948).

13. There is at least one noteworthy recent effort to understand the literary shaping of the Book of the Covenant: Eckart Otto's *Wendel der Rechtsbegründungen in der Gesellschaftsgeschichte des antiken Israel: Eine Rechtsgeschichte des "Bundesbuches" Ex XX 22-XXIII 13* (StudBib, 3; Leiden: Brill, 1988). Otto combines redaction history with form and stylistic criticism, correlated with a developmental history of judicial institutions to arrive at a theory of layers of chiastic structures. It is hard to imagine the rhetorical function of a chiastic arrangement of laws, for chiasmus does not correspond to legal thinking at all. Perhaps Otto is thinking of some hortatory presentation of law, but even in that case the chiastic pairs that he proposes are too far removed from each other to be recognized by an audience. In his analysis, developmental questions seem to override his interest in the

text as a whole is designed to engage its audience. Since ancient
writing was not meant as a substitute for oral language, but to be read
aloud to the intended audience,[14] the question is what audience is
intended and what this language is shaped to do to this audience.

Near the beginning of the Book of the Covenant, in Exod. 21.1,
Moses is commissioned to proclaim the 'judgments' (*mišpāṭîm*) to an
assembly ('them'). One would expect such a public address to be
couched in first person YHWH, second person audience. Practically all
of the material in Exod. 22.20–23.19 does address the audience.
However, the section that immediately follows the commission is
impersonally formulated. One might postulate this impersonal section
as an intrusion, a block of material inserted between the commission
and the personally addressed parts of the document. However, the
term *mišpāṭîm* would appear to be a category term here for the
impersonal laws in Exod. 21.2–22.19. Thus, these too are meant to be
read out before the audience. This is confirmed by the sporadic
appearance of second-person address in the impersonal section (21.2a,
13-14, 23-25, 22.17); these are not mistakes, but reminders of the oral
transaction taking place between the speaker and the audience.

An adequate answer to the question of why the Book of the
Covenant was composed would have to examine each section of the
document to determine its contribution to the rhetorical transaction.
However, simply identifying the document as designed for public
reading is a good start. The audience is not always specified, but when
it is, it is Israel, the people of YHWH (21.13-14; 22.19, 20, 24, 30;
23.9, 13, 14-17, 18, 19). In what setting were they addressed? Nothing
in the document yields that.

The narrative of Exodus 19–24, of course, does give it a precise
setting. One cannot assume, however, that this narrative setting really
is its original historical setting; indeed, it is highly improbable. The
narrative is best regarded as rhetorical history, an account designed to

document as a communication to an audience. I am proposing that we begin with the
rhetorical question and insist that it guide our hypotheses about earlier stages in the
formation of the textual unit.

14. So P. Achtemeier, '*Omne verbum sonat:* The New Testament and the Oral
Environment of Late Western Antiquity', *JBL* 109 (1990), pp. 3-27. I think it safe to
assume that writing in the ancient Near East was also an aid to oral delivery, unless
the writing was not intended for a human audience—either it was for the gods, or
perhaps simply to decorate a monument.

persuade the audience of their obligation to the law enunciated by YHWH. It throws up before the audience an image of their ancestors freely accepting the authority of YHWH to impose laws upon them (e.g., Exod. 19.8, 24.3-8). The drama of that event is so vividly presented that the audience can imagine itself making the same decision.[15]

Was the Book of the Covenant composed to be ensconced in this narrative, or was it once actually proclaimed to the people of Israel in a public ceremony? The latter would be a very lively exchange, for it would involve the people in an actual act of adopting it. Moreover, those texts that portray an actual act of adoption (Exod. 19.3b-8; 24.3-8) have a formal quality about them that suggests they were first performed and then 'historicized'.[16] On the other hand, the historical setting has its own rhetorical power, persuading the people that they owe an obligation to this law by a decision of their ancestors. There is no need to come down on one side or the other of this question. In either case, the setting was an oral exchange in which the people were instructed and motivated in their duty to YHWH.

The ancient Near Eastern codes should be amenable to a similar analysis. The scholar would need to imagine the type of setting for which they were composed to be read aloud from the rhetorical transaction that they are designed to accomplish. They are sufficiently different from the Book of the Covenant in their rhetoric to suggest a different kind of public setting. I will leave it to Assyriologists to pursue the question.

15. Assuming that the event at Sinai-Horeb was already remembered as a momentous one in the history of the people, simply tracing this lawbook to it would increase its authority immeasurably.

16. I set out my case for this some time ago in 'The Covenant Code Source', *VT* 27 (1977), pp. 145-57.

ASPECTS OF LEGAL REFORMS AND REFORMULATIONS IN ANCIENT CUNEIFORM AND ISRAELITE LAW

Eckart Otto

1. Introduction

Ancient oriental law codes, including the law collections in the Israelite predeuteronomistic Book of the Covenant in Exod. 20.24-26; 21.2–23.12* and the predeuteronomistic Deuteronomy in Deuteronomy 12–26, originated from scholarly-judicial traditions of scribal education. In contrast to scholars who even today adhere to the thesis of practical functions of these law codes on court proceedings,[1] B. Landsberger[2] demonstrated that Codex Hammurapi was never quoted as a legal authority in court protocols.[3] F.R. Kraus[4] used this

---

1. See E. Szlechter, 'La "lois" dans la Mésopotamie ancienne', *Revue internationale des droits de l'antiquité*, 3/12 (1965), pp. 55-77; *idem, Codex Hammurapi* (Rome: Pontificio Istituto Biblico, 1977), pp. 7ff.; J. Klíma, 'Zu einigen Problemen der altmesopotamischen Gesetzgebung', in *Festschrift für W. Eilers* (Wiesbaden: Harrassowitz, 1967), pp. 107-21; *idem*, 'La perspective historique des lois hammurabiennes', *CRAI 1972* (Paris, 1977), pp. 297-317; W. Preiser, 'Zur rechtlichen Natur der altorientalischen "Gesetze"', in P. Bockelmann *et al.* (eds.), *Festschrift für K. Engisch* (Frankfurt, 1969), pp. 17-36; G. Cardascia, *Les lois assyriennes. Introduction, traduction, commentaire* (Paris: Cerf, 1969), pp. 28-52; *idem*, 'La formazione del diritto in Assiria', in A. Theodorides *et al.* (eds.), *La formazione del diritto nel Vicino Oriente Antico* (Università di Roma. Publicazioni dell' Istituto di diritto Romano e dei diritti dell' Oriente Mediterraneo, 65; Naples and Rome: Edizioni Scientifiche Italiane, 1988), pp. 52-58; H. Petschow, 'Die §§ 45 und 46 des Codex Hammurapi. Ein Beitrag zum altbabylonischen Bodenpachtretcht und zum Problem: Was ist der Codex Hammurapi?', *ZA* 74 (1984), pp. 181-212; *idem*, 'Beiträge zum Codex Hammurapi', *ZA* 76 (1986), pp. 17-75.

2. See 'Die babylonischen Termini für Gesetz und Recht', in *Festschrift für P. Koschaker*, II (Leiden: Brill, 1939), pp. 219-34.

3. In a paper presented to the 'Internationale Fachgruppe Altorientalische und Biblische Rechtsgeschichte' in Frankfurt on 18 May, 1990, G. Ries (Munich)

fact, together with his observation of formal resemblances between the law codes and the omen-literature, to interpret Codex Hammurapi as school literature without any practical concern. The different approach of J.J. Finkelstein[5] understood the law codes as royal ideology of the king who praised himself as *šar mīšarim* 'the king of justice' before gods and people.[6] But this interpretation accounts only for the framing parts of prologues and epilogues,[7] which were form-critically and traditio-historically independent from the legal corpus proper.[8] Prologues and epilogues used the framed legal collections as royal propaganda so that we are again directed to the scribal school of the E.DUBB.A as the original *Sitz im Leben* of the legal collections. This fact is proved by other judicial texts that were also part of the school curriculum of the E.DUBB.A, such as *ana ittišu*,[9] FLP 1287[10] and YOS I 28.[11] Their redactional techniques show the literary and school

attempted to explain this observation with the thesis that protocols only dealt with *consequences* of criminal cases according to civil law but not directly with cases of criminal law.

4.   See 'Ein zentrales Problem des altmesopotamischen Rechtes: Was ist der Codex Hammu-rabi?', *Genava* ns 8 (1960), pp. 283-96.

5.   See 'Ammisaduqa's Edict and the Babylonian "Law Codes"', *JCS* 15 (1961), pp. 91-104; *idem*, 'A Late Old Babylonian Copy of the Laws of Hammurapi', *JCS* 21 (1967), pp. 39-48; *idem*, 'On Some Recent Studies in Cuneiform Law', *JAOS* 90 (1970), pp. 243-56.

6.   F.R. Kraus (*Königliche Verfügungen in altbabylonischer Zeit* [Studia et documenta ad iura orientis antiqui pertinentia, 11; Leiden: Brill, 1984], pp. 114ff.) converted to this position and interpreted CH like the *mīšarum* edicts.

7.   See G. Ries, *Prolog und Epilog in Gesetzen des Altertums* (Münchner Beiträge zur Papyrusforschung und antiken Rechtsgeschichte, 76; Munich: Beck, 1983), pp. 40-64.

8.   See E. Otto, 'Die Bedeutung der altorientalischen Rechtsgeschichte für das Verständnis des Alten Testaments', *ZTK* 88 (1991), pp. 149-57; *idem*, 'Gesetz', *Bibeltheologisches Wörterbuch* (Graz and Vienna: Styria, 1994), pp. 231-33.

9.   See B. Landsberger, *Die Serie ana ittišu* (MSL, 1; Rome: Editrice Pontificio Istituto Biblico, 1937); C. Zaccagnini, 'La formazione del diritto in Mesopotamia: codificazione regie e consuetudine nel II millenio a.C.', in A. Theodorides *et al.* (eds.), *La formazione del diritto nel Vicino Oriente Antico* (Università di Roma. Publicazioni dell'Idstituto di diritti Romano e dei diritti dell'Oriente mediterraneo, 65; Naples and Rome: Edizioni Scientifiche Italiane, 1988), pp. 40ff.

10.   See M. Roth, *Scholastic Tradition and Mesopotamian Law; A Study of FLP 1287, a Prism in the Collection of the Free Library of Philadelphia* (Ann Arbor: University Microfilms International, 1979), pp. 247ff.

11.   See E. Otto, *Körperverletzungen in den Keilschriftrechten und im Alten*

background of the law collections.[12] In the E.DUBB.A, legal sentences were derived from court decisions, especially from borderline cases, and then scholarly varied.[13] Legal sentences were not the sources of

Testament. Studien zum Rechtstransfer im Alten Orient (AOAT, 226; Kevelaer: Butzon & Bercker; Neukirchen–Vluyn: Neukirchener Verlag, 1991), pp. 26-45.

12.   See H. Petschow, 'Zur Systematik und Gesetzestechnik im Codex Hammurapi', *ZA* 57 (1965), pp. 146-72; *idem*, 'Zur "Systematik" in den Gesetzen von Eschnunna', in J.A. Ankum *et al.* (eds.), *Festschrift für M. David*, II (Leiden, 1968), pp. 131-43; B.L. Eichler, 'Literary Structure in the Laws of Eshnunna', in F. Rochberg-Halton (ed.), *Language, Literature and History. Philological and Historical Studies Presented to E. Reiner* (AOS, 67; New Haven: American Oriental Society, 1987), pp. 71-84; E. Otto, 'Rechtssystematik im altbabylonischen "Codex Ešnunna" und im altisraelitischen "Bundesbuch". Eine redaktionsgeschichtliche und rechtsvergleichende Analyse von CE §§ 17; 18; 22-28 und Ex 21,18-32; 22,6-14; 23,1-3.6-8', *UF* 19 (1987), pp. 175-97; *idem, Rechtsgeschichte der Redaktionen im Kodex Ešnunna und im 'Bundesbuch'. Eine rechtsgeschichtliche und rechtsvergleichende Studie zu altbabylonischen und altisraelitischen Rechtsüberlieferungen* (OBO, 85; Fribourg: Universitätsverlag Freiburg/Schweiz; Göttingen: Vandenhoeck & Ruprecht, 1989), pp. 15-183; *idem*, 'Die Einschränkung des Privatstrafrechts durch öffentliches Strafrecht in der Redaktion der Paragraphen 1-24; 50-59 des Mittelassyrischen Kodex der Tafel A (KAV 1)', in W. Zwickel (ed.), *Festschrift für M. Metzger* (OBO, 123; Fribourg: Universitätsverlag Freiburg/Schweiz; Göttingen: Vandenhoeck & Ruprecht, 1993), pp. 131-66.

13.   See R. Westbrook, 'Biblical and Cuneiform Law Codes', *RB* 92 (1985), pp. 247-64; *idem, Old Babylonian Marriage Law* (AfO, 23; Horn: Ferdinand Berger, 1988), pp. 2ff.; *idem, Studies in Biblical and Cuneiform Law* (CahRB, 26; Paris: Gabalda, 1988), pp. 2ff.; R. Westbrook and C. Wilcke, 'The Liability of an Innocent Purchaser of Stolen Goods in Early Mesopotamian Law', *AfO* 25 (1974–77), pp. 111-21. Cf. the reviews by E. Otto, 'Review of R. Westbrook, *Studies in Biblical and Cuneiform Law (1988)*, TRev* 86 (1990), pp. 284-87; *idem*, 'Review of R. Westbrook, *Old Babylonian Marriage Law* (1988)', *ZA* 81 (1991), pp. 308-14 and R. Yaron, 'Review of R. Westbrook, *Studies in Biblical and Cuneiform Law* (1988)', *Zeitschrift der Savigny-Stiftung für Rechtsgeschichte (Romanistische Abteilung)* 107 (1990), pp. 417-33. See also for the origin of legal sentences P. Koschaker, *Quellenkritische Untersuchungen zu den 'altassyrischen Gesetzen'* (MVÄG 26/3; Leipzig: Hinrichs, 1921), pp. 17ff, 68, 79-80, 83; C. Locher, 'Deuteronomium 22, 13-21. Vom Prozeßprotokoll zum kasuistischen Gesetz', in N. Lohfink (ed.), *Das Deuteronomium. Entstehung, Gestalt und Botschaft* (BETL, 68; Leuven: Peeters, 1985), pp. 298-303; *idem, Die Ehre einer Frau in Israel. Exegetische und rechtsvergleichende Studien zu Deuteronomium 22, 13-21* (OBO, 70; Fribourg: Universitätsverlag Freiburg/ Schweiz, Göttingen: Vandenhoeck & Ruprecht, 1986), pp. 83ff., 90ff.

court decisions but reflected them.[14] They were differentiated and collected in legal collections with sophisticated redactional structures in order to train judges.[15] As the laws referred to court decisions and thus reflected everyday life in a judicial perspective, there was no static 'common law' extending even to ancient Roman law.[16] We cannot renounce the diachronic analysis of ancient Oriental legal texts. There were intensive developments in ancient Near Eastern and Israelite legal history. Legal reforms, that cannot be limited to the *mīšarum* acts,[17] were a decisive aspect of these developments.

2. *Legal Reforms in Cuneiform Law*

In the following sections we will deal with laws of marriage and bodily injuries[18] in Codex Eshnunna (CE), Codex Hammurapi (CH), the Middle Assyrian Laws (MAL) and the Hittite Laws (HL).

a. *Legal Reform of Private Law in Favour of Public Law in the Middle Assyrian Laws*
Tablet A of MAL (KAV 1) consisted of a frame of criminal laws in §§ 1-24; 50-59.[19] They included an originally independent collection

---

14. See R. Westbrook, 'Cuneiform Law Codes and the Origins of Legislation', *ZA* 79 (1989), pp. 201-22.

15. See Otto, *Rechtsgeschichte der Redaktionen im Kodex Ešnunna*, pp. 181-83; *idem, Körperverletzungen in den Keilschriftrechten*, pp. 165-89; *idem*, 'Gesetz', pp. 231-33.

16. Contra R. Westbrook, 'The Nature and Origins of the Twelve Tables', *Zeitschrift der Savigny-Stiftung für Rechtsgeschichte (Romanistische Abteilung)* 105 (1988), pp. 74-121. Against this thesis cf. already E. Volterra, *Diritto Romano e diritti Orientali* (Bologna: Nicola Zanichelli, 1937), pp. 85-173; F. Wieacker, *Römische Rechtsgeschichte*, I (Handbuch der Altertumswissenschaften X/III.1; Munich: Beck, 1988), pp. 10-11, 298-99.

17. Against Westbrook, cf. Yaron, 'Review of R. Westbrook, *Studies*', p. 419 ('auch Rechtsreform wird verneint, wobei mir nicht ganz klar ist, wovon Verf. spricht'). For the *mīšarum* texts see Kraus, *Königliche Verfügungen*.

18. These laws are specially suited for discussion because Westbrook deals with them intensively in several publications. See R. Westbrook, 'Lex talionis and Exodus 21,22-25', *RB* 93 (1986), pp. 52-69; *idem, Old Babylonian Marriage Law, passim; idem, Studies in Biblical and Cuneiform Law*, pp. 39-88; *idem*, 'Adultery in Ancient Near Eastern Law', *RB* 97 (1990), pp. 542-80; *idem, Property and the Family in Biblical Law* (JSOTSup, 113; Sheffield: JSOT Press, 1991), pp. 142-64.

19. See Koschaker, *Quellenkritische Untersuchungen zu den 'altassyrischen*

of marriage laws in §§ 25-38 that was connected with the frame by means of a framework of laws in §§ 39-49. As the frame in §§ 1-24, 50-59 shows, the redactor intended to limit the private criminal law of the *pater familias* by means of the public criminal law of the law courts. §§ 57-59 formed the scopus of MAL.A and dealt with rules of legal proceedings:

KAV 1 VIII 50-53 (MAL § 57)[20]
lu-ú ma-ḫa-ṣu lu-ú a - [. . .] [ša-a ašš] (DAM)-at a['īli (LÚ)] ù gal-lu-li di-e [nu. . .] ša-a [i-na ṭup-pi šaṭ-ru-ú-ni]

KAV 1 VIII 54-57 (MAL § 58)
i-na ḫi-ṭa-a-ni gab-[bi lu-ú na-pa-li lu-ú] na-ka-a-si š[a-a aššat a'īli (DAM-at (LÚ)] ù gal-lu-li di-e-[nu. . .] ki-i ša-a [i-na ṭup-pi šaṭ-ru-ú-ni]

KAV 1 VIII 58-63 (MAL § 59)
uš-šar ḫi-ṭa-a-ni ša-[a aššat a'īli (DAM)-at LÚ] ša i-na ṭup-pi [šaṭ-ru-ú-ni] a'īlu (LÚ) aššas (DAM)-su [i-na aṭ-ṭu] i-ba-qa-an u[z-né-ša] ú-ḫap-pa ú-la-[ap-pat] a-ra-an-šu la-áš-š[u]

MAL.A. § 57
Whether it be beating or. . . of the wife of an *a'īlu*. . . blinding, a court. . . what is written on the tablet. . .

MAL.A. § 58
In all the penalties, either of tearing out or cutting off the wife of an *a'īlu* and of blinding,[21]. . . a court. . . according to what is written on the tablet.

MAL.A. §59
Apart from the penalties for the wife of an *a'īlu*, which are written on the tablet, an *a'īlu* may beat his wife, pluck, bruise the ears, pierce. There is no liability thereupon for him.

§§ 57-59 differ form-critically from the laws standing in front of them which are introduced by *šumma* and consist of the two parts of protasis and apodosis. As explanatory laws ('erklärende Rechtssätze'[22]), §§ 57-59 comment upon §§ 1-24, 50-56. The §§ (57) 58 place the

Gesetzen', p. 65; Cardascia, *Les lois assyriennes*, pp. 42-43, 46-48, 85; Otto, 'Die Einschränkung', pp. 131-66.
    20.   Transliteration and translation by the author. For philological commentaries see Otto, 'Die Einschränkung', pp. 136-37.
    21.   See R. Borger, 'Zu den Asarhaddon-Verträgen aus Nimrud', *ZA* 54 (1961), p. 195; *Akkadische Rechtsbücher* (TUAT, 1.1; Gütersloh: Mohn, 1982), p. 91.
    22.   See Koschaker, *Quellenkritische Untersuchungen zu den 'altassyrischen Gesetzen'*, p. 13.

private laws of severe penalties of mutilation in §§ 4, 5, 8, 15, 24 under the control of public courts. According to § 59 only slight injuries without continuing mutilation are excepted from this control. The redactor intended to limit private penalties by the control of public courts. This intention also becomes evident in the marriage laws in §§ 12-16:[23]

KAV 1 II 14-24 (MAL.A. § 12)

šum-ma aššat (DAM-at) a'īliu (LÚ) i-na re-be-e-te te-te-ti-iq a'īlu (LÚ) iṣ-ṣa-ba-a-sú la-ni-ik-ki-me iq-ṭi-bi-a-áš-še la-a ta-ma-gu-ur ta-ta-na-ṣa-ar e-mu-qa-ma iṣ-ṣa-ba-as-si it-ti-ak-ši lu-ú i-na muḫḫi (UGU) aššat a'īli (DAM.LÚ) ik-šu-du-uš ù lu-ú ki-i sinnilta (MÍ) i-ni-ku-ú-ni še-bu-tu ub-ta-e-ru-uš a'īla (LÚ) i-du-uk-ku ša sinnilti (MÍ) ḫi-i-ṭu la-áš-šu

KAV 1 II 25-29 (MAL.A. § 13)

šum-ma aššat (DA[M]-at) a'īli (LÚ) iš-tu bīti (É-ti)-ša ta-at-ti-ṣi-ma a-na muḫḫi (UGU) a'īli (LÚ) a-šar us-bu-ú-ni ta-ta-lak it-ti-ak-ši ki-i aššat (DAM-at) a'īli (LÚ)-ni i-de a'īla (LÚ) ù aššata (MÍ)-ma i-duk-ku

KAV 1 II 30-40 (MAL.A. § 14)

šum-ma aššat (DAM-at) a'īli (LÚ) a'īlu (LÚ) lu-ú i-na bīt (É) al-tam-me lu-ú i-na re-be-te ki-i aššat (DAM-at) a'īli (LÚ)-ni i-de it-ti-ak-ši ki-i a'īlu (LÚ) ša aš as (DAM)-su a-na e-pa-še i-qa-ab-bi-ú-ni (LÚ)-na-i-ka-na e-pu-šu šum-ma ki-i aššat (DAM)-at a'īli (LÚ)-ni la-a i-de i-it-ti-a-ak-ši (LÚ)-na-i-ka-a-nu za-a-ku a'īlu (LÚ) aššas (DAM)-su ú-ba-ar ki-i lìb-bi-šu e-pa-a[s]u

KAV 1 II 41-57 (MAL.A. § 15)

šum-ma a'īlu (LÚ) iš-tu aššat (DAM)-ti-šu a'īla (LÚ) iṣ-ṣa-bat ub-ta-e-ru-ú-uš uk-ta-i-nu-ú-uš ki-la-al-le-šu-nu-ma i-du-uk-ku-šu-nu a-ra-an-šu la-áš-šu šum-ma iṣ-ṣa-ab-ta lu-ú a-na muḫḫi (UGU) šarri (LUGAL) lu-ú a-na muḫḫi (UGU) dayyānē (DI.KUD.MEŠ) it-tab-la ú-ub-ta-e-ru-ú-uš ú-uk-ta-i-nu-ú-uš šum-ma mu-ut sinnilti (MÍ) aššas (DAM)-su i-du-ak ù a-i-la i-duk-ak-ma šum-ma ap-pa ša aššati (DAM)-šu i-na-ki-is₅ a'īla (LÚ) a-na ša re-še-en ú-tar ù pa-ni-šu gab-ba i-na-qu-ru ù šum-ma aššas (DAM)-s[u ú-uš-šar] a'īla (LÚ) ú-[uš-šar]

KAV 1 II 58-66 (MAL.A. §16)

šum-ma a'īlu (LÚ) ašša[t (DAM-at) a'īli (LÚ) i-na lu-mu-un] pi-i-ša [it-ti-a-ak-ši] ḫi-i-ṭu ša a'īli (LÚ) [la]-áš-[šu] a'īlu (LÚ) sinnilta (MÍ) aššas

---

23. See E. Otto, 'Das Eherecht im Mittelassyrischen Kodex und im Deuteronomium. Tradition und Redaktion in den §§12-16 der Tafel A des Mittelassyrischen Kodex und in Dtn 22, 22-29', in M. Dietrich and O. Loretz (eds.), *Festschrift für K. Bergerhof* (AOAT, 232; Kevelaer: Butzon & Bercker; Neukirchen-Vluyn: Neukirchener Verlag, 1993), pp. 259-81.

(DAM)-su ḫi-i-ṭa ki-i lìb-bi-šu e-em-mi-id šum-ma e-mu-qa-a-ma it-ti-ak-ši ub-ta-e-ru-ú-uš uk-ta-i-nu-ú-uš ḫi-ṭa-šu ki-i ša aššat (DAM-at) a'īli (LÚ)-ma

MAL.A. § 12
If the wife of an a'īlu is passing a public square, an a'īlu seizes her (and) says to her: 'Let me lie with you'. (If) she does not agree and defends herself but he takes her by force, lies with her—whether he is seized upon the wife of an a'īlu or witnesses prove against him that he was lying with the wife—the a'īlu will be put to death. As for the woman, there is no punishment.

MAL.A. § 13
If the wife of an a'īlu comes out of her house and goes to an a'īlu where he is dwelling and he lies with her although he knows that she is the wife of an a'īlu, the a'īlu and the wife will be put to death.

MAL.A. § 14
If an a'īlu lies with the wife of an a'īlu either in a public house or a public square, although he knows that she is the wife of an *a'īlu*: As the *a'īlu* declares that his wife shall be treated, so shall the *a'īlu*, who lay with her be treated. If he lies with her without knowing that she is the wife of an *a'īlu, he who lay with her will not be punished. The a'īlu will charge his wife and will treat her (!)*[24] *as he will.*

MAL.A. § 15
If an a'īlu seizes an a'īlu with his wife and they convict him entirely, they put both of them to death. There is no liability thereupon for him. If he seizes him, either he takes him to the king or to judges, they convict him entirely, the *a'īlu* puts his wife to death, they will put the *a'īlu* to death. If he cuts off the nose of his wife, he shall make the *a'īlu* a eunuch and they shall mutilate his whole face. If he pardons his wife, he shall also pardon the *a'īlu*.

MAL.A. § 16
If an a'īlu lies with the wife if an a'īlu (because of) her deceiving mouth,[25] the *a'īlu* will not be punished. *The a'īlu inflicts a punishment on his wife as he will.* If he lies with her by force and they convict him entirely, his punishment shall be that of the wife of the *a'īlu*.

---

24.   Read *e-pa-a-si* instead of *e-pa-a-su*, which is a scribal error.

25.   See G.R. Driver and J.C. Miles, *The Assyrian Laws with Supplementary Additions and Corrections by G.R. Driver* (Aalen: Scientia Verlag, 2nd edn, 1975 [1935]), pp. 51, 388, 464; Cardascia, *Les lois assyriennes*, pp. 123-25; C. Saporetti, *Le Leggi medioassire* (Cybernetica Mesopotamica. Data Set; Cuneiform Texts, 2; Malibu: Undena Publications, 1979), pp. 39-40; 152; Otto, 'Das Eherecht', p. 264. Against the reading of *ki-i pi-i-ša* by H. Ehelolf (*Ein assyrisches Rechtsbuch. Mit*

§§ 14-16 form a concentric unit. The cases of punishment for the wife and the *a'īlu* in § 14A and § 16B frame the cases of punishment for the wife alone in § 14B and § 16A. § 15, consisting of two parts, forms the centre of this structure. § 15A begins with the direct reaction of the husband *in flagranti delicto*, while § 15B begins with the public criminal proceedings held before king or judges. The redactor mediated the private penalty that the husband imposes on his wife and the public penalty for the *a'īlu*. As a result the penalty that the husband imposes on his wife binds the law court punishing the *a'īlu*. This intention, to combine private and public law, explains this complicated legal sentence. § 15A exempts the husband, who seized the couple *in flagranti delicto* and took them to court, from punishment.[26] Here the redactor used an older law that delivered the husband acting in a case of *in flagranti delicto* from any penalty: 'If an *a'īlu* seizes an *a'īlu* with his wife, he put both of them to death (*i-du-uk-šu-nu*), there is no liability thereupon for him'. In order to mediate private and public criminal law the redactor inserted the public proceedings into the private criminal law in §15A and, conversely, formulated § 15B by inserting the private law into the public court proceedings. In § 15A, although the exegete expects a private penalty because of the motif of *in flagranti delicto*, he is led instead to public court proceedings. In § 15B, similarly, although expecting public proceedings because of the formulation 'he takes him to the king or to the judges', he is led to a private penalty instead. It must be stressed that the private penalty was limited to the woman; the husband had no right to punish the *a'īlu*. Such punishment remained a task of public courts and a matter of public criminal law. Consequently, private law was strictly limited to family members. Others who did harm to the husband were excluded from such private

---

einer rechtsgeschichtlichen Einleitung von P. Koschaker [Berlin: Curtius Verlag, 1922], p. 26) and by R. Borger (*Akkadische Rechtsbücher*, p. 83) see already Koschaker, *Quellenkritische Untersuchungen zu den 'altassyrischen Gesetzen'*, pp. 32-33 n. 2.

26. R. Westbrook ('Adultery', pp. 552-53) tries to harmonize against the text by interpreting § 15A as related to court proceedings *ex post facto* after the husband has killed the wife and the *a'īlu in flagranti delicto*. The text does not say anything about such proceedings. *ubta"erū-š ukta"inū-š* in MAL always means public court proceedings and also excludes an interpetation of § 15A as related to a trial of neighbours by lynch law (so Driver and Miles, *Assyrian Laws*, p. 49).

punishment. If they did so in complicity with a family member, the private penalty imposed upon the family member determined the punishment of the non-family member by the courts.[27]

This intention of the redactor of MAL.A. also explains another peculiarity of §§ 12-16. In their penalties, §§ 12 and 13 differ from §§ 14-16. The former paragraphs are devoted entirely to public criminal law and do not contemplate private penalties. Indeed § 13B contradicts the private penalty in § 16B.[28] The redactor combined laws of different origins. §§ 12 and 13 were concerned with public criminal law. The laws in §§ 14*, 15*, 16*, which were reworked by the redactor (in italics in the translation), were originally concerned only with private law. The redactor mediated both spheres of law by inserting the motif of public criminal law into §§ 14-16, thereby forming a concentric structure out of these sentences and limiting private penalty by public proceedings. In order to make the point that public law takes priority over private law, the redactor placed §§ 12 and 13 at the head of this concentric structure. Concerned with public criminal law, these two laws establish the principle of sanction and thus serve as principle-setting laws. The reformulation of law served its reform.[29]

b. *The Old Babylonian Laws of Bodily Injuries in the Codex Eshnunna and Codex Hammurapi*

The Codex Eshnunna (CE) was mainly composed of the collections of marriage law in §§ 17, 18, 25-28 and of bodily injuries in §§ 42-47 (48), 53-57 (58).[30] Within this latter collection, §§ 42-48 form an independent structural block which the redactor connected with §§ 53-

---

27. The redactor used the same procedure in §§ 14 and 16, where he inserted public proceedings into private law; see Otto, 'Das Eherecht', pp. 265ff.

28. R. Westbrook ('Adultery', pp. 547ff.) harmonizes the text by simply omitting § 12 and § 16 from discussion.

29. MAL.A § 6 confirms how deeply the redactor interfered with his source in MAL.C + G § 9; see E. Otto, 'Die Rechtsintentionen des § 6 der Tafel A des Mittelassyrischen Kodex in Tradition und Redaktion', *UF* 24 (1992), pp. 307-14.

30. See Otto, *Rechtsgeschichte der Redaktionen im Kodex Ešnunna*, pp. 15-183; *idem*, 'Der reduzierte Brautpreis. Ehe- und Zinsrecht in den Paragraphen 18 und 18a des Kodex Ešnunna', *Zeitschrift der Savigny-Stiftung für Rechtsgeschichte (Romanistische Abteilung)* 109 (1992), pp. 475-81. For these laws also see R. Yaron, *The Laws of Eshnunna* (Jerusalem: Magnes Press; Leiden: Brill, 2nd edn, 1988), pp. 172-211, 285-303.

57 by introducing *iššuk-ma* 'he bites' of §§ 56, 57[31] into § 42 thus forming a frame for §§ 42-47 (48) and §§ 53-57 (58).

A III 32-34; B III 17-20 (CE § 42)[32]
šum-ma awīlum (LÚ) ap-pé awīlim (LÚ) iš-šu-uk-ma it-ta-ki-ís 1 ma-na kaspam (KÙ.BABBAR) išaqqal (Ì.LÁ.E) īnum (IGI) 1 ma-na šinnum (ZÚ) $\frac{1}{2}$ ma-na uz-nu $\frac{1}{2}$ ma-na me-he-es le-tim 10 šiqil (GÍN) kaspam (KÙ.BABBAR) išaqqal (Ì.LÁ.E)

A III 35-36; B III 21-22 (CE § 43)
šum-ma awīlum (LÚ) ú-ba-an awīlim (LÚ) it-ta-ki-ís $\frac{2}{3}$ ma-na kaspam (KÚ. BABBAR) išaqqal (Ì.LÁ.E)

A III 36-37; B III 23-24 (CE § 44)
šum-ma awīlum (LÚ) a-wi-lam i-na [sūqim] ís-ki-im-ma qās (ŠU)-su-iš-te-ber₅ $\frac{1}{2}$ ma-na kaspam (KÙ.BABBAR) išaqqal (Ì.LÁ.E)

A III 38; B III 85 (CE § 45)
šum-ma šēp(GÌR)-šu iš-te-ber₅ $\frac{1}{2}$ ma-na kaspam (KÙ.BABBAR) išaqqal (Ì.LÁ.E)

A III 39-40 (CE § 46)
šum-ma awīlum (LÚ) a-wī-lam im-ha-as-ma [kir-ra]-šu iš-te-ber₅ $\frac{2}{3}$ ma-na kaspam (KÙ.BABBAR) išaqqal (Ì.LÁ.E)

A III 40-41 (CE § 47)
šum-ma awīlum (LÚ) i-na [ši-gi-iš]-tim awīlam (LÚ) i-še-el 10 šiqil (GÍN) kaspam (KÙ.BABBAR) išaqqal (Ì.LÁ.E)

A III 42-44; B IV 1.3 (CE § 48)
ù a-na [di-nim] iš-tu $\frac{1}{3}$ ma-na a-di 1 ma-na [dayyānē (DI.KUD.MEŠ)] di-nam ú-ša-ha-zu-šu-ma a-wa-at na-pî-iš-tim a-na šarrim (LUGAL)-ma

CE § 42
If an awīlum bites and severs the nose of an awīlum, he pays 1 mina of silver. For an eye 1 mina, for a tooth $\frac{1}{2}$ mina, for an ear $\frac{1}{2}$ mina, for a slap on the cheek he pays 10 shekels of silver.

CE § 42
If an awīlum severs a finger of an awīlum, he pays $\frac{2}{3}$ mina of silver.

---

31. *ikkim-ma* in § 57 is a scribal error (see A. Goetze, *The Laws of Eshnunna* [AASOR, 31; New Haven: American School of Oriental Research, 1956], p. 133); read *iššuk-ma*; see Yaron, *Laws of Eshnunna*, p. 78.
32. Transliteration and translation by the author.

CE § 44
If an awīlum throws an awīlum to the ground in the street[33] *and breaks his hand, he pays ½ mina of silver.*

CE § 45
If he breaks a leg, he pays ½ mina of silver.

CE § 46
If an awīlum hits an awīlum and breaks his collarbone (?),[34] *he pays ⅓ mina of silver.*

CE § 47
If an *awīlum* injures an *awīlum* in an affray,[35] he pays 10 shekels of silver.

CE § 48
And for a case of ⅓ mina to 1 mina the judges[36] *shall hold court proceedings. A capital delict belongs to the king himself.*

§§ 42-48 show significant signs of legal development. § 42 originally corresponded to § 43: 'If an *awīlum* severs the nose of an *awīlum*, he pays 1 mina of silver'. With the insertion of *iniuria* (offence of honour) as a bagatelle (*meḫeṣ lētim 10 šiqil kaspam išaqqal*) in § 42, the case of unintentional bodily injury (§ 47) was added. These bagatelles were not considered in § 48. The motif of severing a nose in § 42 caused the insertion of other injuries to the head. The original set of laws in §§ 42a, 43, 44-46, 48 (in italics in the translation) regulated the injuries of nose, finger, hand, foot and collarbone or thigh[37] by simple liability for the result (*Erfolgshaftung*[38]). This simple standard of regulation was transformed by the

33.   See CAD S 70; Borger, *Akkadische Rechtsbücher*, p. 37.
34.   See Haddad 116, 5'-6'; M. Roth, 'On LE §§ 46-47a', *Nouvelles Assyriologiques Brèves et Utilitaires* 3 (1990), p. 70; see below n. 37.
35.   See Haddad 116, 7'-8'; Roth, 'On LE §§46-47a', pp. 70-71 and below n. 37.
36.   See B. Landsberger, 'Jungfräulichkeit: Ein Beitrag zum Thema "Beilager und Eheschließung"—mit einem Anhang: Neue Lesungen und Deutungen im Gesetzbuch von Ešnunna', in J.A. Ankum *et al.* (eds.), *Festschrift für M. David*, II (Leiden: Brill, 1968), p. 101.
37.   The order of injuries contradicts the reading *kir-ra-šu*, which is derived from Haddad 116, 5', and confirms the reading *ha-la-šu*, 'thigh'; see Yaron, *Laws of Eshnunna*, pp. 70-71; Otto, *Körperverletzungen in den Keilschriftrechten*, pp. 73-74 n. 3.
38.   See R. Haase, *Einführung in das Studium keilschriftlicher Rechtsquellen* (Wiesbaden: Harrassowitz, 1965), pp. 114-15 for *Erfolgshaftung* in cuneiform laws.

iniuria in § 42 and by §47, which introduced the distinction between accidental and premeditated bodily injuries, that is 'liability by guilt' (*Verschuldensprinzip*).[39]

The law of bodily injuries in Codex Hammurapi (CH) had a starting point identical to those of CE:

CH XVII b 41-44 (§ 195)[40]
šum-ma mārum (DUMU) a-ba-šu im-ta-ḥa-aṣ ritta (KIŠIB.LÁ)-šu i-na-ak-ki-su

CH XVII b 45-49 (§ 196)
šum-ma a-wi-lum i-in mār (DUMU) a-wi-lim úḥ-tap-pí-id i-in-šu ú-ḥa-ap-pa-du

CH XVII b 50-53 (§ 197)
šum-ma eṣemti (GÌR.PAD.DU) a-wi-lim iš-te-bi-ir eṣemta (GÌR.PAD.DU)-šu i-še-eb-bi-ru

CH XVII b 54-59 (§ 198)
šum-ma i-in muškēnim (MAŠ.EN.GAG) úḥ-tap-pí-id ú lu eṣemti (GÌR.NÍG(PAD).DU) muškēnim (MAŠ.EN.GAG) iš-te-bi-ir 1 ma-na kaspam (KÙ.BABBAR) i-ša-qal

CH XVII b 60-65 (§ 199)
šum-ma i-in warad (ÌR) a-wi-lim úḥ-tap-pí-id ù lu eṣemti (GÌR.PAD.DU) warad (ÌR) a-wi-lim iš-te-bi-ir mi-ši-il šīmī (ŠÁM)-šu i-ša-qal

CH XVII b 66-70 (§ 200)
šum-ma a-wi-lum ši-in-ni a-wi-lim me-eḥ-ri-šu it-ta-di ši-in-na-šu i-na-ad-du-ú

CH XVII b 71-74 (§ 201)
šum-ma ši-in-GAG(ni) muškēnim (MAŠ.EN.GAG) it-ta-di ⅓ MA.NA kaspam (KÙ.BABBAR) i-ša-qal

CH XVII b 75-81 (§ 202)
šum-ma a-wi-lum le-e-et a-wi-lim ša e-li-šu ra-bu-ú im-ta-ḥa-aṣ i-na pu-úḥ-ri-im i-na ᵏᵘˢqinnaz (USÀN) alpim (GU₄) 1 šu-ši im-maḥ-ḥa-aṣ

CH XVII b 82-87 (§ 203)
šum-ma mār (DUMU) a-wi-lim le-e-et mār (DUMU) a-wi-lim ša ki-ma šu-a-ti im-ta-ḥa-aṣ 1 ma-na kaspam (KÙ.BABBAR) i-ša-qal

39. Haddad 116, 9'-10' included the fatal injuries into the cases without premeditation.

40. For the transliteration cf. R. Borger, *Babylonisch-assyrische Lesestücke* (AnOr, 54; Rome: Editrice Pontificio Istituto Biblico, 2nd edn, 1979), p. 39; translation by the author.

CH XVII b 88-91 (§ 204)
*šum-ma muškēnum (MAŠ.EN.GAG) le-e-et muškēnim (MAŠ.EN.GAG)
im-ta-ḫa-aṣ 10 šiqil (GÍN) kaspam (KÙ.BABBAR) i-ša-qal*

CH XVII b 92-93; XVIII b 1-3 (§ 205)
*šum-ma warad (ÌR) a-wi-lim le-e-et mār (DUMU) a-wi-lim im-ta-ḫa-aṣ ú-
zu-un-šu i-na-ak-ki-su*

CH XVIII b 4-13 (§ 206)
*šum-ma a-wi-lum a-wi-lam i-na ri-is-ba-tim im-ta-ḫa-aṣ-ma sí-im-ma-am
iš-ta-ka-an-šu a-wi-lum šu-ú i-na i-du-ú la am-ḫa-ṣú i-tam-ma ù asâm
(A.ZU) i-ip-pa-al*

CH XVIII b 14-19 (§ 207)
*šum-ma i-na ma-ḫa-ṣí-šu im-tu-ut i-tam-ma-ma šum-ma mār (DUMU) a-
wi-lim ½ MA.NA kaspam (KÙ.BABBAR) i-ša-qal*

CH XVIII b 20-22 (§ 208)
*šum-ma mār (DUMU) muškēnim (MAŠ.EN.GAG) ⅓ MA.NA kaspam
(KÙ.BABBAR) i-ša-qal*

CH XVIII b 23-30 (§ 209)
*šum-ma a-wi-lum mārat (DUMU.MÍ) a-wi-lim im-ḫa-aṣ-ma ša li-ib-bi-ša
uš-ta-di-ši 10 šiqil (GÍN) kaspam (KÙ.BABBAR) a-na ša li-ib-bi-ša i-ša-
qal*

CH XVIII b 31-34 (§ 210)
šum-ma sinništum (MÍ) ši-i im-tu-ut māras (DUMU.MÍ)-sú i-du-uk-ku

CH XVIII b 35-40 (§ 211)
*šum-ma mārat (DUMU.MÍ) muškēnim (MAŠ.EN.GAG) i-na ma-ḫa-ṣí-im
ša li-ib-bi-ša uš-ta-ad-di-ši 5 šiqil (GÍN) kaspam (KÙ.BABBAR) i-ša-qal*

CH XVIII b 41-44 (§ 212)
*šum-ma sinništum (MÍ) ši«-i» im-tu-ut ½ MA.NA kaspam
(KÙ.BABBAR) i-ša-qal*

CH XVIII b 45-50 (§213)
*šum-ma amat (GEMÉ) a-wi-lim im-ḫa-aṣ-ma ša li-ib-bi-ša uš-ta-ad-di-ši 2
šiqil (GÍN) kaspam (KÙ.BABBAR) i-ša-qal*

CH XVIII b 51-54 (§ 214)
*šum-ma amtu (GEMÉ) ši-i im-tu-ut ⅓ MA.NA kaspam (KÙ.BABBAR) i-
ša-qal*

CH § 195
If a son strikes his father, they cut off his hand.

CH § 196
If an *awīlum* destroys the eye of a *mār awīlim*, they destroy his eye.

CH § 197
If he breaks the bone of an *awīlum*, they break his bone.

CH § 198
If he destroys the eye of a *muškēnum* or breaks the bone of a *muškēnum*, he pays 1 mina of silver.

CH § 199
If he destroys the eye of the slave of an *awīlum* or breaks the bone of the slave of an *awīlum*, he pays half his price.

CH § 200
If an *awīlum* knocks out the tooth of an *awīlum* of equal rank, they knock out his tooth.

CH § 201
If he knocks out the tooth of a *muškēnum*, he pays $\frac{1}{3}$ mina of silver.

CH § 202
If an *awīlum* strikes the cheek of an *awīlum*, who is superior to him, he shall be beaten with 60 lashes of an ox-hide whip in the assembly.

CH § 203
If a *mār awīlum*[41] strikes the cheek of an *awīlum* equal to him, he pays 1 mina of silver.

CH § 204
If a *muškēnum* strikes the cheek of a *muškēnum*, he pays 10 shekels of silver.

CH § 206
If an *awīlum* strikes an *awīlum* in an affray and inflicts a wound upon him, the *awīlum* swears, 'I did not strike intentionally', and pays the surgeon.

CH § 207
If he dies of the striking, he swears likewise; if it is a *mār awīlum*, he pays $\frac{1}{2}$ mina of silver.

CH § 208
If it is a *muškēnum*, he pays $\frac{1}{3}$ mina of silver.

CH § 209
If an *awīlum* strikes the daughter of an *awīlum* and causes her a miscarriage, he pays 10 shekels of silver for the fruit of her womb.

---

41. *awīlum* and *mār awīlim* were identified; contra Westbrook, *Studies in Biblical and Cuneiform Law*, pp. 73ff. See G.R. Driver and J.C. Miles, *The Babylonian Laws*, I (Oxford: Clarendon Press, 2nd edn, 1956), pp. 409-10; Yaron, Review of Westbrook, *Studies in Biblical and Cuneiform Law*, pp. 424-27.

CH § 210
If this woman dies, they put his daughter to death.

CH § 211
If he causes the daughter of a *muškēnum* a miscarriage, he pays 5 shekels of silver.

CH § 212
If this woman dies, he pays $\frac{1}{2}$ mina of silver.

CH § 213
If he strikes the slave-girl of an *awīlum* and causes her a miscarriage, he pays 2 shekels of silver.

CH § 214
If this slave-girl dies, he pays $\frac{1}{3}$ mina of silver.

The traditio-historical basis of the laws of bodily injuries in CH §§ 195-225 was a list of tariff rates in CH §§ 196*, 197*, 200*:

> If an *awīlum* destroys the eye of an *awīlum*, he pays... mina of silver.
> If an *awīlum* breaks the bone of an *awīlum*, he pays... mina of silver.
> If an *awīlum* knocks out the tooth of an *awīlum*, he pays... mina of silver.

The legal-historical development of CH §§ 195-214 took a course which was to a degree parallel to that of CE §§ 42-48. The lists of tariff rates in CE §§ 42-46* and CH §§ 196*, 197*, 200* only differentiated between curable and incurable bodily injuries as rules of pure liability by result. CH §§ 195, 202-205 introduced the *iniuria (meheṣ lētim)* according to CE § 42B. The connection of CH §§ 195-205 with CH §§ 206-208 introduced the differentiation between premeditated and accidental injuries similar to the addition of CE § 47 to CE §§ 42-46.[42] By means of the differentiation between unpremeditated injuries (CH §§ 206-208) and premeditated cases (CH §§ 209-214, also CH §§ 196-200), which latter were originally related to a 'liability by result', the entire series §§ 206-14 was transformed redactionally into cases of a 'liability by guilt'.

Going beyond CE, the bodily injury laws in CH were differentiated additionally according to the structure of Old Babylonian society into cases of *awīlū*, *muškēnū*[43] and *wardū*.[44] Connected with this

---

42. See Otto, *Körperverletzungen in den Keilschriftrechten*, pp. 56-70.

43. For the relation between *awīlum* and *muškēnum* see Kraus, *Königliche Verfüngungen*, pp. 329-31; Yaron, *Laws of Eshnunna*, pp. 132-54.

44. See also R. Yaron, 'Enquire now about Hammurabi, Ruler of Babylon',

differentiation, the redactor introduced a talionic retribution for bodily injuries of an *awīlum* caused by an *awīlum* in CH §§ 196, 197, 200 (210).[45] Both elements, that is, the social differentiation and the talionic retribution in cases of injuries of an *awīlum*, which the prehammurapian laws did not know, were introduced together. The talionic penalties were intended to prevent premeditated injuries within the class of the awīlū.[46] For the lower classes of *muškēnū* and *wardū* (in CH §§ 198, 199, 202, 203, 204) the prehammurapian laws of monetary compensation remained valid. The redactor of CH §§ 195-214 reformed the laws according to the structure of his society. He employed the threat of a talionic retaliation in order to protect the class of *awīlū* from the violence of premeditated injuries.[47]

c. *Legal Reforms in the Laws of Bodily Injuries of the Hittite Laws*
The Hittite Laws (HL) described the reform of older legal prescriptions *expressis verbis*. We exemplify this process of reform by the laws of bodily injuries in HL §§ 7-18.

Tijdschrift voor Rechtsgeschiedenis 59 (1991), pp. 227-28, 230ff.

45. See E. Otto, 'Die Geschichte der Talion im Alten Orient und Israel', in D.R. Daniels *et al.* (eds.), *Festschrift für K. Koch* (Neukirchen–Vluyn: Neukirchener Verlag, 1991), pp. 112-17.

46. The intention to protect societally privileged persons also caused the severe penalties for an *iniuria* against persons of a higher rank in CH §§ 195; 202; 205.

47. R. Westbrook (*Studies in Biblical and Cuneiform Law*, p. 45) harmonizes the laws of CE and CH by the thesis that the talionic penalties could on principle be commuted into money payment and vice versa. It is methodologically impossible, however, to interpolate the Mishnaic interpretation of Israelite talion (Exod. 21.23-25; cf. below) into the Old Babylonian laws of bodily injuries; see E. Otto, Review of R. Westbrook, *Studies*, pp. 285-86. R. Yaron (Review of Westbrook *Studies*, p.422) also rejects the possibility of commuting monetary compensation into talionic retaliation. It is also methodologically inappropriate to argue with the Old Hittite and Middle Assyrian regulations of homicide in Ed. Telepinus § 49 and MAL.B § 2 (one could add MAL.A. §§ 10 [11]; see Otto, 'Die Einschränkung', pp. 152-53), because they are irrelevant for Old Babylonian regulations of bodily injuries. Ed.Tel. § 49 and MAL.B. § 2 are not even part of a 'common law' of homicide; against Westbrook cf. CE § 24 *dīnnapištim = nēpû ša ippû imât*; CE § 26 *dīn napištim = imât*. In CE § 48 (cf. above) a *dīn napištim* of a fatal injury was excluded from monetary compensation.

Ser. I B I 16-18 (HL § 7)[48]

tá-ku LÚ.U₁₉.LU-an EL-LAM ku-iš-ki da-šu-wa-ah-hi na-aš-ma Z[(U₉-Š)]U la-a-ki ka-ru-ú 1 MA.NA KÙ.BABBAR pí-eš-kir ki-nu-na 20 GÍN KÙ.BABBAR pa[(-a-i)] pár-na-aš-še-e-a šu-wa-a-iz-[z]i

Ser. I B I 19-20 (HL § 8)

ták-ku ÌR-an na-aš-ma GÉME-an ku-iš-ki da-šu-wa-ah-hi na-aš-ma Z[(U₉-ŠU)] la-a-ki [(10)] GÍN KÙ.BABBAR pa-a-i pár-na-aš-še-e-a šu-wa-a-iz-zi

Ser. I B 21-24 (HL § 9)

[t]ák-ku LÚ.U₁₉.LU SAG.DU-SÚ ku-iš-ki hu-u-ni-ik-zi ka-ru-ú [(6 GÍN)] KÙ.BABBAR pí-eš-kir n[u?] hu-u-ni-in-kán-za 3 GÍN KÙ.BABBAR da-a-i- A-NA É.GAL^{LIM} 3[(GÍN K)]Ù.BABBAR da-aš-ki-ir ki-nu-na LUGAL-uš ŠA È.GAL^{LIM} pí-eš-ši-it nu-za hu[(-u-ni-in-ká)]n-za-pát 3[GÍN] KÙ.BABBAR da-a-i

Ser. I B I 25-28 (HL § 10)

ták-ku LÚ.U₁₉.LU-an ku-iš-ki hu-u-ni-ik-zi ta-an iš-tar-ni-ik-zi [(nu a-pu-u-u)] ša!-a-ak-ta-a-iz-zi pí-e-đi-iš-ši-ma an-tu-uh-ša-an pa-a-i nu[(É-ri-iš-ši)] an-ni-eš-ki-iz-zi ku-it-ma-na-ašSIG₅-at-ta-ri ma-a-na-aš SIG₅-at-[(ta)-ri(ma)] nu-uš-ši 6 GÍN KÙ.BABBAR pa-a-i ^{LÚ}A.ZU-ᵘa ku-uš-ša-an a-pa-a-aš-pát [(pa-a-i)]

Ser. I B I 29-30 (HL § 11)

ták-ku LÚ.U₁₉.LU-an EL-LUM QA-AS-SÚ na-aš-ma GÌR-ŠU ku-iš-ki tu-wa-a[r-n]i-iz-zi nu-uš-še 20 GÍN KÙ.BABBAR pa-a-i pár-na-aš-še-e-a šu-wa-a-i-iz-zi

Ser. I B I 31-32 (HL § 12)

ták-ku ÌR-na-an na-aš-ma GÉME-an QA-AS.SÚ na-aš-ma GÌR-ŠU ku-iš-ki tu-wa-ar-na-zi 10 GÍN KÙ.BABBAR pa-a-i pár-na-aš-še-e-a šu-wa-a-i-iz-zi

Ser. I B I 33-34 (HL § 13)

ták-ku LÚ.U₁₉.LU-an EL-LAM KIR₁₄-še-it ku-iš-ki wa-a-ki 1 MA.NA KÙ.BABBAR pa-a-i pár-na-aš-še-e-a šu-wa-a-i-e-iz-zi

---

48. For the text see J. Friedrich, *Die hethitischen Gesetze. Transkription, Übersetzung, sprachliche Erläuterung und vollständiges Wörterverzeichnis* (Documenta et monumenta orientis antiqui, 7; Leiden: Brill, 2nd edn, 1971), pp. 17-21. The transliteration of the cuneiform text is reworked according to C. Rüster and E. Neu, *Hethitisches Zeichenlexikon. Inventar und Interpretation der Keilschrift-zeichen aus den Boğazköy-Texten* (Studien zu den Boğazköy-Texten, 2; Wiesbaden: Harrassowitz, 1989); cf. Otto, *Körperverletzungen in den Keilschriftrechten*, pp. 97-98, 103-105. Translation by the author.

Ser. I B 35-36 (HL § 14)
ták-ku ÌR-an na-aš-ma GÉME-an KIR₁₄-še-it ku-iš-ki wa-a-ki 3 GÍN KÙ.BABBAR pa-a-i pár-na-š-še-e-a šu-wa-a-i-iz-zi

Ser. I B I 37-38 (HL § 15)
ták-ku LÙ.U₁₉LU-aš EL-LAM iš-ta-ma-na-aš-ša-an ku-iš-ki iš-kal-la-a-ri 12 GÍN KÙ.BABBAR pa-a-i pár-na-aš-še-e-a šu-wa-a-i-iz-zi

Ser. I B I 39 (HL § 16)
ták-ku ÌR-an na-aš-ma GÉME-an GEŠTUG-aš-ša-an ku-iš-ki iš-kal-la-ri 3 [GÍN)] KÙ.BABBAR pa-a-i

Ser. I B I 40-42 (HL § 17)
[(ták-k)]u MUNUS-aš EL-LI šar-ḫu-wa-an-du-uš-šu-uš ku-iš-ki p[(í-e)]š-[(ši-ya-)]zi [ták-ku] ITU.10.ᴷᴬᴹ 10 GÍN KÙ.BABBAR pa-a-i ták-ku [[-uš]] ITU.5.ᴷᴬᴹ 5 GÍN K[Ù.BABBAR] pa-a-i [pár-n]a-aš-š[e-e-a] šu-wa-a-i[-iz-z]i

Ser. I B I 43-44 (HL § 18)
ták-ku GÉME-aš šar-hu-wa-an[du-u]š-šu-uš ku-iš-ki pi-e[(š-ši-y)]a-zi ták-ku ITU.10.KAM. 5̆(?) GÍN KÙ.BABBAR pa-a-[i]

HL § 7
If anyone blinds a free man or knocks out[49] his tooth, hitherto he gave 1 mina of silver and now he gives 20 shekels of silver; he also spies at his house.[50]

HL § 8
If anyone blinds a male slave or a female slave or knocks out his (her) tooth, he gives 10 shekels of silver; he also spies at his house.

HL § 9
If anyone injures the head[51] of a man, hitherto he gave 6 shekels of silver,

---

49.   See R. Haase, 'Köperverletzung. B. Hethiter', *Reallexikon für Assyriologie* VI (1982), p. 179.
50.   For the formula *parnaššea šuwaizzi* cf. H.A. Hoffner, 'The Laws of the Hittites' (PhD dissertation, Brandeis University, 1963), p. 9; N. Oettinger, *Die Stammbildung des hethitischen Verbums* (Erlanger Beiträge zur Sprach- und Kunstwissenschaft, 64; Heidelberg: Verlag Hans Carl Nürnberg, 1984), pp. 294-98; for Old Babylonian and biblical parallels see E. Otto, 'Die keilschriftlichen Parallelen der Vindikationsformel in Dtn 20,10', *ZAW* 102 (1990), pp. 94-96.
51.   Concerning SAG.DU see R. Haase, 'Regelt § 9 der hethitischen Rechtssamuilung eine leichte Leibesverletzung?', *BO* 19 (1962), p. 116; E. Otto, 'Körperverletzung im hethitischen und israelitischen Recht. Rechts- und religionshistorische Aspekte', in B. Janowski *et al.* (eds.), *Religionsgeschichtliche Beziehungen zwischen Kleinasien, Nordsyrien und dem Alten Testament im 2. und 1. vorchristlichen Jahrtausend. Akten des Internationalen Symposions, Hamburg*

the injured man took 3 shekels of silver, the palace took 3 shekels of silver. And now the king has abolished (the fine due the) palace. Only the injured man takes 3 shekels of silver.

HL § 10

If anyone injures a man and causes him illness, he attends to him. In his place, he provides a man who works in his house until his recovery. On his recovery he gives him 6 shekels of silver. He also pays the fee for the surgeon.

HL § 11

If anyone breaks the hand or the foot of a free man, he gives him 20 shekels of silver. He also spies at his house.

HL § 12

If anyone breaks the hand or the foot of a male slave or female slave, he gives 10 shekels of silver. He also spies at his house.

HL § 13

If anyone bites off the nose of a free man, he gives 1 mina of silver. He also spies at his house.

HL § 14

If anyone bites off the nose of a male slave or a female slave, he gives 3 shekels of silver. He also spies at his house.

HL § 15

If anyone slashes the ear of a free man, he gives 12 shekels of silver. He also spies at his house.

HL § 16

If anyone slashes the ear of a male slave or female slave, he gives 3 shekels of silver.

HL § 17

If anyone causes a free woman a miscarriage; if it is the tenth month, he gives 10 shekels of silver; if it is the fifth month, he gives 5 shekels (of silver). He also spies at his house.

HL § 18

If anyone causes a female slave woman a miscarriage, if it the tenth month, he gives 5 (?) shekels of silver.

§§ 7-18 have a clear redactional structure.[52] §§ 9, 10, 11, 12 regulate the cases of curable injuries, §§ 7, 8, 13-16 the incurable injuries of the loss of an eye, tooth, nose and ear, which are all related

---

17.-2.-März 1990 (OBO, 129; Fribourg: Universitätsverlag Freiburg/Schweiz; Göttingen: Vandenhoeck & Ruprecht, 1993), p. 397.

52. See Otto, 'Körperverletzung', pp. 395-400.

to the head. § 9 is a principle regulation related to all the other curable injuries of the head. § 10 is a principle regulation for all the injuries that do not concern the head and which are not regulated in § 11 and § 12.[53] Both these laws differ from the others because they do not differentiate between the injuries of free persons and slaves. These sentences form the centre of the structure.[54] The framing laws of injuries of the head in §§ 7-9, 13-16 had an independent tradition history before they were incorporated into the redactional structure of §§ 7-18. An older collection, which preceded the reform, listed the four incurable injuries of the loss of eye, tooth, nose and ear. The penalty for destroying an ear was less severe than for the three other cases. In § 9A the case of curable injuries of the head were marked off from the incurable injuries. The penalty for 10 shekels in §§ 8, 12 and 5 shekels in § 18 represents the half of the reform regulations of 20 and 10 shekels as the double (*duplum*) in §§ 7, 11, 17. The laws of the slaves were introduced with the reform regulations.[55] The original collection in §§ 7A, 9A, 13, 15 (in italics in the translation)[56] was a list of tariffs. Into this basis the redactor inserted §§ 7B, 8, 9B, 10-12, 14, 16, 17, 18 and paralleled the penalties of 20 and 10 shekels. This basic tariff list has its closest parallels in CE §§ 42*, 43-46 and CH §§ 196*, 197*, 200. A Hittite reception of this Old Babylonian tradition is possible.[57]

53.   § 10 generally speaks of *ḫūnink-* ('to injure') and *ištarnink-* ('to cause disease' [see Hoffner, 'Laws of the Hittites', pp. 18-19]) without listing injuries of special organs.

54.   The structure of HL §§ 7-18 has its closest parallel in the Israelite collection of bodily injuries in the Book of the Covenant in Exod. 21.18-32; see Otto, *Körperverletzungen in den Keilschriftrechten*, pp. 107, 110, 166-69; *idem*, 'Körperverletzung', pp. 412-14 and below III.a.

55.   See Hoffner, 'Laws of the Hittites', pp. 221-22. The differences of 1 mina and 12 shekels in §§ 13 and 15 and 3 shekels in §§ 14 and 16 result from the fact that the dishonouring aspect of a destroyed nose or ear did not count for the slave.

56.   See Otto, 'Körperverletzung', p. 400.

57.   See V. Korošec, 'Einige Probleme zur Struktur der hethitischen Gesetze', in J. Harmatta and G. Komoróczy (eds.), *Wirtschaft und Gesellschaft im Alten Vorderasien* (Budapest: Akadémiai Kiadó, 1976), p. 294; Otto, 'Körperverletzung', pp. 402-408; for the problem see also V. Korošec, 'Die hethitischen Gesetze in ihren Wechselbeziehungen zu den Nachbarvölkern', in H.-J. Nissen and J. Renger (eds.), *Mesopotamien und seine Nachbarn* (Berliner Beiträge zum Vorderen Orient, 1; Berlin: Dietrich Reimer, 1982), pp. 295-310.

The redactor of the reform collection had three main intentions. He adjusted the tariff list of bodily injuries to the societal structure of free persons and slaves by introducing the slave laws, abolished the payment to the palace ('Zahlung an den Palast') in cases of bodily injuries and improved the compensation for the injured party. § 10 regulated all the curable injuries and stressed the responsibility of the person who caused the injury to provide compensation. In order to limit the damage, he must provide a substitute labourer and payment for the surgeon. With these regulations the redactor expanded the field of regulations from a tariff list, which originally dealt only with injuries to the head, to a list of regulations for all kinds of bodily injuries. § 10 regulated all the curable injuries except those to the head, whereas §§ 11 and 12 differentiated the compensation of 6 shekels in cases of serious but curable injuries. As such, the other regulations of § 10 were also valid for § 11 and § 12. Using a traditional case of the curriculum of the Old Babylonian E.DUBB.A[58] (YOS I 28 §§ 1, 2,[59] UM 55-22-71 §§ 4-5,[60] CH §§ 209-214[61]), the redactor also included women in this set of regulations. HL does not derive, as some have argued, from customary laws that were codified by the redactor of the reform text,[62] but rather from school-traditions

58. See Otto, *Körperverletzungen in den Keilschriftrechten*, pp. 116-17; 'Körperverletzung', pp. 402-408.

59. See A.T. Clay, *Miscellaneous Inscriptions of the Yale Babylonian Collection* (New Haven: Yale University Press, 1915), No. 28; W.H.P. Römer, 'Einige Bemerkungen zum altmesopotamischen Recht, sonderlich nach Quellen in sumerischer Sprache', *ZAW* 95 (1983), pp. 326-27; Otto, *Körperverletzungen in den Keilschriftrechten*, pp. 25-28.

60. See M. Civil, 'New Sumerian Law Fragments', in *Studies in Honor of Benno Landsberger on his 75th Birthday* (Assyriological Studies, 16; Chicago: University of Chicago Press, 1965), pp. 4ff; H. Lutzmann, *Aus den Gesetzen des Königs Lipit Eschtar von Isin* (TUAT 1.1; Gütersloh: Mohn, 1982), pp. 25-26; Otto, *Körperverletzungen in den Keilschriftrechten*, pp. 46-50.

61. See J.J. Finkelstein, 'The Ox that Gored', *TAPhS* 71 (1981), pp. 19-20 n. 11; Otto, *Körperverletzungen in den Keilschriftrechten*, pp. 51-55.

62. So E. Neufeld, *The Hittite Laws* (London: Lusac, 1951), pp. 95ff; H.G. Güterbock, 'Authority and Law in the Hittite Kingdom', in H.M. Hoenigswald (ed.), *Authority and Law in the Ancient Orient* (JAOSSup, 17; Baltimore: American Oriental Society, 1954), p. 21; A. Archi, 'Sulla formazione del testo delle leggi ittite', *Studi Micenei ed Egeo-Anatolici* 6 (1968), pp. 61ff.; *idem*, 'La formazione del diritto nell' Anatolia ittita', in A. Theodorides *et al.* (eds.), *La formazione del diritto nel Vicino Oriente Antico* (Università di Roma. Publicazioni dell'Istituto di diritti

of Old Babylonian origin.[63] HL was a scholarly redacted collection of laws, which reflected the reform.[64]

The distinction between premeditated and unpremeditated injuries is first introduced by the thirteenth-century[65] 'parallel text' KBo VI 4 14-15:

> KBo VI 14-15 (HL § V)
> *ták-ku LÚ-an EL.LUM šu-ul-la-an-na-za ku-iš-ki da-šu-wa-ah-hi 1 MA . NA KÙ.BABBAR pa-a-i ták-ku ŠU-aš wa-aš-ta-i 20 GÍN KÙ.BABBAR pa-a-i*
>
> HL § V
> If anyone blinds a free man as the result of a quarrel,[66] he gives 1 mina of silver. If the hand sins,[67] he gives 20 shekels of silver.

HL §§ 7-10 did not include a regulation of incurable injuries except for those to the head. KBo VI 4 27-29 filled this gap:

> KBo VI 4 27-29 (HL § X)
> *ták-ku LÚ EL.LUM ŠU-SÚ na-aš-ma GÌR-ŠU ku-iš-ki du-wa-ar-ni-iz-zi na-aš ma-a-an kar-ma-la-aš-ša-i nu-uš-ši 20 GÍN KÙ.BABBAR pa-a-i*

Romano e di diritti dell'Oriente Mediterraneo, 65; Naples and Rome: Edizioni Scientifiche Italiane, 1988), pp. 63-64.

63. That the laws of bodily injuries in HL did not know the *iniuria* and the difference between accidental and premeditated bodily injuries shows that the redactor of HL depended upon a tradition that was very near to that of the basic tariff lists in CE and CH; see below n. 70. For a different view see K. Peckeruhn, 'Die Handschrift A der hethitischen Gesetze' (PhD dissertation, Universität Würzburg, 1988),pp. 165ff., who thinks of a nomadic decalogue as the origin of the laws.

64. A. Archi, 'Formazione', pp. 63-64, dates a first redaction of HL to the period of Muršili I and the reform to Hattušili I; V. Korošec (*Keilschriftrechte* [HO, I/3; Leiden: Brill, 1956], p. 183) connects the reform with Telepinus; see also R. Haase, *Texte zum hethitischen Recht. Eine Auswahl* (Wiesbaden, 1984), pp. 19-20.

65. See Haase, *Texte zum hethitischen Recht*, p. 18. E. Imparati (*Le leggi ittite* [Incunabula Graeca, 7; Rome: Edizioni dell' Ateno, 1964], pp. 6-7) dates KBO VI 4 to the period of Tudhaliya IV or Arnuwanda III.

66. In contrast to the *ina risbatim*-motif in OB laws, the motif of the quarrel in the Hittite context signifies a premeditated injury.

67. The formula ŠU-*aš waštai* 'the hand sins' has its parallels in the Hittite oracle-Text KUB V 3 I 3.8; V 4 II 27 (see J. Grothus, *Die Rechtsordnung der Hethiter* [Wiesbaden: Harrassowitz, 1973], p. 15), in Exod. 21.13 and the Twelve Tables VIII 24a (see A. Völkl, *Die Verfolgung der Körperverletzung im frühen römischen Recht. Studien zum Verhältnis von Tötungsverbrechen und Injuriendelikt* (Forschungen zum Römischen Recht, 35; Vienna and Cologne: Böhlau, 1984), pp. 83ff.

ma-a-na-aš U.UL-ma kar-ma-la-aš-ša-i nu-uš-ši 10 GÍN KÙ.BABBAR pa-a-i

HL § X
If anyone breaks the hand or the foot of a free man and they remain stiff,[68] he gives 20 shekels of silver. But if they do not remain stiff, he gives 10 shekels of silver.[69]

The Hittite bodily injury laws, which took their starting point from an Old Babylonian tradition,[70] show a continuous development from the Old Hittite to the New Hittite period.[71] These examples of Assyrian, Babylonian and Hittite legal history show that the legal sentences did not form a static 'common law' but had a history of continuous reformulations. These scholarly refinements reflect the continuous reforming of law in society.

3. *Legal Reforms in Israelite Law*

The legal history of ancient Israel was a history of reforms. We will focus our analysis on developments within the Book of the Covenant and the exegesis of the Book of the Covenant (BC) within Deuteronomy.

a. *Legal Reforms of the Laws of Bodily Injuries in the Book of the Covenant*
The predeuteronomistic BC[72] was redacted out of the collections of the מות יומת-laws in Exod. 21.12-17, the laws of bodily injuries in

---

68. See J. Friedrich, *Hethitisches Wörterbuch. Kurzgefaßte kritische Sammlung der Deutung hethischer Wörter* (Heidelberg: Carl Winter Universitätsverlag, 1952), p. 101.

69. The regulation of serious but curable injuries in KBo VI 4 22-26 (HL § IX), which was formed out of HL §§ 9, 10, was set up from HL § X.

70. A date as early as A. Archi ('Formazione', pp. 63-64) suggests is doubtful; see E. Otto, 'Auf dem Wege zu einer altorientalischen Rechtsgeschichte', *BO* 48 (1991), pp. 9-10. For the Old Hittite 'schwerer Duktus' see A. Kammenhuber, 'Das Ende des typisch alten Duktus im Hethitischen', in J.N. Postgate *et al.* (eds.), *Societies and Languages in the Ancient Near East. Studies in Honour of I.M. Diakonoff* (Warminster: Aris & Phillips, 1982), pp. 150-59.

71. It is too restrictive to limit the reformulation in Hittite laws to the fixing of prices. It has nothing to do with the *mīšarum* acts.

72. See E. Otto, *Wandel der Rechtsbegründungen in der Gesellschaftsgeschichte des antiken Israel. Eine Rechtsgeschichte des 'Bundesbuches' Ex XX 22-XXIII 13*

21.18-32, the שׁלּם-laws in 21.33–22.14 and the court rules in 23.1-8. These originally independent collections, each with a tradition history of its own,[73] became part of the two law collections in 20.24-26, 21.2–22.26* and 22.28–23.12*, out of which the predeuteronomistic BC was formed. This is also valid for the collection of laws dealing with bodily injuries in 21.18-32.[74] The oldest traditio-historical level comprised the laws in 21.18-19, 22*. They are expanded by cases of fatal injuries including the death penalty or compensation, especially in the slave laws (21.20-21, 23, 26-27, 28-32). In the redactional structure of this collection, the laws concerning free persons (21.18, 22-25, 28-31) alternate with those concerning slaves (21.20-21, 26-27, 32), while criminal laws requiring the death penalty (21.20, 23, 29 [31]) alternate with civil laws requiring compensation in 21.18-19, 21, 22, 26, 30, 32. The redactor intended to mark off fatal from non-fatal cases and those requiring the death penalty from those involving compensation. The talion formula in 21.24-25 was an integral part of this structure, as the quotation of 21.24 in 21.26-27 shows.[75] 21.26-27

(Studia Biblica, 3; Leiden/New York: Brill, 1988), pp. 9-56; *idem, Theologische Ethik des Alten Testaments* (Theologische Wissenschaft 3.2; Stuttgart: Kohlhammer, 1994), pp. 19-116. L. Schwienhorst-Schönberger (*Das Bundesbuch (Ex 20,22-23, 33). Studien zu seiner Entstehung und Theologie* [BZAW, 188; Berlin: de Gruyter, 1990], pp. 44-234) counts with an uniform lawbook in 21.12–22.16. For discussion see E. Otto, 'Vom Profanrecht zum Gottesrecht: Das Bundesbuch. Review of L. Schwienhorst-Schönberger, *Das Bundesbuch (Ex 20,22-23, 33). Studien zu seiner Entstehung und Theologie* (1990), *TRu* 56 (1991), pp. 421-27; *idem*, 'Die Kompositionsgeschichte des alttestamentlichen "Bundesbuches" Ex 20,22b-23, 33. Review of Y. Osumi, *Die Kompositionsgeschichte des Bundesbuches Exodus 20,22b-23, 33* (1991)', *WZKM* 83 (1993), pp. 149-65; *idem*, Die Tora in der Rechtsgeschichte Israels. Review of F. Crüsemann, *Die Tora* (1992), *TLZ* 118 (1993), pp. 903-10; L. Schwienhorst-Schönberger, 'Review of Y. Osumi, *Die Kompositionsgeschichte des Bundesbuches Exodus 20,22b-23, 33* (1991)', *Bib* 74 (1993), pp. 275-80.

73. For the collection of שׁלּם-laws cf. E. Otto, 'Die rechtshistorische Entwicklung des Depositenrechts in altorientalischen und altisraelitischen Rechtskorpora', *Zeitschrift der Savigny-Stiftung für Rechtsgeschichte (Romanistische Abteilung)* 105 (1989), pp. 1-31. That the Israelite deposit laws were more archaic than those of the Old Babylonian collections of CE and CH contradicts the thesis of a 'common law' in the Ancient Orient including Israel as to simple.

74. See Otto, *Körperverletzungen in den Keilschriftrechten*, pp. 147-64.

75. See H. Cazelles, *Études sur le Code d'Alliance* (Paris: Letouzey & Ané, 1946), pp. 56-57; J.W. Welch, 'Chiasmus in Biblical Law: An Approach to the

is so firmly connected with 21.20-21 that 21.24-25 cannot be removed from its context by means of literary criticism.[76] The originally independent talion was expanded by the formula נפש תחת נפש in 21.23 and thus connected with the cases concerning fatal injuries.[77] This expanded talion formula formed the centre of this redactional structure of the bodily injury laws in 21.18-32.

What was its function? The surrounding laws concerning fatal injuries in 21.20-29 redactionally confirm the death penalty formula נפש תחת נפש. In contrast, the surrounding laws of non-fatal injuries in 21.18-19, 22, 26-27 stipulate compensation rather than talion. This inconsistency does not mean, however, that we have to misread the talion formula as a tariff list specifying compensation.[78] The redactional structure provides another solution. The redactor intended to mark off cases requiring the death penalty from those of

Structure of Legal Texts in the Bible', *Jewish Law Association Studies* 4 (1990), p. 14.

76. Contra H.J. Kugelmass, 'Lex Talionis in the Old Testament' (PhD dissertation, University of Montreal, 1985), pp. 140ff.; A. Lemaire, 'Vengeance et justice dans l'ancien Israël', in R. Verdier and J.P. Poly (eds.), *La vengeance. Pouvoirs et ideologies dans quelques civilisations de l'antiquité*, III (Paris, 1985), p. 13ff.

77. An original talion formula, which preceded the BC, included the injuries of eye, tooth, hand and foot; see V. Wagner, *Rechtssätze in gebundener Sprache und Rechtssatzreihen im israelitischen Recht* (BZAW, 127; Berlin: de Gruyter, 1972), pp. 5-6. It is not improbable that the formula נפש תחת נפש, which was originally independent of the talion-formula, had a cultic origin; see A. Alt, 'Zur Talionsformel', in *idem, Kleine Schriften zur Geschichte des Volkes Israel* (Munich: Beck, 1953), I, pp. 341-44.

78. So e.g. P. Doron, 'A New Look at an Old Lex', *JANESCU*, 1.2 (1969), pp. 21-27; M.-H. Prévost, 'A propos du talion', in *Mélanges dediés à la mémoire de J. Teneur* (Lille, 1976), pp. 619-29; G. Cardascia, 'La place de talion dans l'histoire du droit pénal à la lumière des droits du Proche-Orient ancien', in *Mélanges offerts à J. Dauvilliers* (Toulouse: Editions Université des Sciences Sociales Toulouse, 1979), pp. 169-83; H.W. Jüngling, '"Auge für Auge, Zahn für Zahn". Bemerkungen zu Sinn und Gestaltung der alttestamentlichen Talionsformel', *TP* 59 (1984), pp. 1-38; E. Lipiński, *'nātau' TWAT*, V (1986), p. 700; Schwienhorst-Schönberger, *Das Bundesbuch*, pp. 85-106. For the origin of this type of interpretation of talion in the Second Temple period, depending upon the interpretation of the Torah as imperial law ('Reichsgesetz'; see K. Koch, 'Gesetz I. Altes Testament', *TRE* XIII [1984], pp. 40, 48-49) under Persian influence, see Otto, 'Die Geschichte der Talion', pp. 101-102, 130.

compensation. By including the talion formula (21.23-25), he confirmed talionic retribution in some cases of fatal injuries and abrogated all kinds of talionic penalty for non-fatal injuries, even if they were incurable. All these cases were to be handled according to 21.18-19. A miscarriage without fatal consequences for the mother (אסון[79]) was to be handled according to 21.22. Talionic punishment for non-fatal bodily injuries was redactionally abrogated without even being mentioned, merely by framing it with the laws of compensation. Talionic punishment for fatal bodily injuries, on the other hand, was retained in some cases.

Individual laws have to be interpreted within their redactional structure. Contradictory laws were intended to be mutually resolved within their redactional structure.[80] The structure of 21.18-32, with the talion formula as its centre, implied a legal reform with partial abrogation of talion in cases of non-fatal bodily injuries. The practical application of talion predates the collection of bodily injury laws in the BC. No text in the Hebrew Bible involves the carrying out of talionic bodily sanctions because Deut. 19.21 and Lev. 24.20 implied the talion formula of the BC and used it to underline the death penalty נפש תחת נפש.[81] We have no direct witness of its function. Similar to

---

79. R. Westbrook ('Lex Talionis', pp. 52-69; cf. also M. Stol, 'Oog om oog, tand om tand: een barbaarse wet?', *Phoenix* 33 [1988], pp. 38-44) tries to harmonize the talion in 21.23-25 with its context by the thesis that 21.22 deals with located responsibility of a known perpetrator (בפללים), whereas 21.23-25 deals with a brawl of an innocent passerby attacked by an unknown person (אסון), so that the injured person has a right to get compensation from the local authorities. But אסון in Gen. 42.37 does not refer to a case of unlocated responsibility. Even if Reuben were responsible for a fatal accident to Benjamin, it would still be an אסון. Responsibility is not a factor within the semantic spectrum of אסון; see Schwienhorst-Schönberger, *Das Bundesbuch*, pp. 89-92. בפללים does not mean 'alone', but is derived from *pālilu(m)*, 'guardian'; see Otto, *Körperverletzungen in den Keilschriftrechten*, p. 120.

80. CH § 6 demands the death penalty for a thief who stole goods of the temple or the palace whereas § 8 demands compensation and envisions the death penalty only if the perpetrator is insolvent. The right approach to this phenomenon is not so much a literary critical operation (contra P. Koschaker, *Rechtsvergleichende Studien zur Gesetzgebung Hammurapis, Königs von Babylon* [Leipzig: von Veit, 1917], pp. 75-76; B.S. Jackson, *Theft in Early Jewish Law* [Oxford: Clarendon Press, 1972], pp. 71-73) as an analysis of the redaction and its structure.

81. See Otto, 'Geschichte der Talion', pp. 121-27; see also Kugelmass, 'Lex Talionis', pp. 133-36.

blood vengeance (2 Sam. 14.11), talion's original intent was to prevent bodily injuries by threatening talionic retaliation by the injured side if perpetrator and injured person came from different communities. At an early stage in Israel, solutions conforming to the casuistic laws of compensation were only possible within the individual community as the societal basis of the local courts. When pre-exilic Judah became a legal unity, talion was replaced by the casuistic regulations of compensation.[82] The latter were more socially convenient than talion because they provided restitution for the damage suffered by the injured person instead of using violence against the violator. The collection of bodily injury laws in BC reflects this pre-exilic Israelite legal reform by reformulating the laws in an artistic redactional structure.

b. *The Theological Interpretation of Laws in the Book of the Covenant*
The redaction of predeuteronomistic BC[83] presupposes an intensive theological interpretation, that points to legal developments within pre-exilic Judah.[84] In the pre-dtr BC, the altar law in 20.24-26 was

82. See E. Otto, 'Gewaltvermeidung und -überwindung in Recht und Religion Israels. Rechtshistorische und theologische Ammerkungen eines Alttestamentlers zu R. Schwagers Entwurf einer biblischen Erlösungslehre', in J. Niewiadomski and W. Palaver (eds.), *Dramatische Erlösungslehre im Gespräch. Ein Symposion (Innsbruck, 25-28.9.1991)* (Innsbrucker theologische Studien, 38; Innsbruck: Tyrolia Verlag, 1992), pp. 97-117. For the history of the local courts see H.J. Boecker, *Recht und Gesetz im Alten Testament und im Alten Orient* (Neukirchener Studienbücher, 10; Neukirchen–Vluyn: Neukirchener Verlag, 2nd edn, 1984), pp. 20ff.; H. Niehr, *Rechtsprechung in Israel. Untersuchungen zur Geschichte der Gerichtsorganisation im Alten Testament* (SBS, 130; Stuttgart: Katholisches Bibelwerk, 1987), pp. 50ff., 63ff.; E. Otto, 'ša'ar', *TWAT*, VIII (1994), pp. 359-408. For a different view, see F. Crüsemann, *Die Tora. Theologie und Sozialgeschichte des alttestamentlichen Gesetzes* (Munich: Chr. Kaiser Verlag, 1992), pp. 80ff.
83. For a discussion of the revisions of BC see Otto, *Wandel der Rechtsbegründungen*, pp. 4-8; N. Lohfink, 'Gibt es eine deuteronomistische Bearbeitung im Bundesbuch?', in C. Brekelmans and J. Lust (eds.), *Pentateuchal and Deuteronomistic Studies. Papers Read at the XIIIth IOSOT Congress Leuven 1989* (BETL, 94; Leuven: Peeters, 1990), pp. 91-113; Schwienhorst-Schönberger, *Das Bundesbuch*, pp. 346-48.
84. Against the view that the literary basis of BC was a religious stratum of divine 'privilege law' (J. Halbe, *Das Privilegrecht Jahwes Ex 34,10-26. Gestalt und*

followed by a frame of social privilege laws with a 6/7-structure in
21.2-11, 23.10-12. They theologically framed the system of laws in
21.12–22.29* and the laws of legal procedures in 23.1-3, 6-8. The
system of laws was framed by laws of involving the death penalty[85] in
21.12-17, 22.17-19a, which included the collection of bodily injury
laws in 21.18-32, the family law in 21.15-16[86] and the collection of
יִשְׁלֵם laws in 21.33–22.14. As result, the pre-dtr BC exhibits the
redactional structure shown overleaf:

Within this structure the altar law in 20.24-26 claimed that each
cultic place, where these laws of the BC were proclaimed, was a
legitimate sanctuary.[87] The frame, consisting of privilege laws in a
6/7-scheme (21.2-11; 23.10-12), interpreted the included systems
theologically. Separation for God in a 6/7-scheme[88] meant assignment
to the reign of God.[89] The redactor interlocked the motif of God's
reign with the requirements of solidarity with the underprivileged in
the slave-, *šemiṭṭa*- and sabbath-laws in 21.2-11, 23.10-12.[90] This
social concern connected the frame to the law system in 21.12–22.29*,

Wesen, Herkunft und Wirken in vordeuteronomischer Zeit [FRLANT, 114;
Göttingen: Vandenhoeck & Ruprecht, 1975]) see Otto, *Wandel der
Rechtsbegründungen*, pp. 6-8; Schwienhorst-Schönberger, *Das Bundesbuch*, pp.
22-27.

85. Although the hypothesis about the origins of law that A. Alt ('Die Ursprünge
des israelitischen Rechts', in *idem, Kleine Schriften zur Geschichte des Volkes
Israel*, I [Munich: Beck, 1953], pp. 278-332) derived from the form-critical analysis
of Israelite law has to be revised, it remains methodologically inappropriate to neglect
form-critical differences within cuneiform and Israelite law. For the state of inquiry
see R. Knierim, 'The Problem of Ancient Israel's Prescriptive Legal Traditions', in
D. Patrick (ed.), *Thinking Biblical Law* (Semeia, 45; Atlanta: SBL, 1989), pp. 7-
14.

86. See E. Otto, 'Körperverletzung oder Verletzung von Besitzrechten? Zur
Redaktion von Ex 22,15f. und §§ 55; 56 des Mittelassyrischen Kodex der Tafel A',
ZAW 105 (1993), pp. 153-65.

87. See Otto, *Wandel der Rechtsbegründungen*, pp. 55-56.

88. See E. Otto, 'šaebă'. šabu'ôt', *TWAT*, VII (1992), pp. 1018-1019.

89. See E. Otto, 'Sozial- und rechtshistorische Aspekte in der Ausdifferenzierung
eines altisraelitischen Ethos aus dem Recht', in *Osnabrücker Hochschulschriften.
Schriftenreihe des FB 3, Bd. 9* (Osnabrück: Ed. Universität Osnabrück, 1987),
pp. 143ff.

90. See G. Robinson, *The Origin and Development of the Old Testament
Sabbath. A Comprehensive Exegetical Approach* (Beiträge zur biblischen Exegese
und Theologie, 21; Frankfurt: Lang, 1988), pp. 111ff.

which latter concludes with social prescriptions (22.20-26*) and
privilege laws in 22.28-29. These laws (22.20-29*) formed the centre
of the predeuteronomistic BC. The privilege laws of the 6/7-scheme
derived this social concern and the system of laws in 21.12–22.29*
and of legal procedures in 23.1-8 from the reign of God.

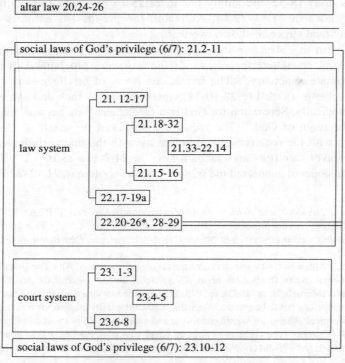

This theological foundation of laws already had forerunners in BC.
The final redaction of the predeuteronomistic BC joined two legal
collections in 20.24-26, 21.2–22.26* and 22.28–23.12*. Both of them
already interpreted the laws theologically. The collection 22.28–
23.12* was framed by privilege laws in 22.28-29, 23.10-12 and had
its centre in the ethical tradition 23.4-5.[91] The theological frame laws
assigned the procedures of law courts to the reign of God, from which

91. See G. Barbiero, *L'asino del nemico. Rinuncia alla vendetta e amore del nemico nella legislazione dell'Antico Testamento (Es 23,4-5; Dt 22,1-4; Lv 19,17-18)*
(AnBib, 128; Rome: Editrice Pontificio Istituto Biblico, 1991), pp. 72ff.

they derived an ethos which transcended all possibilities of law. The structure of this collection became the model for the redaction of the predeuteronomistic BC in 20.24–23.12*. The theological interpretation of the collection in 20.24–22.26* differed from this pattern. This collection, that is legitimized by the social prescriptions in 22.20-26*, was theologically grounded by the concluding sentence כי חנון אני 'for I am compassionate', which referred to YHWH as a divine sovereign who cared for the poor and weak.[92] The theological foundation of laws began with the social crisis of pre-exilic Judah in the ninth and eighth century BC.[93] It tried to unify the broken society by theologically grounding the law as the will of God who demands the integration of the weak and poor into society. This decisive step within Israelite legal history governed the redaction of the BC.[94]

c. *Israelite Distinctiveness and Receptions of Cuneiform Traditions in the Marriage Laws of Deut. 22.22-29*

The final exilic deuteronomistic redaction of Deuteronomy 12–26, which arranged the laws according to the deuteronomistic Decalogue in 5.6-21,[95] used the pre-exilic deuteronomic laws in 19.2–25.12*.

92. See Otto, *Wandel der Rechtsbegründungen*, pp. 38-44; *idem*, 'Recht und Gerechtigkeit. Die Kulturhistorische Bedeutung alttestamentliches Rechtsbegründungen für eine wertplurale Moderne', in F. Hahn *et al.* (eds.), *Festschrift für L. Klein OSB* (BBB, 90; Frankfurt: Verlag Anton Hain, 1992), pp. 63-83. For the connection of this theology with the temple of Jerusalem see *idem*, 'Kultus und Ethos in Jerusalemer Theologie. Ein Beitrag zur theologischen Begründung der Ethik im Alten Testament', *ZAW* 98 (1986), pp. 161-79. For the historical background see *idem, Jerusalem. Die Geschichte der Heiligen Stadt von den Anfängen bis zur Kreuzfahrerzeit* (Urbanreihe, 308; Stuttgart: Kohlhammer, 1980), pp. 61-83.

93. See E. Otto, 'Interdependenzen zwischen Geschichte und Rechtsgeschichte des antiken Israel', *Rechtshistorisches Journal* 7 (1988), pp. 358-66.

94. These kinds of theological interpretations of law differ from those of prologues and epilogues in cuneiform law; see E. Otto, 'Die Bedeutung der altorientalischen Rechtsgeschichte', pp. 153-68; *idem*, 'Gerechtigkeit', in *Bibeltheologisches Wörterbuch* (Graz and Vienna: Styria, 1994), pp. 220-23.

95. See G. Braulik, *Die deuteronomischen Gesetze und der Dekalog. Studien zum Aufbau von Deuteronomium 12–26* (SBS, 145; Stuttgart: Katholisches Bibelwerk, 1991), pp. 23-118 with further literature. In contrast to the view of Braulik it is not possible to find an order of ten laws in Deut. 12–26. The redaction of the Decalogue in Deut. 5.6-21 was not based on the motif of ten laws, which is a late-deuteronomistic motif (Deut. 4.13; 10.4; Exod. 34.28). The Decalogue of Deut. 5.6-21 was structured into five units in Deut. 5.6-10/11/12-15 (centre)/16/17-21; see

The latter were redacted with regard to social responsibility and purity of the people.[96] The deuteronomic redactor, in turn, used a collection of family laws in 22.13-21a, 23, 24a, 25, 27, 28-29, 24.1-4a, 5. The laws 22.22a, 23, 24, 25, 27, 28-29[97] formed a closed structure within the predeuteronomic family laws.[98] 22.23-27* were concentrically redacted[99] and framed by 22.22a, 28-29. The law 22.22a differs from 22.23-27* in that it does not differentiate between adultery and rape. The redactor placed 22.22a as a principle rule at

---

N. Lohfink, 'Zur Dekalogfassung von Dt 5', in *idem, Studien zum Deuteronomium und zur deuteronomistischen Literatur*, I (Stuttgarter Biblische Aufsatzbände. Altes Testament, 8; Stuttgart: Katholisches Bibelwerk, 1990), p. 203. The commandments of the first tablet in Deut. 5.6-15 form a unit that corresponds to the centralization-laws in Deut. 12.2–17.1. The religious commandments of the Decalogue were supplemented by those laws of the constitution of the new Israel after the exile that presuppose the temple. The second tablet in Deut. 5.16-21 corresponds to the judicial and ethical system in Deut. 17.2–26.15. The commandment of obedience to the parents on top of the second tablet reflects the exilic situation of Israel without cultic and political institutions which gives a special importance to the institution of the family. In the constitution of the new Israel after the exile this commandment was supplemented by the order of offices in Deut. 17.2–18.22 that introduce the judicial and ethical system in Deut. 17.2–26.15. For a revision of Braulik's thesis of a decalogue-structure of Deut. 12–26 see E. Otto, Review of G. Braulik, *Die deuteronomischen Gesetze und der Dekalog* (1991), *TLZ* 119 (1994), pp. 15-17; *idem*, 'Von der Programmschrift einer Rechtsreform zum Verfassungsentwurf des Neuen Israel: Die Stellung des Deuteronomiums in der Rechtsgeschichte Israels', in G. Braulik (ed.), *Deuteronomium Studien* (Herders Biblische Studien, 4; Freiburg: Herder, 1995) (forthcoming).

96. See E. Otto, 'Soziale Verantwortung und Reinheit des Landes. Zur Redaktion der kasuistischen Rechtssätze in Deuteronomium 19–25', in R. Liwak and S. Wagner (eds.), *Festschrift für S. Herrmann* (Stuttgart: Kohlhammer, 1991), pp. 290-306. For the deuteronomic redaction in 12.13–26.13* cf. also the following chapter III.d.

97. The בערת-formula (Deut. 22.21b, 22b, 24b) and Deut. 22.26 as an exegesis of 19.2-13 (see M. Fishbane, *Biblical Interpretation in Ancient Israel* [Oxford: Clarendon Press, 1985], pp. 217-20) were deuteronomic-predeuteronomistic additions to the predeuteronomic family laws.

98. See Otto, 'Das Eherecht', pp. 274-81.

99. ‏מצאה‏ :B‎ ,‏מצאה‏ :'B - ‏את הנער המאורשה‏ :'A ;‏כי יהיה נער בתולה מאורשה לאיש‏ :A C: ‏בעיר‏ ;C‎': ‏בשדה‏. This concentric structure precludes a traditio-historical claim that 22.25-27 is a later addition to an original unit in 22.23-24; contra L. Stuhlman, 'Sex and Familial Crimes in the D Code: A Witness to Mores in Transition', *JSOT* 53 (1992), pp. 58-60.

the head of 22.23-29*. This redactional structure of 22.22-29* corresponds to that of the marriage laws in MAL §§ 12-16. This does not mean that these Assyrian and Israelite laws were part of an ancient Oriental 'common law', however. It means, rather, that the redactional techniques of cuneiform law were also known in Judean scholarship. The intentions of the Assyrian and Judean laws were entirely different from each other, even though in tradition history they both started out as private laws. 22.22a was originally a מות יומת law[100] which was superficially transformed into a casuistic form. This מות יומת law of adultery had its parallels in the מות יומת law of Lev. 20.10 and in the prohibitions Lev. 18.20 and Deut. 5.18 (cf. Exod. 20.14). The latter were originally private laws[101] but subsequently became part of the public criminal laws of local courts.[102] Here the מות יומת law of adultery was brought into connection with the casuistic law 22.28-29, its counter-case as a law of compensation.[103] In its tradition history, MAL §§ 14-16* also started out as private law, although directly contradicting Deut. 22.22a. The Assyrian private laws conceded the husband a right to punish his wife the way he wanted. The Israelite private law prescribed the death penalty.[104] This

100. איש שכב עם אשה בעלת בעל מות יומת; see G. Seitz, *Redaktionsgeschichtliche Studien zum Deuteronomium* (BWANT, 93; Stuttgart: Kohlhammer, 1971), p. 120; H.D. Preuß, *Deuteronomium* (Erträge der Forschung, 164; Darmstadt: Wissenschaftliche Buchgesellschaft, 1982), pp. 125-26.

101. See H. Schulz, *Das Todesrecht im Alten Testament. Studien zur Rechtsreform der Mot-Jumat-Sätze* (BZAW, 114; Berlin: de Gruyter, 1969), pp. 34-35, 137; G. Liedke, *Gestalt und Bezeichnung alttestamentlicher Rechtssätze. Eine formgeschichtlich-terminologische Studie* (WMANT, 39; Neukirchen–Vluyn: Neukirchener Verlag, 1971), pp. 130-35. For the prohibitives see J. Halbe, 'Die Reihe der Inzestverbote Lev 18,7-18. Entstehung und Gestaltungsstufen', *ZAW* 92 (1980), p. 87 and E. Lipiński, 'Prohibitive and Related Law Formulations in Biblical Hebrew and in Aramaic', *PWCJS* 9 (Jerusalem, 1988), pp. 25-39. For the Decalogue see E. Otto, 'Der Dekalog als Breunspiegel israelitische Rechtsgeschishte', in H.J. Zobel and J. Hausmann (eds.), *Festschrift für H.D. Preuß* (Stuttgart: Kohlhammer, 1992), p. 61.

102. See E. Otto, *Wandel der Rechtsbegründungen*, pp. 61-66.

103. For the development and social function of these laws see E. Otto, 'Zur Stellung der Frau in den ältesten Rechtstexten des Alten Testaments (Ex 20,14; 22,15f.)—wider die hermeneutische Naivität in Umgang mit dem Alten Testament', *ZEE* 26 (1982), pp. 284-89; Niehr, *Rechtsprechung in Israel*, pp. 44-45, 62-63.

104. See E. Otto, ''Das Verbot der Wiederherstellung einer geschiedenen Ehe. Deuteronomium 24,1-4 im Kontext des israelitischen und judäischen Eherechts', *UF*

was never given up in any phase of the traditio-historical development of 22.22-27*, not even when 22.22a, 28-29 were scholastically expanded by 22.23-27* under the influence of cuneiform laws, especially during the Assyrian period.[105]

It is methodologically necessary to reconstruct the literary history of cuneiform and Hebrew laws, to try to find the points of contact between them and, in the case of Israelite law, to differentiate between distinctive Israelite elements and the reception of cuneiform traditions.[106]

d. *Legal Reform in Deuteronomy by Reformulation of the Book of the Covenant*
Deuteronomy had a decisive role in Israel's legal history which cannot be overlooked if we want to understand the development of Israel's law. The predeuteronomistic Deuteronomy reformulated the BC.[107] N. Lohfink[108] and B.M. Levinson[109] have shown that the deuteronomic centralization-formula and 12.13-28* were exegetical reformulations

24 (1992; publ. 1993), pp. 301-10; *idem, Theologische Ethik*, pp. 39-47.

105. For the cultural climate of this period, see H. Spieckermann, *Juda unter Assur in der Sargonidenzeit* (FRLANT, 129; Göttingen: Vandenhoeck & Ruprecht, 1982), pp. 307-81; B. Halpern, 'Jerusalem and the Lineages in the Seventh Century BCE: Kinship and the Rise of Individual Moral Liability', in B. Halpern and D.W. Hobson (eds.), *Law and Ideology in Monarchic Israel* (JSOTSup, 124; Sheffield: JSOT Press, 1991), pp. 59-91.

106. See E. Otto, 'Town and Rural Countryside in the Ancient Israelite Law. Reception and Redaction in Cuneiform and Israelite Law', *JSOT* 56 (1993), pp. 3-22.

107. See E. Otto, 'Vom Bundesbuch zum Deuteronomium. Die deuteronomische Redaktion in Dtn 12–26', in G. Braulik, W. Groß and S.E. McEvenue (eds.), *Festschrift für N. Lohfink* (Freiburg: Herder, 1993), pp. 260-78; *idem*, 'Rechtsreformen in Deuteronomium XII–XXVI und im Mittelassyrischen Kodex der Tafel A (KAV 1)', in J.A. Emerton (ed.), *Congress Volume of the 14th IOSOT Congress Paris 1992* (VTSup; Leiden and New York: Brill, 1995).

108. See 'Zur deuteronomischen Zentralisationsformel', *Bib* 65 (1984), pp. 327-28.

109. *The Hermeneutics of Innovation: The Impact of Centralization upon the Structure, Sequence and Reformulation of Legal Material in Deuteronomy* (Ann Arbor: University Microfilms International, 1991), pp. 169-220. For a literary analysis of Deut. 12 and its consequences for the development of the motif of cult-centralization see also E. Reuter, *Kultzentralisation. Zur Entstehung und Theologie von Dtn 12* (BBB, 87; Frankfurt: Verlag Anton Hain, 1993), pp. 42-114.

of the altar law of the BC in Exod. 20.24-26. Deut. 12.13-28* and 13.2-18*[110] functioned as principle regulations (Hauptgebote) followed by a framework of social privilege laws in a 6/7-scheme in 14.22–15.23* and 26.2-13*.[111] This frame included the festival system in 16.1-17,[112] the order of courts in 16.18-19*, 17.2-13*, 18.1-8*[113] and the system of laws and ethical rules in 19.2–25.12*. Each of these three systems were concentrically redacted, so that the deuteronomic-predeuteronomistic Deuteronomy of the Josianic period shows the structure shown overleaf, which originates in the corresponding structure of BC.[114]

The cult-centralization propounded by the principal law in 12.13-28* was the hermeneutical key for the exegesis of BC in Deuteronomy

110. See P.E. Dion, 'Deuteronomy 13: The Suppression of Alien Religious Propaganda in Israel during the Late Monarchical Era', in B. Halpern and D.W. Hobson (eds.), *Law and Ideology in Monarchic Israel* (JSOTSup, 124; Sheffield: JSOT Press, 1991), pp. 147-216; E. Otto, 'Review of B. Halpern and D.W. Hobson (eds.), *Law and Ideology in Monarchic Israel* (1991)', *TLZ* 117 (1992), pp. 827-30; *idem*, 'Rechtsreformen in Deuteronomium XII–XXVI'.

111. For the deuteronomistic additions see Otto, 'Vom Bundesbuch zum Deuteronomium', pp. 261-62.

112. For an exegetical interpretation of the predeuteronomistic laws in 16.1-17 see E. Otto, *Das Mazzotfest in Gilgal* (BWANT, 107; Stuttgart: Kohlhammer, 1975), pp. 177-82; *idem*, '*pāsah/paesah*', *TWAT*, VI (1988), pp. 659-82; *idem*, '*šaebă*'. *šabu'ôt*', pp. 1023-1024. For the history of the festival laws see *idem*, 'Feste und Feiertage II. Altes Testament', *TRE* XI (1983), pp. 96-106.

113. See N. Lohfink, 'Die Sicherung der Wirksamkeit des Gotteswortes durch das Prinzip der Schriftlichkeit der Tora und durch das Prinzip der Gewaltenteilung nach dem Ämtergesetz des Buches Deuteronomium (Dtn 16,18–18,22)', in *idem*, *Studien zum Deuteronomium und zur deuteronomistischen Literatur*, I (Stuttgarter Biblische Aufsatzbände. Altes Testament, 8; Stuttgart: Katholisches Bibelwerk, 1990), pp. 305-23; E. Otto, 'Von der Gerichtsordnung zum Verfassungsentwurf. Deuteronomische Gestaltung und deuteronomistische Interpretation im "Ämtergesetz" Dtn 16,8-18,22', in J. Kottsieper *et al.*, *Festschrift für O. Kaiser* (Göttingen: Vandenhoeck & Ruprecht, 1994); *idem*, *Theologische Ethik des Alten Testament*, pp. 193-97. For discussion see also U. Rüterswörden, *Von der politischen Gemeinschaft zur Gemeinde. Studien zu Dt 16,18–18,22* (BBB, 65; Frankfurt: Athenäum, 1987), pp. 89-105; N. Lohfink, 'Review of U. Rüterswörden, *Von der politischen Gemeinschaft zur Gemeinde. Studien zu Dt 16,8–18,22 (1987)*', *TLZ* 113 (1988), pp. 425-30. For the connections within 14.22–16.20* see W.S. Morrow, 'The Composition of Deuteronomy 14,1–17.1' (PhD dissertation, University of Toronto, 1988), pp. 493-500.

114. See Otto, 'Vom Bundesbuch zum Deuteronomium', p. 269.

14–25*. In 14.22–15.23, the laws of slaves and Šemitta in 15.1-18*, which framed the BC in Exod. 21.2-11, 23.10-11, formed the centre of the framework of the privilege laws in Deuteronomy. The laws of tithe and first-born in 14.22-29, 15.19-23, which refer to Exod. 22.28-29 framed 15.1-18* and connected it with the principal laws of cult-centralization in chs. 12, 13* and the festival system in 16.1-17.

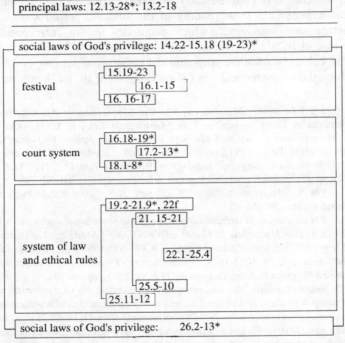

principal laws: 12.13-28*; 13.2-18

social laws of God's privilege: 14.22-15.18 (19-23)*

festival
15.19-23
16.1-15
16. 16-17

court system
16.18-19*
17.2-13*
18.1-8*

system of law and ethical rules
19.2-21.9*, 22f
21. 15-21
22.1-25.4
25.5-10
25.11-12

social laws of God's privilege: 26.2-13*

The court system in 16.18–18.8*, which in 16.18, 19* referred to the court system of the BC in Exod. 23.6, 8, concluded the consequences of the cult-centralization of the court system. In a predeuteronomic period local courts were responsible for all the cases that could be resolved by witnesses. Those cases which could not be cleared up were remitted to the local sanctuary and decided by cultic means (cf. Exod. 22.7-8). With the centralization of the cult these latter cases had to be remitted to court proceedings at the central sanctuary.[115] These stages

115. See Levinson, *The Hermeneutics of Innovation*, pp. 325-404. For literary differentiation between the deuteronomic and exilic-deuteronomistic program in

of legal proceedings were regulated by 16.18–18.8*.

Deut. 19.2-13* was another example of deuteronomic exegesis of the BC. The unusual order of וכי with the following אשר in 19.4b, 5, 11 hints at a direct literary dependence of 19.2-13* upon Exod. 21.12-14.[116] In the BC the general rule of the case of killing in Exod. 21.12 was followed by Exod. 21.13-14, which differentiated between fatal bodily injury and murder. Deut. 19.2-13*[117] reversed the order and placed the asylum regulations at the fore because they were relevant with regard to the hermeneutical key of cult-centralization.

All the laws of the BC were interpreted in Deuteronomy under the aspect of cult-centralization[118] except for the collections of the שׁלֹם-laws and the laws of bodily injuries in Exod. 21.18–22.14. The latter were not incorporated into Deuteronomy but complemented by the family laws in 21.15-21, 22.13-29, 24.1–4.5, 25.5-10 which have no counter-part in the BC. The שׁלֹם-laws and the laws of bodily injuries did not need to be revised under the aspect of cult-centralization. For this reason they could be supplemented by the family laws of Deut. 21.15–25.10*, which in the BC are represented by only a single law (Exod. 22.15-16).[119]

16.18–18.22 see Otto, 'Von der Gerichtsordnung zum Verfassungsentwurf'; *idem, Theologische Ethik*, pp. 193-97.

116. See J.C. Geertz, 'Die Gerichtsorganisation Israels im deuteronomischen Gesetz' (Theol. dissertation, University of Göttingen, 1993), pp. 112-14.

117. 19.1, 2b, 7-9 are deuteronomistic additions; see Otto, 'Vom Bundesbuch zum Deuteronomium', p. 262.

118. For a list of parallels between Deuteronomy and BC cf. G.R. Driver, *Deuteronomy* (ICC; Edinburgh: T. & T. Clark, 2nd edn, 1902), pp. IV-VII; Preuß, *Deuteronomium*, pp. 104-106.

119. For the exilic and postexilic reformulation of BC and Deuteronomy in the deuteronomistic and postdeuteronomistic interpretation of Deuteronomy and in the Holiness Code (Lev. 17–26) see Otto, *Theologische Ethik*, pp. 193-256. With these revisions, an interesting change in the authority of BC and Deuteronomy took place. When BC was revised by the deuteronomic Deuteronomy in pre-exilic Judah, Deuteronomy was to replace BC. When the postexilic Pentateuch redactor, who tried to equalize the deuteronomistic Deuteronomy with the priestly Tetrateuch, interpolated the BC into the Sinai pericope, the BC, which now was directly given by the Lord at Mount Sinai, assumed priority over Deuteronomy, which was only given by Moses. The same happened with the Decalogues; see E. Otto, 'Del Libro de la Alianza al la Ley de Santidad. La reformulación del derecho Israelitica y la formación del Pentateuco', *EstBib* 52 (1994), pp. 195-217; *idem*, 'Das "Heiligkeitsgesetz" Leviticus 17-26 in der Pentateuchredaktion', in P. Hommer and W. Thiel (eds.),

Legal reform and reformulation of laws together represent decisive features of ancient Oriental and Israelite legal history. They represent 'common law' only in this respect: they were continuously changing laws—*leges semper reformandae et reformatae*—because they were a mirror of ever-changing human life in society. 'Law is the life of man seen from a special side' (Friedrich Carl von Savigny).

Festschrift für H. Graf Reventlow (Frankfurt: Lang, 1994), pp. 65-80. Together with the BC, the Decalogue in Exod. 20 and the Holiness Code in Lev. 17–26, which was a priestly exegesis of Deuteronomy BC and D (see Otto, *Theologische Ethik*, pp. 240-53), also gained a higher status than Deuteronomy. A comparison of the exegetical methods in Deut. 12 as an exegesis of the altar law of the BC and of Lev. 17 as an exegesis of Deut. 12 can show the development of the authority of a text as *traditum* in relation to a text as *traditio*; see E. Otto, 'Gesetzesfortschreibung und Pentateuchredaktion', *ZAW* 107 (1995) (forthcoming).

CONTRIBUTORS

Martin Buss is Professor of Religion at Emory University. He has had a long-term interest in biblical law with its relation to world-wide issues of law and ethics. His most current involvement is with the nature and development of the study of form, with special reference to the way concerns with generality and particularity appear within it.

Samuel Greengus is the Julian Morgenstern Professor of Bible and Near Eastern Literature at the Hebrew Union College-Jewish Institute of Religion in Cincinnati. He received an MA in Judaic Studies and a PhD in Assyriology from the Oriental Institute of the University of Chicago. His research areas are social and economic institutions in ancient Mesopotamia and the analysis of biblical law, society and culture in their ancient setting.

Sophie Lafont is a Professor in the Faculty of Law at the University of Angers, France. She wrote her dissertation, 'Women in Criminal Law in the Ancient Near East' (1990) with Professor Guillaume Cardascia (Faculty of Law, University of Paris). She specializes in comparative legal history and is currently writing an article for a volume on feudalism. She is also preparing a collected edition of Professor Cardascia's articles.

Bernard M. Levinson, Assistant Professor of Near Eastern Languages and Cultures at Indiana University, Bloomington, chairs the Biblical Law Group of the Society of Biblical Literature. His research interests include biblical and cuneiform law, inner-biblical exegesis, Deuteronomy and the history of interpretation. He is currently working on his book, 'Scripture Subverting Scripture: The Hermeneutics of Legal Innovation in Deuteronomy'. He has published articles on the current literary approach to biblical studies and on the hermeneutical issues associated with revising authoritative texts. His most recent publication is ' "But You Shall Surely Kill Him": The Text-Critical and Neo-Assyrian Evidence for MT Deuteronomy 13:10', in G. Braulik (ed.), *Deuteronomiumstudien 1993* (Herders Biblische Studien, 4; Freiburg: Herder, forthcoming in 1995).

Victor H. Matthews, PhD, Brandeis University (1977) in Near Eastern and Judaic Studies, is a Professor of Religious Studies at Southwest Missouri State University in Springfield, Missouri, where he has served since 1984. He is currently the editor of the *ASOR Newsletter*, Convener of the Conference of Regional Secretaries for the

Society of Biblical Literature, and Regional Secretary for the Central States Region of SBL/ASOR. He is the author of *Pastoral Nomadism in the Mari Texts, 1830–1760 B.C.E.* (ASOR Dissertation Series, 3; Cambridge, MA: ASOR, 1978); *Manners and Customs in the Bible* (Peabody, MA: Hendrickson, 1988, 1991); and co-author with Don C. Benjamin of *Old Testament Parallels: Laws and Stories from the Ancient Near East* (Mahwah, NJ: Paulist Press, 1991), and of *The World of Ancient Israel: A Cultural Anthropology* (Peabody, MA: Hendrickson, 1993).

William Morrow is Assistant Professor of Hebrew and Hebrew Scriptures at Queen's Theological College which is affiliated with Queen's University in Kingston, Ontario, Canada. He has written on various problems concerning the composition of biblical Hebrew texts (e.g., Deut. 15.1-3; Job 42.6; and the Ketib/Qere notes in the Masora). He is the author of a book length study on the composition of Deut. 14.1–17.3, forthcoming from Scholars Press.

Eckart Otto, Professor of Old Testament and Biblical Archaeology at the Johannes Gutenberg-University in Mainz, Germany, specializes in cuneiform and biblical legal history, the history of the Israelite cultus, and the archaeology and historical geography of Israel. He chairs the Fachuntergruppe Altorientalische und Biblische Rechtsgeshichte of the Wissenschaftliche Gesellschaft für Theologie (Germany) and is co-editor of *Studia et Documenta ad Iura Orientis antiqui pertinentia* (Leiden: Brill). Among his most recent books concerned with biblical law are: *Wandel der Rechtsbegründungen in der Gesellschaftsgeschichte des Antiken Israel* (1988), *Rechtsgeschichte der Redaktionen im Kodex Ešnunna und im «Bundesbuch»* (1989), *Körperverletzungen in den Keilschriftrechten und im Alten Testament* (1991), *Theologische Ethik des Alten Testaments* (1994). He is preparing a commentary on Leviticus for the new commentary series Herders Theologischer Kommentar zum Alten Testament (Freiburg: Herder).

Dale Patrick is Professor of Bible at Drake University. He traces his scholarly lineage to James Muilenburg, Claus Westermann and James Barr, but gives primary credit for whatever he knows about law to members of the Biblical Law Group, particularly Martin Buss, Jacob Milgrom, Ron Hals, Tikva Frymer-Kensky and Rolf Knierim. No one can be blamed for his idiosyncrasies, which derive from an effort to expand and modify form criticism to encompass the conceptual system and the rhetoric of the text. His publications include *Old Testament Law: An Introduction* and the editing of *Thinking Biblical Law, Semeia* 45 (1989).

Raymond Westbrook holds degrees in law from Oxford University and from the Hebrew University of Jerusalem as well as a PhD in Assyriology from Yale University. He is Professor of Ancient Law in the Department of Near Eastern Studies at the Johns Hopkins University where he teaches cuneiform law and diplomacy, biblical law and Roman law.

INDEXES

INDEX OF REFERENCES

OLD TESTAMENT

INDEX OF AUTHORS